No. 832
$9.95

THE ELECTRONIC MUSICAL INSTRUMENT MANUAL

a guide to theory and design

ALAN DOUGLAS

Sen. Mem. I.E.E.E.
Associate, Incorporated Society of Organ Builders
President, Electronic Organ Constructors Society
Formerly Senior Scientific Officer, British Iron and Steel Research Association

SIXTH EDITION

TAB BOOKS

Blue Ridge Summit, Pa. 17214

SIXTH EDITION

FIRST PRINTING—JUNE 1976

Copyright © Alan Douglas 1968, 1976

Printed in the United States
of America

Hardbound Edition: International Standard Book No. 0-8306-6832-2

Paperbound Edition: International Standard Book No. 0-8306-5832-7

Library of Congress Card Number: 76-15887

Contents

Preface to the Sixth Edition

This is not a constructional book; its object is to start the reader right at the fundamentals of sound, and progressively work up to examples of current organs. However, we have not forgotten the thousands of owners of valve organs, and from both this and the historical aspect, have devoted some space to these original techniques from which the modern instrument developed. And from this, we look forward to many experimental possibilities in the last chapter, for this art never stays still; see, for example, *Electronic Music Production* by the same publishers.

The author is again indebted to several manufacturers for new data, notably C. G. Conn Ltd; The Hammond Organ Co.; The Allen Company; Harmonics Ltd; Philips Gloeilampenfabrieken; The Wurlitzer Company; and Nippon Gakki Co., Japan.

Alan Douglas

1 Sound

When one hears sound mentioned, the mind at once thinks of the ear. This is natural, since the ear is the organ especially provided to pass on the sensation of hearing to the brain; but what is the origin and meaning of sound? Any object which is capable of vibrating can initiate sound waves. The ear cannot detect vibrations below a certain rate or above a certain rate, but both very low and very high vibration rates may cross the border between sound and feeling, and if sufficiently intense may give rise to pain. That with which we are concerned is therefore a range of vibration rates, but first let us see how these vibrations, which may be induced and maintained by many means, reach the ear.

Sound can travel only through a medium; it cannot be conveyed through a vacuum. The medium we are most concerned with is air, but later on it will be shown that the conveying, reflecting or absorbing powers of other media have very important effects on the nature of the vibrations before they reach the ear.

It is convenient to imagine the air between the vibrating body and the ear as consisting of a series of layers, like the concentric skins of an onion, and as being perfectly still. When an object (a tuning fork is usually chosen, since this produces vibrations of a regular and simple nature) vibrates, imagine it to start from rest and to move to the right. Each layer consists of a vast number of individual particles. The particles in the immediate proximity of a leg of the fork move to the right, so producing a pressure which energizes the next layer to the right, and this in its turn, causes the next layer to move; and so on until the pressure wave reaches the ear, the receiving member of which will also be displaced to the right. When the movement of the tuning fork reverses, exactly the opposite effect takes place and a reversal of the pressure wave takes place, because the air is elastic, so that, by the same means as before, the ear is eventually made to reverse its diaphragm position and all the particles return to rest until re-energized.

Now a tuning fork vibrates in a perfectly regular and even manner and it is thus easy to draw a picture of how the layers of air behave. The layers follow the shape of the mode of vibration exactly, but as the waves proceed in straight lines, it is rather difficult to draw their progression through the alternations of compression and rarefaction exactly in this form; consequently, being a simple harmonic motion (page 20), this is more easily understandable if converted into a *curve*.

Thus in Fig. 1 it can be seen that when the fork, starting from rest, moves to the right a rise of pressure is created in one direction, which we may call positive. It increases to a maximum when the fork has moved to the limit, and this point is $+p$. The fork now reverses its movement, and the pressure reduces until it comes to where it started, which is where the horizontal line cuts the curves. Movement of the fork continues in the opposite direction, causing a reversal of pressure which again reaches a maximum value at $-p$. The process is repeated so long as the fork is kept in vibration and so the wave form of the fork is as shown in Fig. 1. The quantities shown are assigned to any simple wave and form its essential characteristics. The

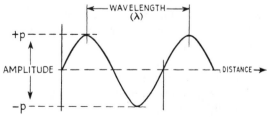

Fig. 1 Simple sine wave with quantities shown

frequency of a wave is the number of complete vibrations passing a certain point per second.

If the air between the fork and the ear is in layers it must be clear that at any one instant all the layers cannot be travelling in the same direction; this is true, for the first layer starts to move before the second one, and so on. Thus in any complete cycle of operations some layers will be out of phase with others.

In practice the ear is unable, or unwilling, to detect small differences in phase, but conditions can arise where the effects of phase can be serious. The instance of destructive interference, as it is called, is always qualified in practice by the fact that any two notes of identical frequency (or pitch) and amplitude (or loudness) practically never occur. Nonetheless, as will be described later, there are effects from this type of phase difference. As has been pointed out, in the pressure wave train caused by the layers of air some points are out of phase with others. If two tuning forks of exactly the same pitch and loudness sound together, it is possible to find a point distant from the forks where the waves arrive 180° out of phase. Therefore no sound is heard at the point of observation since, as the vibrations are of identical loudness but in opposite phase, they cancel out.

It is not necessary to conduct an elaborate experiment to prove this point, in which it must be observed that it is not the *ear* which does the cancelling, for the pressure waves are already cancelled before they reach the ear and so the ear cannot hear anything. A simple experiment, and one of considerable significance in organ building, is to mount two tuning forks of identical pitch and loudness close together, and to cause them to sound. The movement of air-pressure waves from one fork interferes with the direction of the pressure waves from the other, so that very soon they settle down in such a way that their vibrations are out of phase; thus no external layers of air are energized and the ear hears nothing. Yet each fork vibrates with its normal amplitude, as can be perceived by the eye if the pitch is low. This is destructive interference.

Conversely, if a point is found where the waves are exactly in phase, the sound will now be loud and clear; indeed the energy will be not twice that of the single fork, but four times. For it is a general law that the energy of a vibration is proportional to the square of the amplitude.

Thus it can be seen that a succession of simple sound waves may arrive from different distances at different degrees of loudness—but not pitch. The kind of vibration which has been discussed is only of very small amplitude, and if this is the case, all portions of the wave, and the source initiating the waves, will be moving at the same speed at any one instant. In the tuning fork, where this condition obtains in normal use, the pitch of the vibrations is always the same, whether they are loud or soft. This is a most important property, for it can clearly be seen that if there was any tendency for the pitch of any instrument to vary with loudness it would be quite impossible to give any expression to music.

It is known that the degree of vibration does affect the pitch of certain instruments, but this is for other reasons and at the moment we are considering only simple vibrations of small amplitude, so as to form a clear picture of the mechanism of sound propagation.

Another fact of equal importance is that the rate of travel is the same for all pitches. It does not substantially matter if we are near the sound source or far from it, the order in which the various sounds arrive being always the same for any distance. So far as musical sounds are concerned, the rate of travel is also the same for any degree of loudness. This is approximately 1130 ft/s in air at ordinary room temperatures; but the effect of temperature on the speed of sound is very marked, the rate increasing by just over one foot a second per Fahrenheit degree. This of course has a marked influence on the constancy of tune of musical instruments, most of which tend to alter in pitch from moment to moment. Any shift in pitch of an electronic music generator would cause the rise or fall to be uniform for the whole instrument at any instant of time. This might have some significance where several *kinds* of instruments were playing together, some of which might be more prone to remain in tune than others, but in fact no instance worth commenting upon has been reported, although detailed observation has been made by a prominent research laboratory.

The process of transmitting simple sound waves having been examined, it is interesting to examine what happens to the large number of vibrations in all directions before they reach the ear, for of course the source excites all the layers of air in contact with it and they pass on the movement to many other layers. Thus the sound will be travelling in other directions as well as towards the ear of the listener.

Most listening is done in an enclosed space. For this reason we will disregard conditions in the open air, and the falling off in energy with distance is not really significant except in very large concert halls. The matters now to be discussed may, however, largely offset that effect, which of course is due to the fact that any one unit of sound energy has to excite a quantity of air progressively greater with distance.

The conditions qualifying the reflection and absorption of sound in rooms are extremely complex. Exact evaluation of the energy distribution is possible by means of electrical analogies, but it is not necessary for the purpose of this book to do more than condense the sequence of events between the departure of the air-pressure wave from the source and the impact on the ear of the listener.

As stated, when sound waves leave the source they spread in all directions. Fig. 2 shows an observer O and a sound source S. The distances between the observer, the sound source, and the walls, ceiling, and floor are not the same. If we assume that all these surfaces reflect all sounds of any pitch 100 per cent, it is clear that some sounds will go to and fro between different walls several times before they reach the ear. This means that the ear will hear the same sound at different inter-

vals, and from the dimensions of the room and the speed of sound it is easy to find these different times, at least the principal ones.

Usually the time difference in small rooms is also small, and the effect is almost unnoticed; but in large concert halls the effect may be most marked. Since the effect on any one ear is different for other positions in the room, the position of the listener will produce different effects on him; but in any event where there is reflection the listener will hear a louder sound than the original sound because the sound which would have gone elsewhere is now collected by the walls etc., and returned to the ear to augment the directly-received sound.

We are still considering simple wave forms and assuming that all pitches are 100 per cent reflected, but this condition never exists in practice. All materials used for building partly reflect and partly absorb. If the reflection is 70 per cent, the absorption is 30 per cent. There is almost negligible transmission through the material, owing to the high mechanical resistance to the small power of an arriving sound wave. Obviously by proper construction it is possible to adjust the degree of reflection to a known extent; but this is greatly complicated by the differing degrees of reflection (or absorption) for varying pitches. Nearly all suitable substances have some discrimination against certain frequencies, and whilst this is of small significance in the home it is most difficult to adjust in large rooms; particularly as it is possible for a wall or other structure to vibrate at its own resonant frequency, thus re-radiating some of the energy reaching it not only into the room containing the sound source, but into other parts of the building. The abridged table on page 4 clearly shows the effect on sounds of equal loudness but different pitches, covering most of the useful musical range, as also does Fig. 3.

It must be remembered that although sound is reflected in a manner similar to light, the reflecting surface must be large in relation to the wavelength of the sound. Therefore, a reflecting surface of a given size will reflect sounds above a certain frequency, while sounds of a lower frequency will be diffracted or spread out. To reflect fully the lower tones of an organ a reflector thousands of square feet in area is necessary. This, together

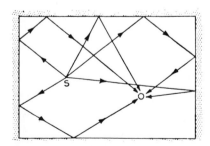

Fig. 2 Observer and sound source in enclosed space

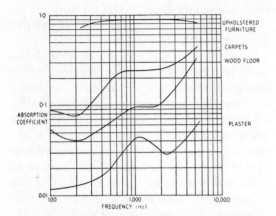

Fig. 3 Variation of absorption coefficient with frequency

with the data in the table below, explains why identical tone colours produced in different enclosures will sound very different to the ear.

In practice the sound source has a finite size and if this is very small, e.g. a loudspeaker, special problems are encountered which affect even the smallest room. These are examined in Chapter 6.

Table of Absorption of Sound by Different Materials at Various Pitches

Material	CC	C	C¹	C²	C³	C⁴	C⁵
Wood blocks		0·05	0·03	0·06	0·09	0·10	0·22
Thick carpet		0·09	0·08	0·21	0·26	0·27	0·37
Bare brick wall	0·02	0·02	0·02	0·03	0·04	0·05	0·07
Tiles	0·01	0·01	0·02	0·03	0·04	0·05	0·05
Wood panels		0·09	0·17	0·17	0·15	0·15	0·15
Human being*	0·35	0·72	0·89	0·95	0·99	1·00	1·00

* Very variable.

The proportions and construction of a room that will prolong the sound, but not to such an extent as to produce a separate image of it at a later time, are such as to cause *reverberation*. If the physical dimensions are so great that the original sound is heard separately first and an image of that sound some time later, the room is said to have an *echo*. Clearly this latter state must be avoided at all costs, since after a few cycles of wave trains everything becomes a meaningless blur. The length of time that it takes for a loud clap of the hands to reappear will give the time of the echo, and a reasonable and widely-used estimate of the reverberation time can be formed from the time taken for the clap to die away until it is just inaudible.

The exact reverberation time can be calculated by means of the formula—

$$T = \frac{0 \cdot 05V}{a}$$

where T = reverberation time in seconds,
V = volume of room in cubic feet,
a = total sound-absorbing power of the material exposed to the sound waves.

The formula is accurate provided that the damping is not excessively high, e.g. a room with heavy curtains all round the walls.

The result of many observations and tests has established that for music and speech there are desirable maximum reverberation times for the cubic content of the hall, assuming reasonable geometry of shape (see Fig. 4).

It is, of course, the degree of reverberation which imparts the richness of tone to massive sources of sound, such as the orchestra and organ. They tend to sound thin and ragged without this acoustic reinforcement. And the excellence or otherwise of the room properties for this purpose is extremely well illustrated by broadcasts from halls built for listening; the microphone picks up a true picture of the acoustic conditions whilst the subconscious control exercised by the brain over the ear may modify the exact proportions of the direct and reflected sounds. The characteristics are thus

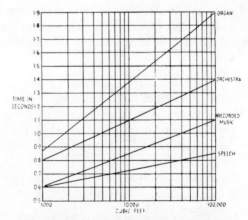

Fig. 4 Desirable reverberation times for rooms

more accurately defined by remote listening, other things being equal, and it is of course true that many halls which are acceptable to an audience actually in the hall require acoustic correction for broadcasting.

Since all electronic musical instruments use one or more loudspeakers to convert the electrical wave forms into air-pressure waves, the special conditions relating to such sound sources are dealt with later on in the text; but at the outset it must be made quite clear that no musical instrument, physical or electronic, can sound satisfactory in a perfectly 'dead' room and it will be found that under conditions of this kind, much more power will be required for apparently equal loudness.

The foregoing observations will be sufficient to indicate the more important factors influencing the kind of sound which finally reaches the ear, and it is obvious that it consists of part direct and part reflected sound. What now happens inside the ear? The theory of hearing is largely conjectural; how the vibrations of the eardrum and its subsequent chain of nervous mechanisms really function is not known, but the construction of the ear is interesting and will be briefly described.

Firstly it should be borne in mind that in spite of possibly great expenditure of power to initiate the air-pressure waves at the source, the actual amount of energy available in the sound waves is incredibly small. This is principally due to the very poor coupling with the air of the various vibrating media, in other words they cannot move a sufficiently great amount of air. Hence the ear is an extremely sensitive device. Since it is not known how much energy is required to stimulate the hearing nerves, it is not possible to say whether any amplifying action takes place. Not all the sound waves arriving at the ear need to be air-pressure waves, for hearing may be induced by mechanical vibration of the bone structure of the ear. There is some loss of higher frequencies in this latter process, so that sounds tend to be muffled.

The ear consists of a roughly conical collector, from which a small channel conveys the sound to the eardrum. This is very small and approximately oval in appearance, and consists of a skin diaphragm about 0·003 in. thick, tightly stretched over a bone surround. Behind the eardrum lies a chain of small bones, touching the diaphragm at one end and in contact with another small membrane at the other end. This membrane is in contact with a fluid which fills the remainder of the ear structure, and in which is immersed a minute but extremely complex grid of tightly stretched fibres. These are of different lengths and they have been compared by Jeans with the strings of a piano. It is indeed probable that they have a selective function in separating sounds of different pitches.

Immersed in the fluid mentioned is the prodigious number of 24 000 minute stimulating machines, each of which has a conducting nerve to the brain. This amazingly intricate device is developed to respond to a greater pitch or frequency range in man than in any other animal. Though many animals can hear sounds of much higher pitch and smaller intensity than human beings, the cut-off at the lower end of the scale is much more extensive.

It may well be thought that all this mechanism would ensure the accurate interpretation of all sound waves impinging on it, but the ear does not hear notes of all pitches with equal loudness. Indeed, it is very insensitive at the extreme upper end of the frequency range, and even more so at the lower end. A hearing response curve is shown in Fig. 5. In this the pressure in dynes per square centimetre is plotted against frequency, and this clearly shows the average minimum pressure required to produce any sense of hearing, as well as the pressure at which hearing becomes unbearable and rapidly causes a sensation of pain.

It will also be observed that there is a range of pitch over which the ear is very sensitive. Only a small sound energy is needed to be intelligible in this band. Conversely an enormous amount of energy is required at the lower end of the pitch scale. Thus to provide equal loudness, the slightest touch of a high violin note will balance with the full output of an organ pipe thirty-two feet long and perhaps two feet or more in width. The relative amounts of energy required to excite these two producers of sound may vary by several million times to one, to produce equal loudness, as is clearly seen from Fig. 5.

Thus it will be seen that the power required to produce an equal sense of loudness will vary

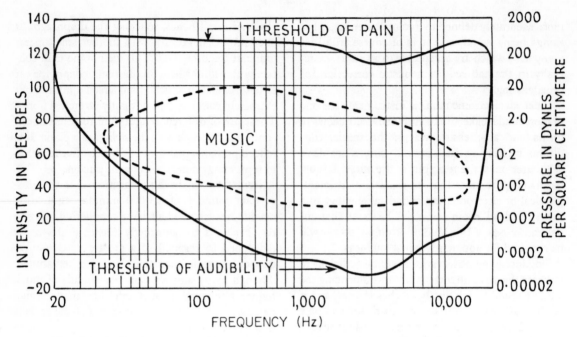

Fig. 5 Limits of hearing and range of frequency and intensity required for utmost fidelity in music reproduction

throughout the pitch range, and this is an important factor in the design of electronic musical instruments, especially in relation to loudspeaking equipment.

Moreover, the ear has the remarkable power of producing notes of its own and adding to or subtracting from the original sound. Part of this process is a psychological one, the ear altering its appreciation of received sounds because it wishes to; and part is due to the fact that the diaphragm does not vibrate in a quite linear fashion. If the forward and backward motion of the air-pressure wave is symmetrical, for the diaphragm to follow this motion it is necessary that the same force should act on both sides of it. This is not so, because on one side is air, on the other is the mechanism transmitting the vibrations to the nerve network. Thus the diaphragm follows one half of the wave with accuracy, but the other half with slightly less amplitude. This results in an unsymmetrical wave and, as is shown in Chapter 2, this must contain some overtones or harmonics.

The original sound is thus altered and this produces what are known as difference tones. The theories underlying the exact procedure are complex, and it will suffice to say that the most common effect of this non-linear response is slightly to brighten the original sound. But this is much modified by the degree of loudness of the sound. It should be noted that the ear does not instantly respond to a pulse of sound, estimates of the time taken varying from one-fortieth to one-twentieth of a second. It takes longer than this to *identify* a particular sound.

The last point to be considered in this section is the question of intensity. If a steady tone is gradually increased in loudness, the ear cannot at once perceive the increase; it is only after a time that it is noticed. The experience of many investigators has shown that about 25 per cent increase in energy is required to produce a perceptible difference. Fechner's law states that 'The intensity of our sensation of hearing does not increase as rapidly as the energy of the exciting cause, but only as rapidly as the logarithm of this energy.' Thus changes in hearing are multiplications and not additions of the sound energy.

This led to the adoption of a convenient unit for measuring these increases in loudness. The change in intensity resulting from an increase of ten times in the energy is known as a 'bel'. This can conveniently be subdivided into smaller steps, each of which will approximate to the 25 per cent increase in loudness which represents the smallest change perceived by the ear.

Each step must represent exactly an increase of $^{10}\sqrt{(10)}$, which is equal to $1 \cdot 2589$. These steps are known as 'decibels', and this is the unit generally used to indicate changes in sound intensity. Thus if the intensity at the threshold of hearing is taken as the zero point, and we call it 1, then

Unit of Energy		Decibels (dB) Sound Intensity
1	is equal to	0
1·26		1
1·58		2
2		3
4		6
8		9
10		10
100		20
1000		30

2 Music and Noise

We have seen in Chapter 1 how sounds originate and how they may be altered in character before they reach the ear. All these remarks apply to sounds of the kind we are accustomed to hearing, and with which our ears are familiar. For the sake of simplicity, it has so far been assumed that the sound waves discussed have been of a simple form and regular progression.

We can now examine the kind of sounds which we are more likely to encounter, and which form the subject-matter of this book. Whilst some of the remarks apply to other kinds of sound, such as speech, no consideration will be given to them because we are primarily interested in music. But first it is important to understand the difference between music and noise. Both these forms of sound are the result of vibrations, but they produce very different effects on the ear.

The predominant characteristics may be condensed into the statement that music consists of a series of vibrations recurring in an orderly and controlled manner, so as to form a cyclic pattern within prescribed frequency bands; whereas noise is an 'unpitched' series of discontinuous vibrations in which the energy is more or less uniformly spread over an infinite frequency range in a random and non-cyclic manner.

A characteristic of noise is that if the upper frequency components are very pronounced it produces a sense of irritation, even at low levels of loudness. It is reasonable to suppose that the ear tends to anticipate the content of the regularly-recurring wave forms of musical sounds, and certainly prefers them, but is frustrated by the sudden pulses of discrete shock waves and registers annoyance. Noises do, of course, have restricted frequency bands; for instance, heavy gunfire is quite different from striking a match, but unless the noise is very loud, the lower frequency components

do not cause the same sense of irritation which accompanies high frequency noises. Apart from the very complex frequency spectrum of such high-pitched noises, the sound may be of too short a duration or even too complex in character to be analysed by the ear; under these circumstances there is no doubt that the irritation value is greatly increased.

It is of interest to note that there is a noise range accompanying the musical response of many instruments. It always lies at the upper end of the frequency band and is illustrated in Fig. 6, to which further reference will be made. Though small in amplitude, if omitted from the wave spectrum the sound loses much of its freshness.

To transfer our attention now to musical sounds. It has been stated that these are characterized by a well-ordered wave form development of a regularly-recurring nature. This does not mean that the waves necessarily have simple shapes. Indeed if the wave form is too simple and regular, the sense of monotony induced causes loss of interest in the sound.

Thus even if the pitch or frequency range of simple sounds is constantly varying, it is desirable

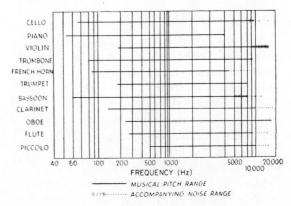

Fig. 6 Noise range of musical instruments

that there should be some further characteristic of these vibrations embodying more than a pitch change. This introduces the most important aspect of sound waves, on the correct interpretation of which is founded every method of electronic tone production.

It is obvious to the most casual observer that a note of the same fundamental pitch sounds quite different if produced by a violin, a trumpet, and a flute. This is not because of any difference in loudness, but because all musical instruments produce notes of other frequency along with the fundamental pitch notes. These other notes are known as harmonics, overtones or partials. Harmonics are notes which are an exact multiple of the fundamental pitch; other notes are known as overtones or partials. The character which the presence of these harmonics imparts to sound is known as timbre.

Now we are principally interested in percussion and sustained-tone instruments, and the factors which cause the harmonics to appear differ according to whether the sound is produced by strings or by the action of wind. The reason we must look into these matters briefly is that, as will be explained later, it is possible to analyse the combined wave forms and find out the number and magnitude of their individual components; and, as was discovered by Helmholtz many years ago, by producing and combining a number of pure waves of equivalent pitches and amplitudes an exact replica of an original sound may be obtained. It is because of this fact that synthetic tones produced by electrical means are possible.

Sound produced by strings

Let us first look at a stretched string. It does not matter, as far as its mode of vibration is concerned, whether it is on a violin or a piano or indeed on any instrument at all. If the string is tuned to a definite pitch, a tuning fork of that pitch will cause the string to vibrate and assume the appearance of *A*, Fig. 7. If a series of forks of increasing frequency is applied, we shall find that the string will not now be set in motion until a fork of twice the original frequency is applied, when the string will appear as in *B*. The process can be repeated and it will be found that all the frequencies at which the string

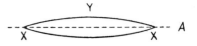

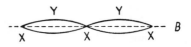

Fig. 7 Stretched string—fundamental and second harmonics

will vibrate are multiples of the primary number: 2, 3, 4 times etc. The amplitudes of the respective vibrating parts decrease as the frequency increases.

Correspondingly, if a set of strings mounted close to each other is tuned to the above frequency multiples, then when one is excited the remainder will also vibrate. It is to be observed that no other strings will vibrate; only the multiples described. Thus, apart from the fundamental, the following harmonics will appear—

2, 3, 4, 5, 6, 7, 8, and so on.

Now not all of these are concordant; if the fundamental is C^1, the seventh harmonic is $B\flat^3$, which is discordant in relation to the other harmonics. Fortunately, the strength of the upper harmonics decreases rapidly, but it is possible to eliminate this harmonic, which occupies only a very small length of the string, by bowing it at this point. This is a usual position for the hammer of a piano, the felt being made sufficiently wide to prevent the seventh from appearing, the practice being modified a little according to the maker's design; but it should be noted here that whilst this and certain other harmonics are objectionable in string tone, they are most essential to the production of many reed tones.

It has been assumed so far that energy has been continuously supplied to the string, so that the wave form is constant in amplitude. But if the string is struck or plucked once only, the energy is soon dissipated in overcoming the force tending to restore the wire to its position at rest and the vibrations are then said to be damped. Later it will be shown that electrical circuits can be made with similar characteristics, and this forms the basis of an important class of electronic musical instruments.

The points X in Fig. 7 are known as nodes and the points Y as loops. The middle point of a string is a node for all harmonics of even number and a loop for all odd harmonics; so if the string is struck in the middle, all even harmonics will be eliminated. If, however, the string is struck at a position one-third of its length, the even harmonics will be heard, but not the odd ones. Clearly, then, there is great control over the harmonic development obtainable from a string, and this can be used to produce tone colours ranging from clear, smooth and brilliant to nasal and hollow.

Here we are assuming a perfect string, with constant mass per unit length and quite rigid end-supports; in such a case, the fundamental frequency will be

$$f = \frac{1}{2l}\sqrt{\frac{T}{M}}$$

where T = tension in dynes,
   M = mass in grammes per unit length,
   l = length of string in centimetres.

In practice the exact harmonic development is somewhat modified, because the bow has a width comparable to the length of some of the upper harmonics and because the above considerations assume a perfectly flexible string.

Sound produced by wind instruments

Before describing how the harmonic content of a complex sound wave can be analysed (Chapter 5), we will examine the production of steady tones by means of wind instruments. All sounds of this nature are also characterized by harmonic development, but they are produced in a different way.

The commonest example is the familiar organ pipe. It is also an acoustic generator of a type in which we are very much interested. A column of air is capable of vibrating with the same frequency ratios as a stretched string. In organ-pipe construction the special conditions necessary to realize this state cannot easily be met, but if the pipe has a very small diameter compared with its length there is little loss; of course it is undesirable to produce this kind of tone from many organ pipes. There are many ways of altering the harmonic development of pipes by design, but at the

moment we are only concerned with the principles of pipe speech. The mechanism of flue organ-pipe tone production is based on the properties of edge tones, allied with suitable resonators to reinforce the required vibrations sufficiently.

If a stream of air strikes a sharp edge, as for instance the edge of a sheet of metal, small eddies are formed which occur at regular intervals and can give rise to a musical note. If the metal edge is arranged in association with a resonating tube of the correct length for the frequency, then we have a flue organ pipe as in Fig. 8.

The fundamental resonance of an open pipe is

$$f = \frac{C}{2l}$$

where l = length of pipe in centimetres,
   C = velocity of sound in centimetres per second.

The open pipe produces a series of even and odd harmonics, 1, 2, 3, 4 etc. The edge tones start vibrations of the air column in the pipe and if the pipe resonates truly there will rapidly be a large radiation of energy from the pipe itself. Once the column of air is in full vibration the amount of energy available will tend to draw the edge tone

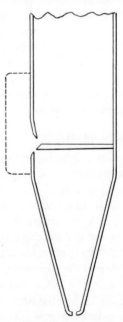

Fig. 8 Flue organ pipe

into resonance with the more powerful vibrator, as is the case with any coupled vibrating systems. It is a special characteristic of organ pipes that they are *pulse* generators, that is, the initial edge tones are a series of puffs.

This is not a treatise on pipe organs, and therefore no detailed description of the various means by which the characteristic tones are produced will be given. But there are one or two further observations of interest. The air, on admission to the pipe, will not at once build up to the full velocity. Thus for a brief interval we may hear edge tones of another frequency. This produces a 'starting tone', which is a characteristic of many organ pipes and which will assume differing degrees of importance with the speed of the passage being played.

Another important class of organ pipe is one which is stopped at the top end of the pipe. The distinguishing character of this class of pipe is the predominance given to odd harmonics. This follows because if the end of the pipe is stopped no air can move and so it must be a node; at the mouth a loop exists. The pipe will therefore sound harmonics of the order 3, 5, 7, 9 etc., as well as its fundamental.

The fundamental resonance of a stopped pipe is

$$f = \frac{C}{4l}$$

where the symbols have the same meaning as above.

There remains one other vibrating generator of interest to us—the reed. These are of two types and can be used in two ways. Firstly there is the free reed, in which a springy metal blade or tongue moves to and fro in a slotted block under the influence of wind (Fig. 9). On wind being admitted to the reed, the tongue is driven upwards until the elastic restoring force operates to return it against

the wind pressure. In doing this it attains momentum which causes it to overshoot its original position until this is expended, when once again the wind drives it upwards. The reed is tuned to a given resonant frequency and rapidly vibrates at that rate.

The natural frequency of a vibrating reed tongue is found from

$$f = \frac{1}{2\pi} \frac{x}{L^2} \sqrt{\frac{E}{\Delta(1 + 4 \cdot 1K)}}$$

where L = length of tongue in centimetres,
$\quad x$ = breadth of tongue in centimetres,
$\quad E$ = modulus of elasticity of material in dynes per square centimetre,
$\quad \Delta$ = density of material in grammes per square centimetre,
$\quad K$ = ratio of mass at end of tongue to mass of tongue itself.

In reed organs it is usual for the reeds to taper in width and thickness, and an extremely complicated formula is required to calculate their frequency. These shaping processes are an attempt to reduce the discordant harmonics or overtones. For electrical generators, parallel reeds are more satisfactory. Such reeds are used to a large extent in harmoniums and were also to be found in the Aeolian Orchestrelle instruments.

The moduli of elasticity for some suitable materials are

Aluminium	7×10^{11} (dynes/cm²)
Brass (average)	10×10^{11}
Phosphor bronze	12×10^{11}
Steel	19×10^{11}

Brass is the most frequently used material for reeds of the kind used in certain electronic generators. The composition of typical brasses is given here

Percentage Copper	Percentage Zinc	Tensile strength (tons/in.²)
90	10	17
60	40	25

Another mixture is iron 1·7 per cent, aluminium 0·4 per cent, lead 0·5 per cent; tensile strength = 27 dynes/cm².

Fig. 9 Free reed

Typical overtones for a free reed (clamped at one end) are

Number of Tone	Number of Nodes	Distance of Nodes from free end in terms of length of reed tongue	Frequencies as a ratio of the fundamental
1	0	—	f
2	1	0·2261	6·267f
3	2	0·1321, 0·4999	17·55f
4	3	0·0944, 0·3558, 0·6439	34·39f

These overtones are clearly not harmonic; the first has a higher frequency than the sixth harmonic.

All reeds are liable to alter their elasticity for some time until aged. Thereafter they settle down with repeated reversals of stress (when vibrating) in accordance with Fig. 10.

Reed tongues must be very carefully contoured; any abrupt change in section causes a serious reduction in the safe range of stress. The surface finish also has a decided effect on the fatigue range; the finer the surface, the greater the range. The *rate* at which reversals take place does not seem to have any effect on the fatigue range. Such 'free' reeds are used in harmoniums and American organs, and in spite of the apparently undesirable harmonic content, which of course cannot be controlled in these instruments and causes the acoustic output to assume a harsh and somewhat 'snarling' tone, there are some ways of using free reeds for electronic tone production which are highly effective. One commercial musical instrument employed wind-driven reeds (Chapter 7) and there are many experimental possibilities (Chapter 8).

In pipe organs the reed may be of the striking or beating type. Here the tongue cannot pass through the slot and strikes it at each half cycle. The striking reed produces a more biting and brilliant tone. In order to increase the strength of the fundamental tone, a resonating pipe is coupled to the reed chamber, so that the tone is clear and powerful.

Since many sounds produced by the pipe and electronic organ are imitative of some orchestral instruments, it will be interesting to look at the special features of the more important of these.

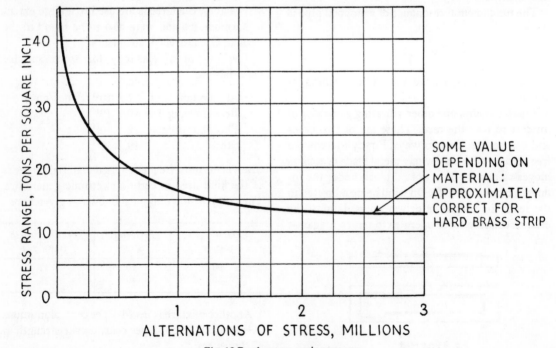

Fig. 10 Reed-tongue ageing process

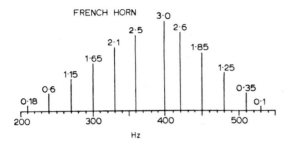

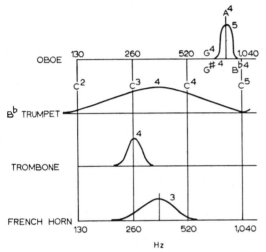

Fig. 11 Formants of some orchestral instruments. Those shown in the lower diagram are generalized; a more exact analysis for the French Horn is shown above, giving the component frequencies. The figures above indicate the relative amplitudes

The majority of the tonal differences in orchestral wind instruments of the same pitch range are due to the materials of which they are constructed. If an air column is set into vibration at its resonant fundamental frequency, owing to the increased rate of travel of sound waves through solids as compared with air, there will be a tendency for certain groups of harmonics to sound at a loudness level unrelated to the expected amplitude for their harmonic number. Such group reinforcement is known as a formant, and the interesting characteristic is that the fixed band of frequencies constituting this is substantially the same for all notes in the essential tonal range of the particular instrument. The formant group may not operate outside this range. By way of example, the formant band in a trumpet can be clearly heard if a soft mop is tightly inserted into the bell of the instrument;

most of the fundamentals are damped out, that is, the major resonances of the metal tube and the air column, but the formant group remains and can clearly be heard as a tone something like the familiar 'paper comb'.

This group reinforcement can be simulated by electrical means, and this enables us to reinforce the oscillations of certain electrical generators by formant circuits to produce similar accentuation, and is an essential feature of several instruments described in Chapter 7.

Fig. 11 shows the formants for certain instruments. As may be deduced, the magnitude of the formant increases with the complexity of the tone. The figures over the formant ranges give the intensity of the notes in the formant in relation to that of the fundamental. It is clear that this is a form of broad resonance, and it is a property of the utmost importance in tone-forming circuits of an electrical nature.

Special features of musical sounds

Now that the properties of acoustic generators of the kind that most concern us have been briefly considered, there are several special features of all musical sounds which raise peculiar problems when they have to be simulated electrically.

Most of the previous remarks in this chapter assume that a continuous tone is supplied. But this sound must be started. Since all vibrating bodies which generate harmonics must take time to start the full range of vibrations, there is often a starting tone which is quite characteristic. It is usually of very short duration and is often not completely audible, but in the case of certain sounds it is almost as important as the steady or running tone. Some instruments possessing this feature to such a marked extent as bells, gongs, tympani etc., are not within our province, but many organesque sounds are characterized by a distinct starting tone. Indeed eminent organists have found difficulty in positively identifying well-known pipe sounds when the starting tone has been suppressed.

Analysis by modern sound analysers suggests that there is quite a large inharmonic content in both the starting and running tones and it is furthermore quite possible that the edge tone of an organ flue pipe is reacted upon by the vibrations of the upper air column (at any rate under some conditions of voicing) so as to produce asymmetry in the supply of energy; this is not really surprising when one realizes that a flue pipe is not symmetrically open at all. One end is partially shaded by the mouth, and there is reflection from the languid, whilst the other end is subject to a length correction factor of from $0 \cdot 66$ to $0 \cdot 82r$, where r is the radius of the pipe. Thus the pipe becomes an unsymmetrical pulse generator, in which the pressure wave is started quickly but decays slowly. Under these conditions, which produce very strongly characterized tone colours, exact synthesis by electrical means is impossible, in spite of the expenditure of much ingenuity; the means by which some control of the start may be obtained are discussed in Chapters 7 and 8. The nearest we can approach is only an approximation, but it is better to concentrate on other more easily reproduced tone colours, to which, in the absence of the original, the ear will quickly adjust itself.

The effect of the absence of any starting tone is to give a general sense of smoothness to the sound, except in cases where the speed of attack is greater than the ear has been trained to accept (see Fig. 12).

Musical scales

This chapter may be concluded with a brief reference to musical scales, that is, the sequential arrangement of notes, and their relationship to other intervals in the scale, which is known as tuning.

A number of surveys of the historical development of the musical scale have been published, but the present-day equal temperament scale dates back to the sixteenth century, although it was not used here until less than a hundred years ago. In this scale the twelve semitones of the octave progress in the ratio $1:\sqrt[12]{2}$, a ratio of $1 \cdot 05946$. This gives an exactly equal division for every semitone, all of which are slightly imperfectly tuned in all keys. But the very small disparity is not in any way discordant and the ear is now trained to accept it. Nevertheless the accurate subdivision of intervals by violinists does occasionally cause some of their notes to sound sharper than those of the accompanying piano or orchestra, an effect which most of us have heard.

There are two other points of interest, the permissible degree of departure from this tuning, and pitch. It is essential that every octave be exactly in tune, but within the octave very slight departures from tune are permissible.

If the tuning is quite accurate, then the frequency ratios within the octave, on the basis of $C = 1$, are

$C = 1$	$E = 1 \cdot 2599$	$G\sharp = 1 \cdot 5874$
$C\sharp = 1 \cdot 05946$	$F = 1 \cdot 3348$	$A - 1 \cdot 6818$
$D = 1 \cdot 1225$	$F\sharp = 1 \cdot 4142$	$A\sharp - 1 \cdot 7818$
$D\sharp = 1 \cdot 1892$	$G = 1 \cdot 4983$	$B - 1 \cdot 8877$
		$C^1 - 2 \cdot 0000$

Experience has shown that fundamental frequency errors of the order of $0 \cdot 1$ per cent are just tolerable. This point is of great importance in the design of electronic instruments which do not have mechanically-coupled generators. The frequency error should, of course, be kept smaller, if possible, because of the possibility of forming beats (Chapter 4) with other notes; at the same time there are some who prefer the 'stretching' of fourths and fifths as practised by piano tuners. This is possible with independently-tuned note generators.

At one time there were many pitches to which instruments could be tuned, but from our point of view it is best to fix the tuning at $A = 440$ Hz ($C = 523 \cdot 251$) as this is now the standard international pitch.

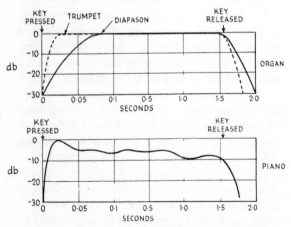

Fig. 12 Average rate of attack and decay of sound in pipe organs and grand piano

The frequencies of other significant harmonics which will be required for understanding tonal synthesis are given in the table below. Further reference will be made to this later on.

Harmonic Deviation Table

Fundamental A = 55 Hz

Harmonic	Natural Frequency	Nearest Note E.T.S.	Frequency E.T.S.	Deviation Hz	Percentage Error
1	55	A^1	55	0	0
2	110	A^2	110	0	0
3	165	E^3	164·81	− 0·19	0·115
4	220	A^3	220	0	0
5	275	$C\sharp^4$	277·18	+ 2·18	0·79
6	330	E^4	329·63	− 0·37	0·112
7	385	G^4	392	+ 7	1·820
8	440	A^4	440	0	0
9	495	B^4	493·88	− 1·12	0·23
10	550	$C\sharp^5$	554·37	+ 4·37	0·795
11	605	$D\sharp^5$	622·25	+ 17·75	2·85
12	660	E^5	659·26	− 0·74	0·112
13	715	F^5	698·46	− 16·54	2·320
14	770	G^5	783·99	+ 13·99	1·820
15	825	$G\sharp^5$	830·61	+ 5·61	0·680
16	880	A^5	880	0	0
17	935	$A\sharp^5$	932·33	− 2·67	0·286
18	990	B^5	987·77	− 2·23	0·226
19	1045	C^6	1046·50	+ 1·50	0·147
20	1100	$C\sharp^6$	1108·73	+ 8·73	0·793
21	1155	D^6	1174·66	+ 19·66	1·700
22	1210	$D\sharp^6$	1244·51	+ 34·51	2·850
23	1265	$D\sharp^6$	1244·51	− 20·49	1·620
24	1320	E^6	1318·51	− 1·49	0·113
25	1375	F^6	1396·91	+ 21·91	1·59
26	1430	F^6	1396·91	− 33·09	2·31
27	1485	$F\sharp^6$	1479·98	− 5·02	0·338
28	1540	G^6	1567·98	+ 27·98	1·815
29	1595	G^6	1567·98	− 27·02	1·69
30	1650	$G\sharp^6$	1661·22	+ 11·22	0·681
31	1705	$G\sharp^6$	1661·22	− 33·78	1·980
32	1760	A^6	1760	0	0

3 Conventional Multinote Instruments

In order properly to appreciate the principles involved in designing electronic instruments, we should bear in mind that such instruments are imitative in nearly all cases. Where a direct simulation of known musical sounds is not attempted, some other reason for electrical conversion will be apparent: a change in the loudness or dynamic range, or the production of a purely melodic (i.e. single note at a time) instrument. Melodic instruments fall into a class of their own, and are dealt with separately in Chapters 7 and 8.

By far the greatest appeal of the electronic instrument lies in the class of instrument using playing keys of normal design, e.g. the pianoforte and organ. Other keyboard instruments, such as the harpsichord, have also been simulated. The appeal lies not only in the extended measure of control and expression, as compared with melodic instruments, but also in the fact that they are much more satisfactory to manipulate.

Construction of the piano

As it is desirable briefly to detail the main functions of the piano and organ, let us look at the construction of a piano. All such instruments operate in the same way, by the impact of a hammer on a single or multiple wire. Many ingenious mechanisms have been evolved to enable the hammer to develop sufficient force with a small pressure on the key, and to regulate the speed of movement of the hammer. The essential feature of all striking mechanisms is that however the key is manipulated, the hammer can only momentarily strike the wires and cannot remain in contact with them; otherwise the vibrations would be rapidly damped out. The wires are stretched over a metal frame of great rigidity, and at one point pass over a wooden bar known as the bridge. This enables the vibrations of the string to pass to the wooden soundboard, which is large in area and thus effectively couples the vibrating string to the air, for without it no sound from the strings would be audible. The large area of the soundboard can set a quantity of air in motion and the sound is thus made audible. The whole of the soundboard must vibrate in phase, and for this reason is frequently made from Norway spruce; in this wood sound travels at a speed of 16 000 ft/s and therefore the time taken for any frequency to be radiated is infinitesimal.

Since, as we know, a great increase in energy is required to radiate low notes, the soundboard will increase in size towards the bass end and may attain very considerable proportions in a large grand piano. Such an instrument is necessary in a concert hall where the bass notes must travel a long way with as little loss of energy as possible. The small amount of energy lost by absorption in the material of the soundboard can be reduced by heavily varnishing the wood so as to increase its reflecting power.

Now the form of the vibrations in a piano is very interesting; there is no other instrument quite like it, and it cannot be exactly simulated by electrical means. The principal reason for this is the very strong characteristic starting tone which is almost of a transient nature, having a very steep front containing many frequencies (Fig. 13). Immediately after the wires are struck they vibrate in phase, but soon they vibrate in opposition, because perfect tuning is impossible. But this cannot account for the transients, because there are no frequency components of sufficiently high pitch. The typical piano starting transient is due to a rotational displacement of the bridge on applying a torsional stress to the wire (Fig. 14). This movement dies down almost instantly, but is the principal factor in producing the characteristic attack of the piano.

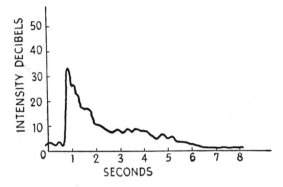

Fig. 13 Form of piano wave

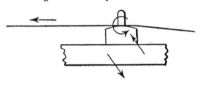

Fig. 14 Rotational movement of bridge

It is essential to retain the order in which the vibrations of the strings are related to the starting tone if the sound is to be like a piano. The same combination of fundamentals and harmonics may be present if Fig. 13 is reversed, but the sound will not be the same because the attack has disappeared; the wave form if reproduced the wrong way round (e.g. a gramophone record of a piano played backwards) will sound more like an organ although the composition of the wave form is the same. This suggests that electrical methods might be used to produce new tones from stringed instruments, and that is the case (see Chapter 7).

The characteristics outlined above apply to notes of all pitches and it will be clear that to synthesize piano tone electrically is extremely difficult. This is borne out in practice, the difference in the rates of attack and decay of electronic pianos proving particularly confusing to a professional. But some new sounds of considerable attraction and following a very similar sequence of initiation and decay may be produced by suitable electrical circuits (see Chapter 7).

Construction of the organ

The organ is essentially, and by contrast, a sustained-tone instrument. It is not touch-responsive like the piano, and variations in loudness can be obtained only by altering the number of pipes or reeds in use, or by enclosing them in a chamber fitted with movable apertures. Again by contrast, the sound continues as long as the keys are held down, and does not die away as in the piano. The power to produce this energy comes from the apparatus supplying the wind, and for continuous sound we must provide continuous energy. The organ is probably the most popular instrument for simulation by electrical means, and since it is desirable that the design of any such electronic instrument should enable conventional organ-playing technique to be used a condensed description of the pipe organ is given.

Organs possess one or more keyboards, each having a compass of five octaves, and generally a pedal keyboard of thirty or thirty-two notes. Each clavier (pedal or keyboard) is provided with an associated range of sets of pipes. These are conventionally known as stops, because when the appropriate control device is put 'off', it stops the wind from entering the pipes.

The sets of pipes are designed to produce different tone colours, which fall into general groups of the flute, diapason, string and reed classes. For any group the pitch range may vary very considerably. Normal pitch is known as 8 ft, because that is the length of an open pipe necessary to produce CC in that pitch. Thus, pipes of, say, fluty character may have pitches of 16, 8, 4 and 2 ft. The effect of playing these all together is obviously the extension of the normal pitch of 8 ft, downwards one and upwards two octaves.

Some or all of the pipes may be enclosed in sound-constraining chambers known as swell boxes (because the sound 'swells out' when the shutters with which these chambers are fitted are opened) and in addition there are usually means for mechanically coupling the various claviers together. There is frequently a mechanism associated with some of the sets of pipes which causes a cyclic change in wind pressure, thus producing an undulating or vibrato effect. Since some of the sets of pipes are rather lacking in harmonic development, but produce a bold and full foundation tone, it is usual to provide special sets which supply the missing harmonics.

It is obvious that an infinite variety of sound

combinations may be obtained according to the size and complexity of the organ, but for reasons to be examined later it is not yet possible to obtain such a wide range of tonal effects from electrical generators. We can, however, go a long way, and the foregoing notes are merely to indicate the conventional arrangement for the benefit of those not acquainted with the constitution of an organ. Fig. 15 shows a cross-section of a normal organ console. There are broadly accepted standards for some parts, whilst there is a great deal of latitude for others. For example, a legitimate organ always has keyboards of 61 notes compass, or five octaves; but many electronic makes have keyboards from 37 notes upwards. Obviously this will prevent the proper interpretation of standard pipe-organ works, but will not matter much for popular or rhythmic music where, in any case, registration (or the proper choice of stops) can rarely be attained.

We often find abbreviated pedalboards with only 13 notes, C to C. This is useful for an elementary bass but prevents correct pedalling technique, and even for popular tunes it is a retrograde step, for in any other key than C it is practically impossible to provide a proper bass line.

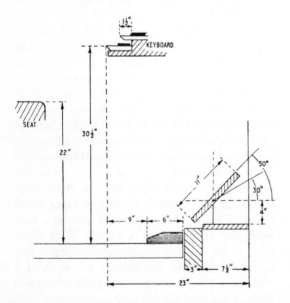

Fig. 15 Recommended console layout (mid C of pedals under mid C of manuals)

The correct balance of the body is most important for comfort, and this is different for two, three or four manual consoles. Since the amateur is generally interested in two manuals, we show preferred dimensions for the major part of this.

Naturally, space is at a premium with electronic instruments, whereas the console is usually remote from the organ proper where pipes are used; but this is no excuse for cutting down the proportions to the extent sometimes encountered. Transistorization enables the whole generator to be mounted in a minute space; but is this of any import at all? There must be minimum dimensions for the case, and these cannot be less than 52 in. long, 43 in. high and 20 in. deep. So there is ample space for either valve or transistor generators and, in fact, the servicing requirements are much better met in a large console.

Electronic organs are frequently full of strange mechanisms; not all of these can be bought, but all parts of standard organ consoles can be; so the prospective constructor is strongly advised to stick to the measurements which have proved so successful for so many years, as far as possible.

One or two points may be noted which are of assistance when the design of electronic instruments is considered. The ear is comparatively insensitive to the harmonic content of very low notes, unless there are very powerful harmonics. The pitch is the principal criterion, and it is therefore fairly simple to design a satisfactory generator for low pitches.

Equally, the harmonic development of complex tones such as reeds and strings need not be fully carried out at the upper end of the scale since, in general, significant harmonics will be above the normal limit of audibility; indeed it is customary to make the upper octave or so of organ reed pipes from ordinary open flue pipes of small scale, which completely satisfy the ear. Thus there can be an economic limit to the number of electrical generators employed.

The harmonic content plotted against intensity is illustrated in Fig. 16 for several characteristic organ tone colours. Further examples will be found in the next chapter. Very much simpler harmonic structures suffice for more elementary organs, in particular those intended for domestic use.

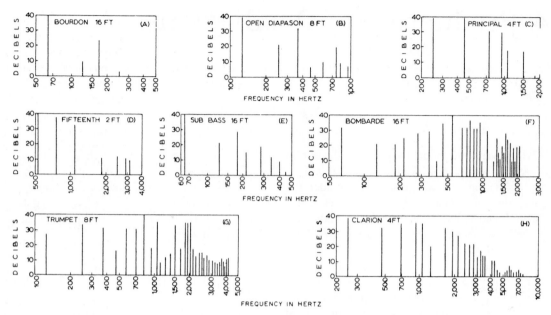

Fig. 16 Harmonic content for several characteristic organ-tone colours plotted against intensity

4 Production of Oscillations

Having given some thought to the general question of sound waves produced by mechanical or physical vibrations, we must now consider the production of similar wave forms by electrical means. It can be stated generally that it is quite immaterial whether the vibrations are caused by a mechanical force or by an electrical means: provided that they have the required shape or contour it is only necessary to find a means of converting them into air-pressure waves of the same form, for the same ultimate sound to be radiated to the ear.

Thus if it is more convenient for a simple wave such as that of the tuning fork to be manufactured by some form of electrical circuit, if the electrical oscillations can be converted into corresponding air-pressure waves the resultant sound heard will be identical with that of the tuning fork.

The nature of oscillations

Before we proceed to the possible methods of producing the oscillations, which for our purpose may be understood to be the same as vibrations (as in the case of all electrical generators they are of very small amplitude), we must see how the complex final series of oscillations which represents the complete tone colour is constituted. We know that they are complex and not simple waves because they have the characteristic quality of timbre. This must include some harmonic content. The work of Helmholtz and Fourier has proved that any wave form, no matter how complex, may be resolved into its individual frequency components by mathematical means. Not only the frequencies but their amplitudes can be calculated.

We shall not explore the rather complex mathematics of the method but shall content ourselves with a simple explanation and one or two examples. The pitch of the fundamental wave fixes the period of time within which all other waves must be present. Fig. 17 represents a simple sine wave as might be produced from a tuning fork. Now a sine wave is the simplest form of regularly-recurring wave movement, and represents simple harmonic motion.

Imagine a particle of elastic matter to be at rest at some point on a straight horizontal line. Then if it is moved along this line, there is a force due to elasticity which tends to restore it to the starting position. This force is directly proportional to the amount of displacement, so that if the particle is now released it will vibrate to and fro along the line with *simple harmonic motion*. Note that the vibrations repeat regularly, and that it rests for a moment at each reversal of movement. The particle also accelerates towards the central position, and slows down towards the points of reversal.

If the harmonic motion is that produced by, say, a swinging pendulum, and this draws a line on a sheet of paper travelling at right angles to the direction of swing at a uniform speed, then the trace is drawn out into a simple harmonic or sine curve. Since the time axis is constant, this is the form in which the vibratory conditions of any sound or electric wave are denoted, conveniently, for the purpose of analysis or synthesis (see Fig. 17).

The *amplitude* is the height of a peak from the

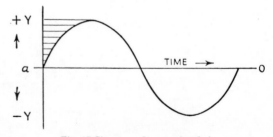

Fig. 17 Sine wave from tuning fork

20

axis; the *period* is the time for one complete curve; the *frequency* is the number of complete curves per unit time (always taken, for this class of wave, as seconds). The *velocity* is the wavelength times the number of waves per second.

The energy, or intensity, of a sine wave varies as the square of the amplitude, with constant frequency; and as the square of the frequency with constant amplitude. If both amplitude and frequency vary, the intensity varies as the square of the product of amplitude and frequency, i.e.

$$I = f^2 a^2$$

The phase of a sine wave is the fraction of a period (one complete vibration) which has elapsed since the point last passed through its starting position (in a positive direction).

Whilst one often sees a complete wave form drawn to illustrate the composition of some complex sound, an analysis of a number of such cycles shows that in fact the different frequency components are not necessarily in the same phase; for example in Fig. 29 (page 25), if the fundamental wave (1) is examined, it will be seen to have started before the vertical line *D* which forms one of the boundaries for analysis. One complete wavelength equals 360°, and in this case the fundamental has already travelled through 76° of the 360° before it meets the boundary *D*. Its phase is therefore 76°.

Thus the correct position for the start of the fundamental, that is, where it crosses the time axis, is 76/360 of its wavelength which, being measured from crest to crest, is to the left of the line *A*. The phases of the other harmonics can be found in the same way, remembering that each one must be measured in terms of its own wavelength.

The ability to compound similar curves of waves of this nature greatly simplifies harmonic analysis.

It is desirable to understand the significance of the above quantities.

We can now revert to the simple wave from the tuning fork shown in Fig. 17, and so to the further elementary examples.

One complete cycle of operations extends from *a* to *o*. Within this distance must lie any harmonics which may be present in one cycle of a complex sound wave. The effect of adding another simple wave one octave higher (second harmonic) is

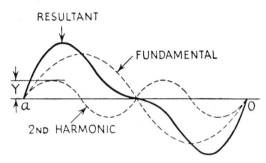

Fig. 18 Addition of second harmonic

shown in Fig. 18. This wave is given an intensity or amplitude *Y*. The original wave, now shown dotted, is changed in shape because of this addition and will assume the appearance of the heavy line. Note that the contours of the sides and the top have altered. The complete wave is no longer symmetrical along the time base *ao*; if it were, i.e. if it contained exactly similar positive and negative loops, it could not contain even harmonics. The addition of the second harmonic has caused the centre of the wave to move slightly to the left, because this is the middle of a loop at second harmonic frequency.

Let us now see what happens if we add a third harmonic only to the sine wave. The effect of this is shown in Fig. 19 from which it can be seen that the composite wave is now symmetrical in each half, and clearly this is because the third harmonic has a node at this point on the time base instead of a loop. The further effect of adding a fifth harmonic can be seen in Fig. 20.

If now we take a case where the frequency difference is much greater, and extend it to cover a series of waves, we can see the effect more clearly.

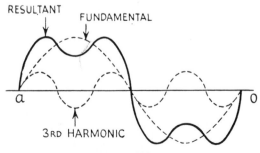

Fig. 19 Addition of third harmonic

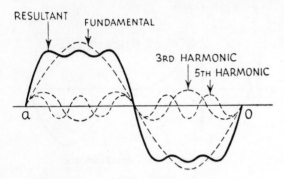

Fig. 20 Addition of fifth harmonic

wave is exceedingly useful in musical synthesis, as all 'hollow' sounding tones consist principally of odd harmonics. Several circuits for producing such wave forms either directly or from some other kind of wave are shown later in this chapter. The harmonic intensity of a symmetrical square wave is shown in Fig. 23. If the square wave is not symmetrical on the time axis, i.e. if it is off for longer than it is on, the harmonic content alters. An example is given in the table showing amplitudes for two rectangular waves. Note the difference in the harmonic content.

Fig. 21 shows the composite wave form resulting from the addition of a fundamental frequency and another frequency of ratio $6\frac{1}{4}$ to 1. This is not a particularly musical sound.

It has previously been stated that the very rapid steeply fronted characteristic of a transient sound contains a wide band of frequencies. Such a wave form, if sustained for a time, might be represented by Fig. 22. When the form shown is symmetrically repeated, this is known as a square wave. Its special property is that it contains only *odd* harmonics in addition to the fundamental. The square

A special case is shown in Fig. 24. If the midpoint of a string is stretched we obtain a 'curve' with approximately straight sides. Nevertheless

Harmonic Amplitudes for Two Rectangular Wave Forms

Order of Harmonic	Pulse Width	
	A 10/90	B 50/50
1	0·197	0·637
2	0·187	0
3	0·172	− 0·213
4	0·150	0
5	0·127	0·127
6	0·101	0
7	0·073	− 0·09
8	0·046	0
9	0·021	0·07
10	0	0
11	− 0·017	− 0·057
12	− 0·031	0
13	− 0·039	0·049
14	− 0·043	0
15	− 0·042	− 0·04
16	− 0·037	0
17	− 0·03	0·037
18	− 0·02	0
19	− 0·01	− 0·03
20	0	0
21	0·009	0·03
22	0·017	0
23	0·02	− 0·027
24	0·025	0
25	0·025	0·025
26	0·023	0
27	0·019	− 0·02
28	0·013	0
29	0·006	0·02
30	0	0

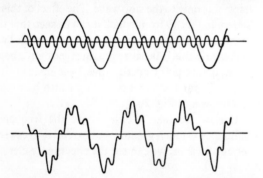

Fig. 21 Addition of two waves of widely differing frequencies

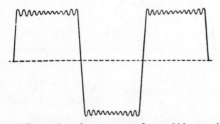

Fig. 22 Formation of square wave from odd harmonics

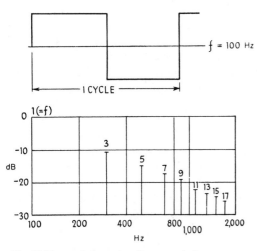

Fig. 23 Harmonic intensity of symmetrical square wave

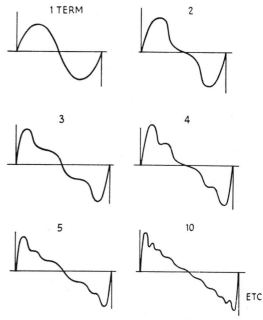

Fig. 25 Formation of a sawtooth wave

this can be resolved into its constituent harmonics and the analysis is shown in the figure. The height of the wave crests is exaggerated for clearness. As we have already seen, if the vibrations are such as to be exactly similar in each half, no even harmonics can be present.

Another wave form of great value in electrical tone synthesis is the triangular wave known as the sawtooth; in fact it might be said that the successful imitation of orchestral tone colours demands both square and sawtooth wave forms, as well as sine waves.

The sawtooth contains both odd and even harmonics, and if suitably generated, those up to at least the thirtieth will be usable; and what is more important, each harmonic will be at the correct amplitude in relation to all other harmonics in the complete wave.

The analysis of a sawtooth from its individual sinusoidal components is shown in Fig. 25, and the harmonic intensity is plotted in Fig. 26.

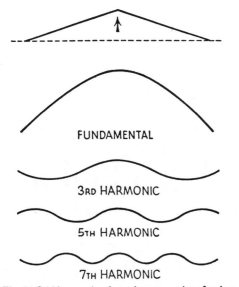

Fig. 24 Odd harmonics through centre point of string

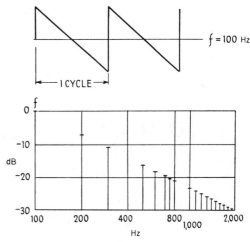

Fig. 26 Harmonic intensity of sawtooth wave

Note that although the triangular wave depicted by the stretched string in Fig. 24 looks like a double sawtooth, it cannot be interchanged as it contains only odd harmonics.

In order to show the results of harmonic análysis in terms of the relative intensities of the individual harmonics, these should be plotted on a logarithmic scale. Such a scale is one where the distances between the ordinates (vertical lines) are in proportion to the ratios of the frequencies.

An ingenious method of doing this is due to the late Prof. D. C. Miller. In Fig. 27 the vertical lines correspond to the notes on a piano keyboard. All such notes are logarithmically related. The different pitches are thus obvious at a glance.

Taking a horizontal strip of card, vertical lines ·e drawn on this to correspond with the fundamental and, say, thirty harmonics. This is drawn in one key only, when the relationship will be found to hold for any other key.

By then providing a wave form drawn to the correct size, and placing this on the chart so that the fundamental lies on the correct vertical pitch line, the other vertical rulings on the horizontal scale,

when projected on to the vertical scale, at once give the correct frequencies for the other harmonic components of the wave form.

The vertical height indicates the relative intensity of that particular harmonic.

As an example, the organ-pipe wave form in Fig. 29 is shown plotted in Fig. 27. It will be realized that this is the composition and energy distribution for one note only; other notes throughout the compass will probably have quite different energy contents, which at once suggests the difficulty in synthesizing tones electrically by any fixed or non-adjustable system of filters or formant circuits operating over a range of notes. Notice, for instance, the differences in energy distribution for notes played at different strengths on the same instrument (Fig. 28).

Numbers of other examples of organ tones are given in the appropriate figures (Figs. 29, 30, 31 and 32), and from the foregoing examples, taken in conjunction with Fig. 16 in Chapter 3, the requirements for synthesis of most musical sounds can readily be understood.

Two points should be noted in the foregoing

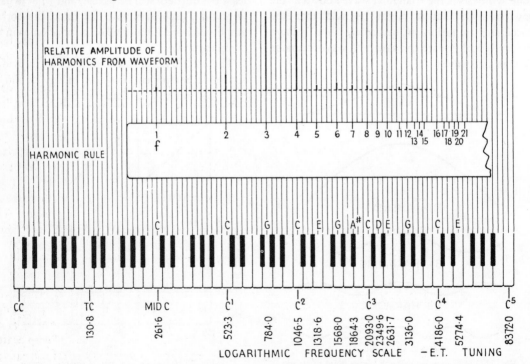

Fig. 27 Method of plotting harmonic content

examples. The *individual waves* which are used to compound the mixed wave form must in themselves be perfectly pure waves. The *proportions* of fundamental and other harmonics may vary over wide limits, since the amplitude as well as the number of the waves greatly influences the character of the final tone. This can clearly be seen from Fig. 16 where the amplitudes of the components are plotted in such a way as to indicate the relative intensities very easily.

Note that experiments in compounding complex waves cannot be tried on a piano, because the wave form of each note is complex and changing; this quite prevents the proper relationships being obtained.

Now there is another very important characteristic of related waves, which applies to electrical

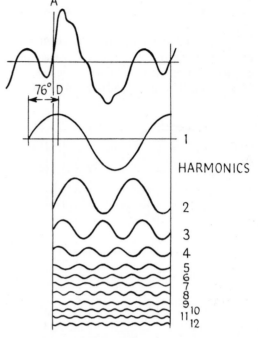

Fig. 29 Analysis of organ reed pipe tone

tone generation as well as to acoustic means. It is the effect due to oscillations sounding simultaneously and of nearly, but not quite, the same pitch. If two such notes sound together, the one of higher pitch will complete a cycle of operations before the lower pitched one. In the course of a number of such cycles there must be moments when the two vibrations travel in the same direction at the same instant, when they travel in different directions, and so on, at regular intervals. This will cause the respective frequencies to add at one time, be equal at another, and be in opposition to each other at yet another instant.

This gives rise to an undulating sound of frequency equal to the degree of difference, and known as a beat. The frequency of the beats is

$$f = n_1 - n_2$$

where n_1 and n_2 are the two beating frequencies.

Fig. 33 shows the appearance of two vibrations of 8 and 9 per second, forming a beat tone as at *a* and *b*, and practically cancelling at *c*. These beats are very important because their effect can range from pleasing to interfering. It is a general rule that

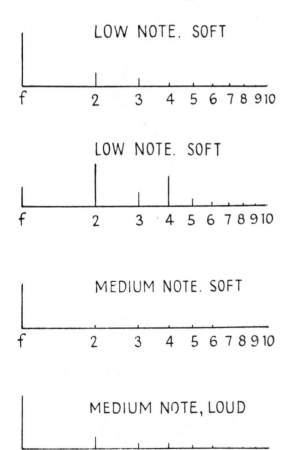

Fig. 28 Analysis of flute tone

beats sound displeasing when the number is comparable with the frequency of the fundamental tone.

Beat tones do, in fact, contribute much more to music than is generally realized. For example, the ear detects a fundamental tone in the lower notes of a violin. The real fundamental is extremely weak, because it lies below the fundamental resonance of the violin body, and any sound output lower in pitch than the resonance is very small. Adjacent, strong, upper harmonics produce the beat tone which sounds to the ear like the actual fundamental or pitch note of the sound being produced.

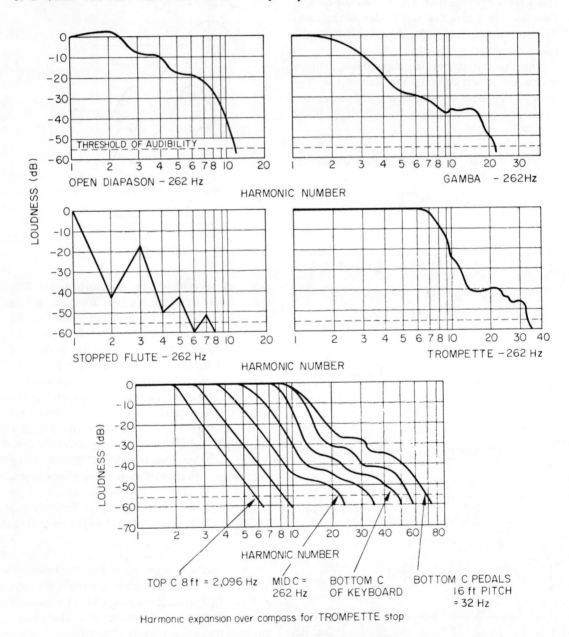

Fig. 30 Further examples of harmonic analysis

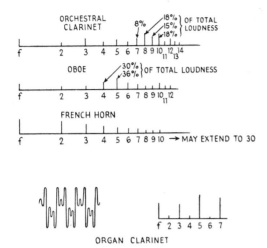

Fig. 31 Analyses of imitative tone colours

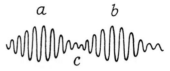

Fig. 33 Formation of beats

Beats are commonly introduced into an otherwise steady tone to form a vibrato or tremulant. Such beats are very slow; the frequency difference being great, the separate pulsations modulate the main tone as an easily distinguishable wavering of the tone and are an essential ingredient of vocal music. If, on the other hand, a means is provided for injecting a beat tone into each separate tone of a frequency bearing some fixed relation to each note, then the effect is much more subtle and rich; this is found in the pipe

organ in the double rank of pipes known as a *celeste*. It also obtains in the orchestra, where players of instruments covering a limited pitch range each introduce a vibrato of their own choosing at rates related to the range of notes of the particular instrument they are playing, e.g. the vibrato rate of a violin is faster than that of a violoncello; the combination of these many main tones so modulated is responsible for the extraordinary richness of a string orchestra, and the effect can be produced electrically as described on page 143.

If one of the sound sources is much more powerful than the other, this one may tend to pull the other into step and cause a note of nearly equal frequency to be heard. This is yet another form of interference which, together with the destructive interference mentioned in Chapter 1, makes it necessary for the organ builder to position his pipes very carefully.

These remarks indicate that design of electrical oscillation generators must be very carefully carried out to prevent the formation of beats.

Producing electrical oscillations

Having established that complex vibrations can be formed by combining simple vibrations (which as stated must all independently be pure sinusoidal vibrations), we can examine the several satisfactory means by which such vibrations can be generated. When electrical methods are employed the vibrations are called oscillations.

Now there is an infinite variety of ways by which electrical oscillations can be produced. Indeed the possibilities are endless, but there are several important limiting factors. The principal one is cost; the next, complexity; we must first of all find out what is required of the generators. These functions vary with the class of instrument, but we can place them in three distinct classes—

1. Generators in which pure sinusoidal waves are produced.

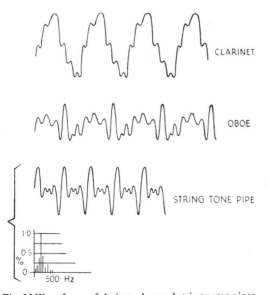

Fig. 32 Wave forms of clarinet, oboe and string organ pipes

2. Generators in which some harmonic content is designedly present.

3. Generators which mechanically determine the initial wave form, such as struck strings or wires.

It is rather difficult properly to subdivide the relative types, as in some cases they may perform dual functions. However, we can define them broadly according to whether the composite final waves are formed in the generator or by a subsequent circuit arrangement. The few really suitable generators can be extracted from the very many possible methods and segregated into four main types—

1. Those using oscillating valves, gas tubes, or semiconductors.

2. Those using rotating or vibrating electromagnetic systems, for which a mechanical driving source is required.

3. Those conforming to the second type, but operating by electrostatic means.

4. Those conforming to the second type, but operated by photoelectric means.

Valve and transistor oscillators

Since the first edition of this book was published, many far-reaching developments in the design of oscillators for music generators have taken place and since the last edition, the transistor has largely replaced the valve. But since the circuit principles are the same for valves and transistors, the same simple explanation will serve for both methods. It is hardly possible to separate the elements into valve and transistor, so in this introduction both methods are mixed up; but later on, we deal with transistors in much greater detail. Let us first look at valve and gas tube circuits.

An oscillator for our purpose is just a means of producing an alternating current from a d.c. supply. At this time it is necessary to decide on a particular circuit configuration, because there are many ways in which the same principle can be applied but each requires explanation; it has been decided to use what is the most popular configuration for music sources, the *LC* Hartley circuit (Fig. 34). We may, reasonably enough, be sure that when J. V. L. Hartley invented this circuit in 1917, he had no thought of music in his mind!

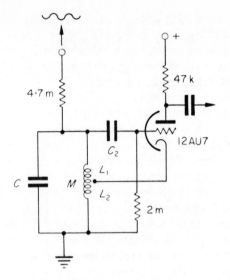

Fig. 34 Basic *AF* Hartley oscillator

All such oscillators split into two parts: the inductance L with its tuning capacitor C, forming the resonant or tank circuit; and the active element, a valve (or transistor), forming the maintaining or driving amplifier. On switching on, a pulse of current will be applied to L and C, and since these are connected in parallel, this current will divide equally between the L and the C; therefore, their reactances must be equal, i.e. $2\pi fL = 1/2\pi fC$. By re-arrangement we get the well-known formula for resonance—

$$f_r = 1/2\pi \sqrt{(LC)}$$

where $f_r =$ frequency of oscillation.

Left to itself then, and supposing that neither L or C had any resistance, the current would alternate between flowing through the coil, reversing in sign and charging C; then again discharging into L and so on for ever, at the frequency fixed by the formula above. Of course this condition cannot exist, there must be electrical resistance in the circuit or the oscillations would soon die out. The rate at which this takes place is governed by the 'goodness' of the coil, that is, the reactance divided by the resistance, and is called Q. The voltage across any generator supplying this coil will be increased by Q times. Therefore the better the Q value, the less loss there will be in the oscillatory circuit and the smaller the current required from the maintaining amplifier to overcome the circuit loss and keep it oscillating. A high Q is obtained by using a low-resistance wire and a high permeability core; and we can say that if the Q is less than1, the circuit cannot oscillate. Between 10 and 100 are preferred values.

The duty of the amplifier is to give a small 'kick' as it were to the oscillatory circuit at the correct time to revitalize the tuned circuit and maintain oscillations. This it can do if it has a gain greater than 1 and the input and output circuits are in the correct phase relationship to ensure positive feedback. This will make the amplifier oscillate. In the Hartley circuit shown, phase reversal is brought about by the coil centre tap, like the centre tap on a push–pull output transformer for an audio amplifier. If the coil is wound in the same direction for the two sections, it is impossible to connect it wrongly. One might suppose that once the amplifier started to oscillate, it would continue to build up indefinitely, but this is not so because there is always some non-linear characteristic of the active device which acts as a limiter. Of course, the anode or collector current of the device may be distorted, but it is interesting to note that the current in the actual oscillator coil will still be sinusoidal—unless the circuit is deliberately driven into a heavily overloaded state; one can therefore obtain a good sine wave from the top of the tank circuit, as used in another book by the same author for a home-constructed organ. This saves filtering, for in fact the wave is not absolutely pure but contains minute traces of higher even harmonics which brighten the tone.

The ratio of the two parts of the coil L_1 and L_2 makes no difference to the frequency, the net inductance being $L_1 + L_2 + M$, M being the mutual inductance; but since it affects the feedback, it will have an influence on maintenance conditions; the tap can then be set to give the best degree of coupling without upsetting the frequency. With valves, this would result in a 50 : 50 turns ratio; with transistors, possibly 25 to 30 per cent of turns in the emitter-base section would be more satisfactory. The blocking capacitor C_2 is to allow a.c. to circulate, but to prevent d.c. short-circuits.

This capacitor, called the grid capacitor, plays an important part in the function of the circuit. If it is too large, it will not be able to discharge quickly enough in a cycle of oscillations, and may eventually make the grid so negative that oscillations stop for a time until the charge drains off; thus the proper frequency of oscillation will be interrupted cyclically, causing 'squegging' or clicking and making the circuit useless for music purposes. If the capacitor is too small, the grid may never reach a stable potential, and the frequency can wander; so for each frequency there is, in theory, an exact optimum value of capacitor (and resistor to earth; for it is the total time constant of these elements which determines the amount of grid potential). In practice, one set of values will easily cover one octave of frequencies in the audible range.

But if the amplifier can be so connected that it can oscillate, then the actual form of the frequency-determining circuit need not be LC. Anything which causes the correct phase difference by feedback could be used, so it is possible to use resistors. At the very low frequencies required for vibrato (5–8 Hz), inductances would be very bulky and costly, so the multi-section RC oscillator is commonly used and has become almost standard for simple electronic vibratos. Such a configuration is called a phase-shift circuit (Fig. 35). Several sections have to be employed to get enough phase shift and there is attenuation due to the resistors, consequently a gain of at least 29 is required. The

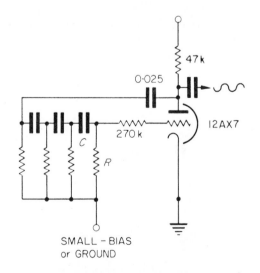

Fig. 35 Basic phase-shift RC oscillator

calculations are tedious but the formula for the oscillation frequency, if all R's and all C's are equal, is

$$f = \frac{1}{2\pi\sqrt{(6RC)}}$$

Such oscillators are not stable enough for tone generators, but the exact vibrato frequency is not critical; indeed, it may be an aesthetic advantage if it is slightly variable. We therefore have these two classes of oscillator, with very different duties in an electronic musical instrument.

An experimental phase-shift oscillator in which only one element need be varied is described in Chapter 8.

To obtain a sine wave, the gain should be just sufficient to maintain oscillation; for example, an electronic vibrato requires that the wave should be symmetrical at each reversal of sign, or harmonic components will be introduced into the signal, causing cross-modulation and an objectionable form of distortion.

It is also dangerous to impose any load on such an oscillator, therefore it should be followed by another valve acting as a buffer or separator stage; this is added on from the oscillator anode as in Fig. 36. Sine waves can of course be produced from many complex waves by sufficient filtering and this system is used in some commercial organs.

Closely allied to the phase-shift oscillator is the parallel T or twin-T circuit. Possibly the original application was by Wien in his well-known bridge circuit, but simplified versions have been used with limited degrees of success in the days of germanium transistors; however, now that silicon

planar transistors are cheap and metal film resistors are getting that way, there are distinct possibilities for the twin-T oscillator. It is cheap and light in weight and both these considerations weigh heavily with the amateur constructor.

Basically the circuit consists of a transistor with two balanced RC bridges connected in parallel between the collector and the base. Each bridge is designed to give 180° phase shift, and one is a high-pass filter whilst the other is a low-pass one (see page 68). The essential circuit elements are shown in Fig. 37 and a table of values for the range of organ frequencies is given on page 31. It is important that the transistor used should have a high gain, about 100 minimum; and the buffer stage should also have a good gain. An interesting point is that the higher the oscillation frequency, the greater must the gain be. Signals may be taken off at several points, but are best removed as shown from the buffer collector load.

A modification of this circuit from which two different wave forms can be extracted without altering the frequency is given in Fig. 38. Note the extra circuit elements to allow of this and the shapes thereby obtained. The transistor here should be of even higher gain, about 200. As the reader can see, we are now beginning to think of

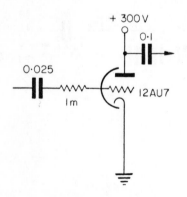

Fig. 36 Buffer stage for Fig. 35

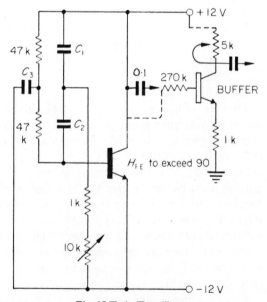

Fig. 37 Twin-T oscillator

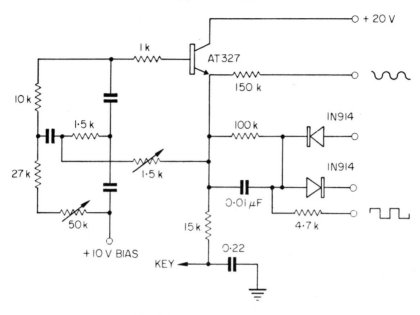

Fig. 38 Improved twin-T oscillator

wave shapes other than sine, and this leads us to the main types of oscillator in use today; for the number of strictly sine organs is very limited, for reasons which we will try to explain as the problems are approached.

Frequency (Hz)	$C_1 C_2$	C_3
27–70	$0.1 \mu F$	$0.5 \mu F$
42–111	0.05	0.5
69–150	0.05	0.25
110–220	0.02	0.25
133–330	0.02	0.1
250–390	0.01	0.1
390–700	0.01	0.05
680–1,600	0.005	0.01
1,250–2,600	0.0033	0.005
2,000–4,300	0.0015	0.005
3,700–5,000	680p	3900p
4,500–7,100	680	2000
7,000–10,000	470	1000

Sawtooth-wave-form generators

As we know, because all known musical sounds consist of a number of independent sine waves put together in various ways, if circuits can be found which in themselves generate harmonically rich wave forms, it may be more convenient or economical to use these and get rid of unwanted harmonics by circuitry; especially because it is found that all such possible circuits provide far more harmonics than are ever required. Now on page 23 we see that sawtooth waves have all the harmonics in their proper order. This kind of oscillator is therefore capable of great accuracy in forming imitative tones. There are several ways of generating sawtooth waves; at the moment we are of course not dealing with transistors to any extent. The simplest basic arrangement is to apply a high enough potential across the electrodes of a gas tube; at some value of this, the gas will 'ignite' and conduct a current across the tube; in fact, it will become almost a short-circuit, so a limiting resistor is required. Once the tube is 'lit', it will remain conductive to the same extent even if the voltage is reduced; but at some point, of course, it will cease to conduct; this is often about half the ignition voltage. In a suitable circuit these properties can be made use of to generate oscillations. Fig. 39 (*A*) shows a basic circuit in which the capacitor *C* is charged through a resistor from the d.c. line *Eb*. The capacitor does not charge linearly but in an exponential manner as shown in Fig. 39 (*B*). When

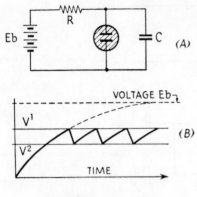

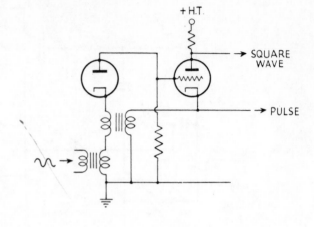

Fig. 39 Neon tube oscillator
A = oscillator; B = wave form

the voltage across the capacitor reaches the ignition voltage of the tube, this conducts and almost immediately discharges the capacitor. The process then repeats at a frequency determined by the values of C, R and Eb. Since any load across the tube changes the frequency, distorts the wave form and may even stop oscillations, a buffer valve must follow this simple circuit; but in general the deficiencies of simple gas tubes outweigh their advantages, and they are not now used as prime frequency sources; all the same, many interesting experiments can be carried out with such inexpensive and simple arrangements as shown.

There are no other very easy circuits for the hobbyist which will produce a sawtooth direct, but there are several ways of turning other kinds of wave shape into a sawtooth, and this is the way in which it is done today—that is, for music generators. Certainly, if the cost and complication are of little account, as in a high-grade oscilloscope for instance, then direct production of sawtooth waves justifies the quite complex circuits required.

Since we are concerned only with music generators, we know from pages 48–71 that a square wave has many uses in organs. It is true to say that over 90 per cent of current small organs use this wave shape although it is never actually generated as such; it is obtained by some circuit arrangement which, since the advent of transistors, has become very much easier than with valves. We therefore just show, in passing, Fig. 40, which is a gating device which clips a sine wave to give two different types of output wave. Before we

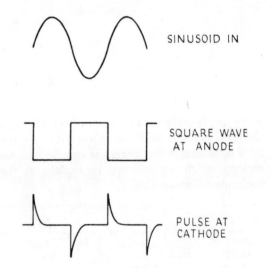

Fig. 40 Square-wave and pulse-shaping circuit and wave shapes

leave valve prime wave form sources, there are two circuits which produce wave shapes which are neither sawtooth nor square, but which have many random harmonics as well as a good fundamental frequency. These are illustrated in Fig. 41 and have both been very successful commercially. A further variant is given in Fig. 42 which has been extensively used by amateur constructors. As the figure shows, it is possible to remove a sine wave from A, very useful pulses from C and D, a square wave from B and a triangular wave from E. Direct keying and the possible formation of a second note from the same circuit are other advantages of this circuit.

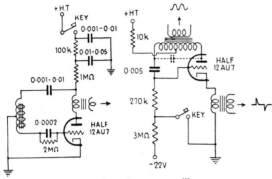

Fig. 41 Complex-wave oscillators

Generally speaking the inductances for such circuits are wound to give a near approximation to the required frequency with some standard value of capacitor, then the fine tuning to obtain exact pitch is done by moving part of the iron core of the coil assembly. This is done in one of the ways shown in Fig. 43 (or if a pot core, by the screwed slug). The foregoing represent the really useful valve oscillators for organs, but since the valve is now almost obsolete as a prime tone source, we do not show the many other possible circuits; that of Fig. 42 is the most useful and stable of those described.

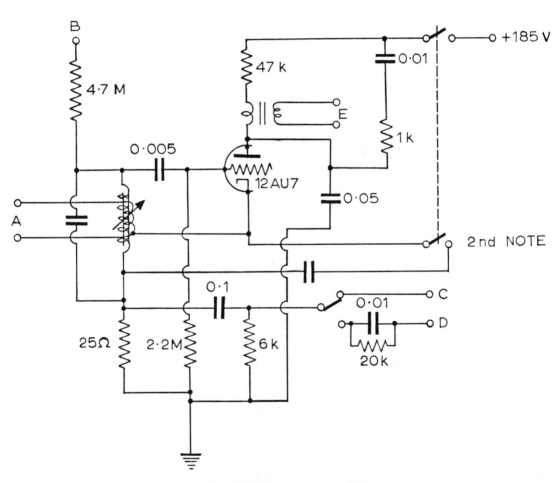

Fig. 42 Multiple wave-form oscillator

A = sine wave; B = square wave; C = sawtooth wave;
D = modified sawtooth wave; E = triangular wave

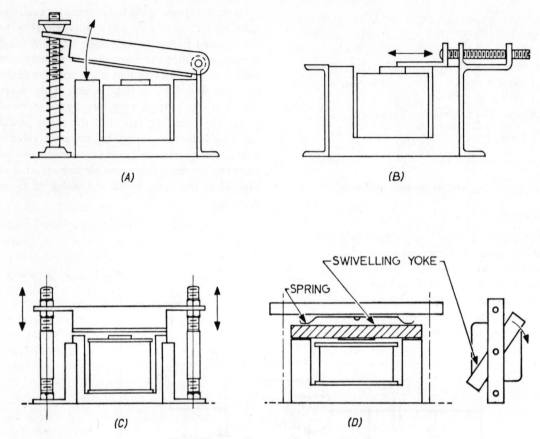

Fig. 43 Tuning adjustments for iron-cored coils

One or two physical aspects should be considered; firstly the matter of temperature. It is the copper which is the main offender, but the inhomogenous nature of a laminated core makes it contribute to the drift which may be of the order of 40 parts in a million per degree Centigrade change. The more regular molecular structure of ferrites will bring this figure down to about 25 parts, and if the iron content is abolished and we are left with only the copper, as in an air-core coil, it can be as low as 6 parts. There are also losses in the tuning capacitors but with luck these can be made to almost neutralize the losses in the inductance; most modern capacitors have negative temperature coefficients. Polystyrene is one of the most satisfactory substances to date.

An interesting point arises from the use of laminations as opposed to ferrites. Because of the random distribution of iron and silicon particles in the mass of the sheet from which these are stamped out, and the irregularity of orientation when stacking the laminations within the coil bobbin, the flux distribution will never be exactly the same for any two coils; thus, if the oscillators are fractionally over-driven, there will be slightly varying harmonics set up in different coils, and it is this which accounts in great part for the richness of sound from organs having independent oscillators, so-called 'free-phase' organs. Where the oscillator itself is not a prime source of tone oscillations but only a triggering or timing device, then this property is of no account and ferrite cores are much better from a manufacturing aspect.

Another important feature is that of decoupling. If a number of oscillators take their power from a common supply line, the voltage drop due to the current drawn may alter the impedance of the supply line and cause transfer of energy from one circuit to another; this can result in the formation of spurious frequencies and so each oscillator should be isolated from the common power source by a decoupling filter (Fig. 44). The impedance of the bypass capacitor should not be higher than about 10 per cent of the resistor with which it is associated. The impedance of a capacitor in ohms is—

$$X_c = \frac{10^6}{6 \cdot 28 fC}$$

where f = frequency in Hz, C = capacitance in μF.

Blocking oscillators

This kind of oscillator is capable of both running freely to act as a prime source, or of being synchronized to run at some sub-multiple of the injected frequency; it is thus also suitable as a divider, and this is how it is usually employed. Essentially it may be thought of as a circuit which over-drives itself into a state of paralysis, so that only one oscillation, or perhaps only a part of one, is generated until the circuit restores itself. This is usually brought about by adjusting the rate of discharge of a capacitor which is charged up when the valve first conducts, so that the restoration of the correct grid potential to allow the valve to start operations again depends on the leakage rate of this capacitor; the rate being, of course, controlled by the time constant of the RC circuit, hence one or other of these elements can be set to give the frequency rate required. Such blocking circuits were used in many valve organs and one such form is described in *Transistor Electronic Organs for the Home Constructor* (Pitman), where full constructional details are given. It might be noted that the pulse currents are high, and excellent insulation for the windings is required. The wave shape derived is rather like a sharpened sawtooth and is not only very useful in itself, but is eminently suitable for driving any form of frequency divider;

all such circuits require an input wave form having a steep leading edge—they will not trigger from a sinusoidal wave form (see Fig. 45).

Introduction to transistors

In this section we deal with the three-element transistor; the diode as a rectifier; and a special form of diode, generally known as a Zener diode, which can be used to provide a constant voltage over a range of currents. As a matter of interest, some comparisons are made with similar characteristics of valves, but we cannot devote space to the theory of semiconductors to any extent and the reader is strongly advised to obtain one or more of the books readily available. For the same reason, it is not possible to explain the many different processes by which transistors are made, since in a book of this kind the principles of operation must assume a very much simplified form.

Let us begin with a word of caution. Habits of thought induced by long experience with valves are likely not only to be wrong but costly when applied to transistor circuits. Semiconductors are not the answer to every problem; indeed, they have some great disadvantages. But in the course of time these will be overcome, just as they were with valves. We would also ask the reader to remember

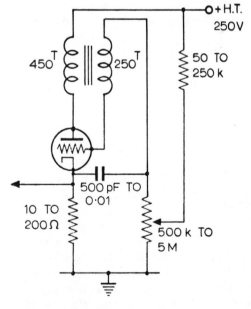

Fig. 45 Blocking oscillator

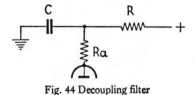

Fig. 44 Decoupling filter

that it is only the applications to music generators with which we are concerned, so that their suitability or limitations in other ways are not discussed.

The experimenter whose experience has been confined to valves will find the techniques of using transistors very different; for not only are the principles different, but also the circuit constants.

No attempt has been made in previous editions to explain the theory of the valve, nor is any space given to this now; but to compare the action of semiconductors it is essential to outline the main differences between the two systems.

The two basic differences are: in a valve there is complete isolation between any and all elements unless deliberately overcome by the application of signals or potentials and currents; and the operating voltages are high, the input impedance is high, power is required to heat the cathode before any action is possible.

In a semiconductor there is leakage between all elements which cannot be avoided; currents flow at room temperatures, so obviating the need for heaters; the impedances are relatively low; and so are the working voltages.

In somewhat greater detail, the valve structure serves only to support the grid, anode and cathode/heater assemblies and does not contribute to the action of the system except for the activated surface of the cathode. The whole of the elements are supported from the base in such valves as are used in musical instruments and this results in a somewhat elastic arrangement which can vibrate in some circumstances, giving rise to microphony which is unpleasant. Electrons only can flow from cathode to anode and are completely controllable by potentials applied to the grid—which does not, however, draw any current. Comparatively high temperatures are needed to raise the cathode surface to a useful figure and this means that heat is radiated from the glass envelope of the valve, a possible cause of drift in adjacent circuit elements. Also, extra current must be provided for the heaters. This is low-voltage a.c. and is not rectified or smoothed, therefore there is often the possibility of picking up hum in the valve or external wiring. Much ingenuity has been expended on means to reduce this annoying effect, for whilst in

ordinary broadcast programme material it is possibly not so serious, with the sustained tones of an organ it produces most unpleasant modulation and discords.

Anode voltages of 50 to 300 V are commonly required to pull the electrons across from the cathode through the vacuum which insulates the respective parts from each other, since all are separated by quite appreciable distances physically.

This is a kind of rough structural picture of the valve used as an amplifier or oscillator, the other main application being that of a rectifier for our h.t. supply. In this case, the same structure is used but the grid is omitted since no control is required. The parts are larger because this valve must carry current for the whole system. Considerable heat is evolved and care must be taken in siting this component to avoid damaging electrolytic capacitors, etc. Once again, we need quite a heavy heater current to obtain enough emission, and this sometimes leads to difficulties with the heater/cathode insulation.

Consider now the semiconductor. We said that the theory of operation would not be explained in detail, but it is such a vastly different device from the valve, both physically and electrically, that some simple explanation of its working must be given.

The name indicates that these devices rely on materials which are neither perfect insulators nor perfect conductors. Physically, we find that a piece of silicon or germanium is treated chemically or metallurgically to have certain properties, and is in intimate contact with another piece of the same substance, treated in a different way. There may, in fact, be an intermediate wafer of extreme thinness. To ensure overall contact, the mating faces are actually diffused into each other, although there are other methods of manufacture.

The outstanding difference in function between valves and semiconductors is that in the latter, current is carried by positive as well as by negative carriers. The positive carrier is called a hole, and it has a positive charge exactly equal to the negative charge of an electron. Being of opposite sign, an electron and a hole can attract each other and the electron may fill the hole. This is a state of equilibrium when neither can then take any part in carrying current.

The predominance of holes or electrons in the same basic material is determined by adding very small quantities of alkali metals, so that the general tendency is for holes or electrons to form the major charge content of the material. If positive, it is called p-type; if negative, n-type. But there are always some carriers present of opposite sign, as in Fig. 46 (*A*), and because they are relatively few, they are called minority carriers. The additive process, or doping, can be made to produce transistors of two types, p-n-p or n-p-n.

The three-element transistor therefore consists of one electrode, a centre electrode, and a further electrode. These are not quite the same in physical size and although reversible transistors are obtainable, the connections are nearly always indicated, namely, emitter, base, collector. These represent the cathode, grid, and anode of the valve in general terms.

Before looking at the transistor in a circuit, it will be easiest to see what happens in a semiconductor diode of the junction type. Starting with two separate blocks of germanium or silicon appropriately doped to have predominantly negative or positive charges, when the two parts are brought into contact, there appears at the junction a gradient of electron and hole densities which results in migration across the junction; there are more electrons in the n-type material than holes, so electrons diffuse into the p-type material, whereas at the same time, holes diffuse from the p-type into the n-type material. This leaves the n-type side with a net positive charge and the p-type side with a net negative charge. So there is an electric field or potential barrier set up across the junction in such a direction that it inhibits further carrier movement and an equilibrium condition exists so that no steady net flow takes place after an instant. Any flow of, say, electrons can only be possible if these acquire energy from somewhere which enables them to overcome this barrier. Suppose now an external e.m.f. is applied as in Fig. 46 (*B*), the barrier potential is reduced at the junction and a net current flows across the junction and through the external circuit. This current consists of holes which are injected from the p-type into the n-type and of electrons injected from the opposite side. Although the particles flow in opposite directions, their currents add because of the opposite sign of their charges.

But if the external voltage is reversed in polarity, as in Fig. 46 (*C*), the height of the barrier potential is increased and the electrons and holes find it almost impossible to migrate, save for a few thermally-generated carriers which are randomly present in the material. A very small net current flows.

The point contact diode is also encountered; in this, a metallic wire or point is connected to the germanium base. By a variety of methods, a small p-type area is formed under the point, and since the base material is n-type, rectification can take place at this boundary. These diodes are inexpensive and extremely suitable for small-signal circuits—they will not handle any power.

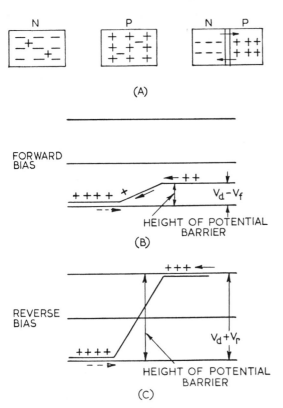

Fig. 46 Applying an external e.m.f.

V_d = junction voltage; V_r = reverse diode voltage; V_f = forward diode voltage

Since an alternating current swings firstly positive and then negative, clearly the junction diode will conduct the positive excursion of the signal but will suppress the negative half cycle; thus the device acts as a rectifier. This property is again useful for various forms of music signal control, quite apart of course from its common function as a mains rectifier.

All the materials used to make semiconductors are temperature-sensitive. This must be so if they are able to emit electrons at room temperature and without auxiliary heaters (such as are required to produce emission in a valve).

There is an important structural difference as compared with valves, due to the size of the heat-conducting surfaces. The semiconductor is a poor heat conductor and the junctions are buried in the structure. So the limiting factor is, where any degree of power is concerned, the junction temperature or the heat sink area. In the case of the small current carried by a diode when reverse biased, this will have a fixed value if the temperature is also fixed. After the reverse voltage is increased to some figure depending on many factors, the reverse current will suddenly increase and may destroy the diode. During experiments by Clarence Zener, it was found that provided certain characteristics were produced in the diode, a large range of currents could be utilized over a very small voltage range. This property is known as the Zener effect, although it is not strictly true once a certain current is exceeded.

Note that whilst for normal rectification purposes it is the forward conduction characteristics of the diode which are of importance, the Zener action is confined to the reverse conduction properties. It enables one to hold a constant voltage for considerable changes in current and can thus form an economical type of stabilizer for many purposes. Because of the influence of temperature on diodes, those made for regulating purposes are always silicon, which ensures not only a small change of reverse leakage current at normal temperature but also enables such diodes to be used at much higher temperatures than would be possible with germanium.

The typical reverse conduction properties of a crystal diode are shown in Fig. 47. It can be seen

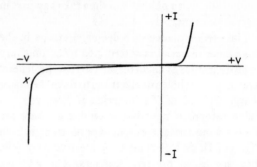

Fig. 47 Reverse conduction properties of a crystal diode

that for a forward positive voltage, the current rapidly increases beyond the 'knee' or region of zero conduction. But in the reverse direction, for a negative voltage, there is hardly any change in current for quite a range of voltages.

This can be used to provide regulation to a circuit drawing varying current loads. If we expand the sketch of Fig. 47 into that of Fig. 48, it can be seen that a supply voltage (of at least twice the working voltage of the Zener diode) is connected through a series resistor which produces the voltage drop XY. YZ is the voltage drop across the diode (-6 V in this example). If the resistor brings the current to I_0 on the 'Zener' curve, then a load line can be drawn as in the figure. If, now, the supply voltage should increase, the load line will move downwards towards I_m (since the current in the diode must also increase). But the change in voltage between the conditions I_0 and I_m is almost nil, though clearly this depends on the slope resistance, easily ascertained from the makers' data sheets. The care we must exercise is to make quite sure that under the worst condition, i.e. at I_m,

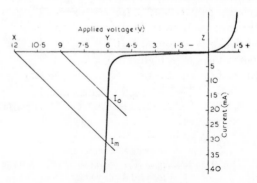

Fig. 48 Expansion of Fig. 47

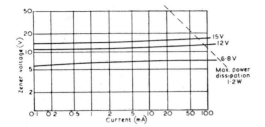

Fig. 49 Typical Zener characteristics

the diode is not overloaded. Some typical Zener characteristics are shown in Fig. 49.

Before leaving the diode, it should be mentioned that when an a.c. wave form, such as one might obtain from a music generator, is applied to any suitable diode it is *rectified*, which means of course that its harmonic content is completely changed and this may make it unsuitable for tone forming. On the other hand, this method can be used for deliberately distorting wave forms for musical synthesis, and we will see examples of this later on.

The simplest way to describe the action of a three-element transistor is by means of Fig. 50. This is a theoretical section of a p-n-p junction transistor, so called because the emitter, base and collector are joined together by a diffusion process over a considerable relative area. The emitter is connected to the positive end of the battery and the collector to the negative end. The base is shown connected to an intermediate point, but this must be negative with respect to the emitter. Other ways of providing the base bias will be shown later. Positive holes from the emitter cross into the base region and, since the collector is still more negative outgoing, they increase the collector current. The transistor amplifies partly because current flowing between emitter and base controls current of greater power between base and collector; but gain is principally accomplished by delivering power from a low- to a high-impedance level. For instance, if the input resistance R_i was 50 Ω and the

load resistance R_l was 50 000 Ω, then since $G = \alpha^2 R_l / R_i$, there is a power gain of 1000. (α will be observed to be taken as 1, but is more generally about 0·9 and in any case cannot exceed 1 for a junction transistor.) Or, looked at in another way, if the base-emitter input signal is 20 μA and the resulting collector current swing 1·05 mA, then the gain is

$$\frac{1·05 \times 10^{-3}}{20 \times 10^{-6}} = 52·5$$

a little over 50 : 1.

Many practical examples of the use of amplifying transistors are given throughout this book, for the present the above will suffice. Conventional symbols for the usual three-element transistor are shown in Fig. 51, but before leaving this introduction, mention must be made of another important design which is now assuming significance: the field effect transistor. Several forms of this exist, the main advantages being very high input impedance, control by voltage instead of current, low noise and a power gain approaching that of a valve. In short, most conventional valve circuit techniques can be used with the field effect transistor, which was first designed by W. Shockley in 1952.

The action of these devices is complex but we can simplify the idea by looking at Fig. 52, which shows the source, gate and drain—new expressions for the electrodes. If the correct material is used, a voltage applied at the source can flow across to the drain. If a bias voltage is applied to the gate, the flow is modified so that a family of

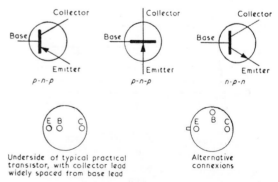

Fig. 51 Conventional symbols for the three-element transistor

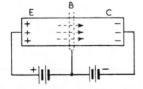

Fig. 50 Current flow in p-n-p transistor

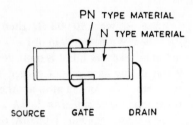

PN TYPE MATERIAL

N TYPE MATERIAL

SOURCE   GATE   DRAIN

Fig. 52 Field effect transistor

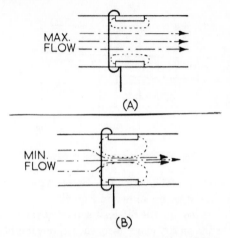

MAX. FLOW

(A)

MIN. FLOW

(B)

Fig. 54 Action on flow when gate bias is altered

conduction curves can be drawn, as in Fig. 53. These can be seen to be very similar to those of a valve, devoid of the sharp turnover voltage or current typical of the transistor.

The action of the gate can best be described by Fig. 54 (*A*) and (*B*), where alteration in the gate bias performs a throttling action on the flow of current and the net effect is almost that of a variable resistor as the depletion layer extends farther into the body of the device. The transfer of energy is thus almost entirely voltage controlled and this means that small currents are drawn and therefore high impedances can once more be employed; the input capacitance can also be low. The operating voltages are comparable with those of normal transistors, although if this is so, the input signal must also be small. Higher voltages can be used with later types as indicated in Fig. 53. Since the method of connection is almost identical with that of a valve, we show in Fig. 55 how this device is connected in a small general-purpose amplifier. Note that with an n-p-n transistor as an output stage, the supplies etc., are exactly the same as for a valve amplifier.

Later forms of this device may have appeared by the time this edition is published, e.g. the G.E.C. D5KI complementary unijunction transistor, but there will be much further development in this field with new materials for the field effect transistor lacking the shortcomings of germanium or silicon.

There are a number of precautions to be observed when handling semiconductors of any type. Firstly, make certain that the polarity of the supplies is correct. Next, when soldering do not heat the leads within about an inch of the transistor body; it is surprising how many electric soldering irons either leak from the heater to the case, or produce a strong electric field around the tip; either condition can damage or destroy the transistor; it is therefore a good idea to connect all the leads of the transistor together temporarily and this indeed is essential with many integrated circuits. The actual bit can well be connected to earth as a further precaution; a pair of pliers makes an effective heat sink to protect the unit. Lastly, when

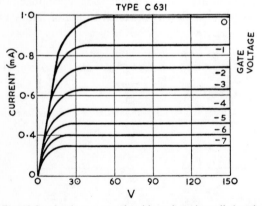

TYPE C 631

GATE VOLTAGE

0
−1
−2
−3
−4
−5
−6
−7

Fig. 53 Conduction curves when bias voltage is applied to the gate

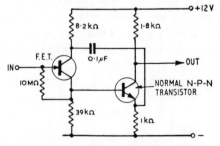

Fig. 55 Small signal amplifier using field effect transistor

handling power transistors, obey the instructions carefully about the area of heat sink required. Some information on this is given in Chapter 6, with further details of Zener diode stabilizers. Remember that overheating of any transistor will result in thermal runaway which will instantly destroy the transistor without warning. Precautions in the matter of power supplies are given in Chapter 6.

With this brief introduction to semiconductors we can now return to the subject matter of this chapter; but there are many other circuit considerations to be borne in mind when using semiconductors, and these will be explained when necessary in the text.

Transistor oscillators

All oscillators using valves can be transistorized. As has already been explained, there are two major types; those for sine waves and those for complex wave forms. Since the wave shape is dependent on the way in which the potentials or currents are applied and their magnitude, it is possible to use most oscillators for either purpose. We find therefore that the frequency range to be covered usually determines the type of circuit to be preferred.

For very low frequencies the phase-shift oscillator is more suitable, since no inductances are required. In the case of a vibrato oscillator, for example, the coils would be very large and costly and only a small frequency variation is called for. Such a circuit is shown in Fig. 56. The frequency can be varied from 3 to 8 Hz by the 1·5 k potentiometer and the depth by the 20 k potentiometer. Any transistor having a current gain of 50 or so works well, but it will be noted that as the 2 μF

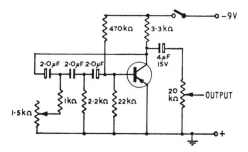

Fig. 56 Phase-shift oscillator circuit

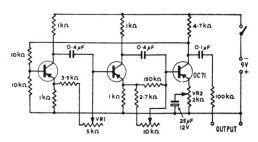

Fig. 57 Wide range phase-shift oscillator

capacitors are polarized, it is necessary to use a paper one for the centre position. A convenient feature of this oscillator is that since the current consumption is only 1 mA, a small dry battery can be used, so that if the remainder of the instrument requires some voltage other than 9 V there will be no difficulties in the way. In addition the use of a separate battery supply may greatly reduce interaction and coupling between the various parts of the generating circuits.

A rather ingenious phase-shift oscillator is shown in Fig. 57. A quick examination of these circuits shows that, if the frequencies are to be appreciably altered, it is necessary to vary three elements simultaneously. In this circuit a range of 3 : 1 can be covered by the simple adjustment of one resistor. It can be used, for instance, to produce pedal notes for an organ, since the wave form is nearly sinusoidal.

Two other types of sine-wave oscillators are shown in Fig. 58 (*A*) and (*B*). These employ normal coils and may have frequency ranges of from 65 to 8000 Hz. Because of the lower impedance of suitable transistors as compared with valves, the centre tap should be moved down to give about two-thirds winding above it and one-third towards the low potential or earthy end—usually the lower end in the diagrams. Such oscillators have good stability and could be used for additive mixing or tone forming as explained later.

In general, a complex wave is best provided by a second transistor functioning as a shaper and following the actual oscillator. This also has the merit of isolating the oscillating circuit from the load. Very many circuits could be used in this connection, but the Hartley configuration is now almost the only one to be found and no other is so simple or inexpensive for music generators.

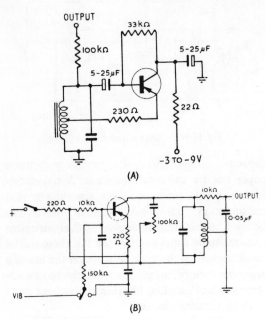

(A)

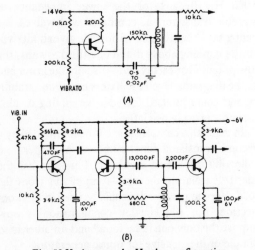

(B)

Fig. 58 Two other types of sine-wave oscillators

Such variants of this circuit as exist are usually due to the desire to use standard resistor and capacitor values throughout the organ or for some other reason of manufacture. Two examples are given here, each of which is suitable for practically any form of keyboard instrument, either as independently tuned circuits for each note, or master oscillators feeding a chain of dividers. Transistors of the ACY 20 or 22 types, or the equivalents of other makers, are suitable. (Fig. 59 (A) and (B).)

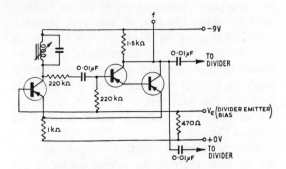

Fig. 60 Master oscillator of high stability

Note that final tuning cannot be done unless the vibrato isolating resistors are connected; but Fig. 59 (B) uses a reactance stage which is a much better way of introducing vibrato modulation.

Another extremely useful oscillator for driving frequency dividers is shown in Fig. 60. This is more unusual in that the inductance coil is not centre-tapped, therefore it is easier to wind and still only one capacitor is required to tune it. The use of two transistors in the buffer stage should be noted. The types required are obtainable from Newmarket Transistors Ltd, Exning Road, Newmarket, Suffolk.

This is also a good prime source and is easily modulated for vibrato—which is not always such a simple matter. Blocking oscillators can of course be used as previously described for valves, a good circuit being shown in Fig. 61, and this gives a very good approximation to a sawtooth wave. However, the bistable circuit known as the multivibrator could also be used. This will give a square wave, devoid of even harmonics, but from which good flute and clarinet or stopped diapason tones can be produced (see Fig. 62). All circuits of this kind which do not have an inductance require a fully stabilized power supply or the frequency

(A)

(B)

Fig. 59 Variants on the Hartley configuration

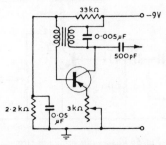

Fig. 61 Circuit using blocking oscillator

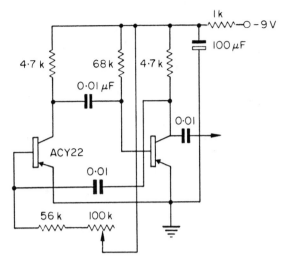

Fig. 62 Multivibrator

will drift. Chapter 6 deals with this matter in detail. Another oscillator is interesting because it can be made so very small; this is shown in Fig. 63. Here we see a small composite transistor, type TAA320BIFET (Philips) in association with a Vinkor transformer. Since it is possible to attain a Q of nearly 400 with this efficient ferrite, the Q of 10 necessary to get the circuit to oscillate is easily

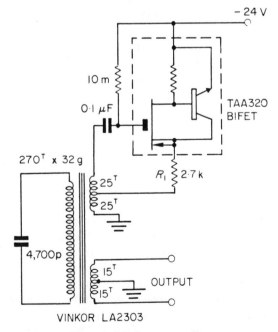

Fig. 63 Stable sine-wave oscillator

obtained. In common with most oscillators using an inductance, the stability is good, indeed changes in supply of up to 25 per cent hardly produce any measurable drift. As shown, the circuit will deliver 1·5 volts r.m.s. into a load of 3000 ohms. In passing, the TAA320 can withstand 100-volt transients on the gate, and will drive a high-voltage output transistor such as the BD 115, giving a very simple 2-watt audio amplifier suitable for high-impedance inputs like a crystal microphone or pickup, etc. The purity of the sine wave from this circuit is very good indeed and physically the size is under two cubic inches. A 24-volt supply is required, the resistor R_1 might have to be adjusted to pass the correct current but in general is not critical. As is evident, the TAA320 is a field effect transistor and an ordinary bipolar one, combined in a T018 can. Further examples of transistor oscillators will be found in Chapter 8.

Frequency division

The great majority of small organs use this technique to derive lower octaves from an oscillator tuned initially to the highest note of that sign—e.g. C might be 8372 Hz when, if applied to a chain of bistable dividers, we would obtain the next C, 4186, then the next, 2093, and so on until we get right down to pedal notes of perhaps 32·7 Hz. As previously explained, this system leads to simplification in tuning and lowering of cost for the whole generator.

Since the interval of the octave has a ratio of 2 : 1, then this is the division ratio required of the dividers; for it is possible to divide by all kinds of ratios, and indeed the value of this will be seen later for other systems. A divider of the kind in which we are interested is really a high-speed switch, in which the two transistors are each turned on for some period of time, and then turned off. Each input pulse causes the circuit to change from one state to the other, i.e. one side fully conducting, the other side cut off. There is then one complete cycle of the bistable circuit for every two input pulses. Therefore the repetition rate from either collector is half that of the input frequency; so division by two has taken place. One or two points must be watched. All dividers have to be jerked into action, as it were, by a shock and this is accomplished by the steep wave front of the input triggering signal. Equally, every divider must change its state very rapidly, not only to trigger the next stage, but to give what we are after, a good square wave. This means that the rate of transition or switching must be high, and this is controlled by the time constants of the collector/base *RC* networks. Not so long ago various subterfuges were necessary to regulate this and other factors in such circuits, but with the advent of silicon planar transistors there is no need to go to the expense of steering diodes or bias supplies. Fig. 64 shows the components of a modern silicon divider, satisfactory for all organ applications where dividers can be used at all. An excellent point is that the same component values and layout are used for each divider, regardless of the frequencies involved. However, we can only obtain a square wave from this kind of circuit, and quite often it is found desirable to have a sawtooth, possibly as well as the square one. A converter stage as in Fig. 65 can follow any divider of the bistable type, and some component values are given for the normal organ range of frequencies. Fig. 66 gives the details of a Wurlitzer divider which is not too critical as to component values. It has the important advantage that two separate signal outputs are available from the one input, and

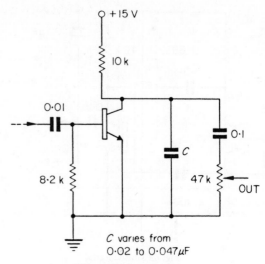

Fig. 65 Sawtooth converter

normally one output would go direct to the tone-forming devices, whilst the other would be treated for percussive effects. This is done by holding one of the anodes at a negative potential until the percussion key is pressed, when this is changed to +300 volts. The valve then conducts and a signal is developed across the 1 megohm load resistor. The $0.0047\,\mu F$ capacitor to earth reduces any key click. To sustain such a signal, the $0.22\,\mu F$ capacitor is charged by the lower rod, rotating and so earthing this unit. When a key is released, the +300 V is removed and the $0.22\,\mu F$ capacitor keeps the valve conducting until it discharges and the − voltage cuts the valve off. The component values shown will of course require some adjustment for the different input frequencies.

The upper frequency limit is about 20 kHz, so it falls within the useful range for musical instruments. Sometimes a small negative bias may be required, depending on the type of tube. Division stability is good and changes in heater and anode supply voltages do not much affect this circuit. Division up to 10 : 1 is possible, so that 16 ft pedal notes are easily within its compass.

A very successful gas-tube frequency divider which overcomes the deficiencies of the simple tube described on page 45 is illustrated in Fig 67, which shows two gas tubes in series, with series timing capacitors C_5 and C_6. This capacitive voltage divider isolates the output so that loading

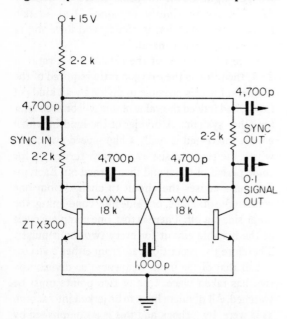

Fig. 64 Silicon frequency divider

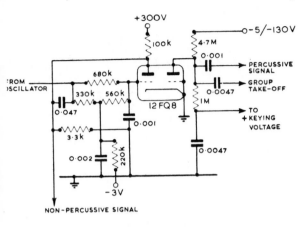

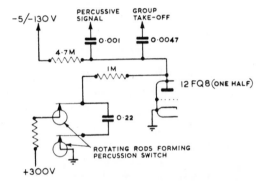

Fig. 66 Wurlitzer frequency divider and percussion circuit

does not affect the frequency. The two tubes have a high impedance to earth. Capacitors C_3 and C_4 in another divider are 1/100th of the values of C_1 and C_2. As their midpoint is connected to that of V_3 and V_4, the proportion of the output of the first stage at the second stage is nearly proportional to the values of the two capacitors.

Assuming that the negative flyback pulse of the first stage appears before the charge on C_5 and C_6 is high enough to ionize V_3 and V_4 and is applied to the junction of V_3 and V_4, the lower electrode of V_3 then becomes sufficiently negative to ignite it. A higher positive potential then appears on the upper electrode of V_4 and that tube ignites. Capacitors C_5 and C_6 quickly discharge and extinguish V_3 and V_4. Capacitors C_5 and C_6 begin to recharge to produce the rising portion of the second stage output wave. So the first stage triggers the second. Any divided signal fed back to the output of the first stage (a common failing with single tube dividers) must pass through the high-impedance

voltage divider (C_3 and C_1 in series) and the low-impedance shunt divider C_2. Very great attenuation of the fed-back signal is achieved.

Notwithstanding these precautions, a good deal of artificial ageing of cheap neon tubes is necessary to stabilize their performance. Thereafter their behaviour depends to a great extent on how often they are used. Long periods of dis-use frequently result in inability to start and means must be provided to adjust the free-running frequency of such oscillators.

To equal the long-term stability of valve oscillators, it is really necessary to use high-quality gas tubes, which increase the cost. Even so, there remain certain difficulties which can be overcome by replacing the lower gas tube by a silicon diode, e.g. Philips type BA100.[*] This provides a very low resistance path when the gas tube is conducting, so that the capacitor discharges extremely rapidly. But when the tube is not conducting, there will be a very high resistance path so that with the small coupling capacitors a high synchronizing voltage can be injected to the cathode of the gas tube. Germanium diodes are unsuitable because of their high leakage. This causes a reduction of the pulse duration so that synchronization may be lost due to 'jitter', that is, fluctuation of the discharge voltage.

Despite the prevalence of other forms of sawtooth oscillator or frequency divider, the gas tube remains an inexpensive and accurate method of generating this form of wave, which is so useful for synthesizing imitative tone qualities in organ generators. We will note one or two features of the tube itself which determine whether or not the result will be effective.

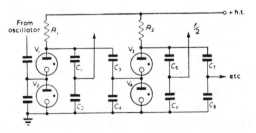

Fig. 67 Gas tubes in series with capacitive voltage dividers

[*] H. van de Kerckhoff, N. V. Philips Gloeilampenfabrieken.

When the supply voltage to the tube is raised to the point of ignition, the gas is ionized and a current flows. The voltage then drops to the maintaining voltage, which is less than the voltage needed to cause ignition. In this condition the tube has a negative resistance and thanks to this property oscillation can take place when a capacitor is connected in parallel with the diode.

For some small increase in current now, the discharge will spread farther over the cathode whilst the voltage will remain nearly constant; the resistance is very low. If this process continues, so that the whole cathode is covered by the glow, the voltage across the electrodes will rise. The correct maintaining voltage is of the utmost importance because the frequency depends on it.

Also, the ignition delay must be short in relation to the period of the sawtooth; a high value of delay will lead to jitter, so that the amplitude of the sawtooth will vary statistically with time. The delay can be made short by treatment of the electrode and gas filling or by applying a strong synchronizing pulse—one exceeding the ignition voltage.

Then the highest frequency of which the tube is capable depends on the de-ionization time of the charge carriers in the gas. It is difficult to provide equal recombination times over a very wide frequency range, so the gas is further treated to have a slow time at low frequencies, thus avoiding jitter. Also, there must be a relationship between the supply voltage and timing resistor for various values of capacitor. Some of these points are shown in Fig. 68 (A), (B) and (C).

Thus, unless good-quality gas tubes are used, there will be a high percentage of tubes which will not synchronize or will fall out of synchronism with time. But, given tubes with suitable gas filling and electrodes of good purity, this circuit is an excellent example of a sawtooth frequency divider.

Another device, the silicon unilateral switch, can be used to produce a good sawtooth wave as in Fig. 69. These elements require a stabilized supply line, but give excellent wave forms with no interference. An oscillator is of course required to drive the chain; here we show one consisting of a field effect transistor, which is very simple; but any other circuit would do as well.

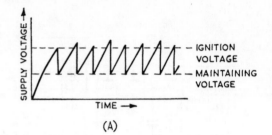

(A)

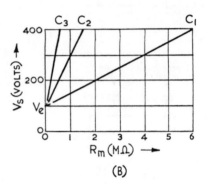

(B)

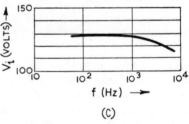

(C)

Fig. 68 (A) The phenomenon of jitter in which the amplitude of the sawtooth signal fluctuates regularly; (B) The relationship between the minimum resistance R_m and the supply voltage V_s at a certain value of the capacitance: $C_1 = 100$ pF; (C) The dynamic ignition voltage V_i as a function of frequency

If, however, a true square wave is required, then to form accurate tone colours there must be sharp edges to the wave; this is also true of square waves as triggers; to ensure that there is no loss of time, the coupling resistors must be shunted by small capacitors as shown in Fig. 71, where the effect is illustrated.

It will be clear from the previous few pages that to form a good square wave by frequency division is very easy; but to form a good sawtooth, there is

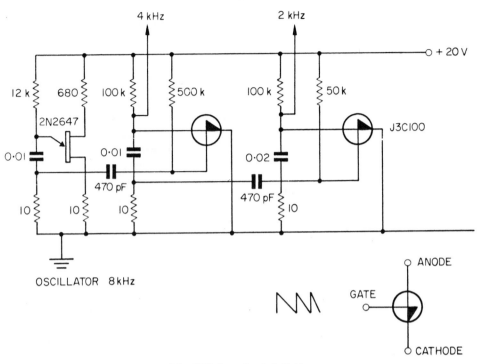

Fig. 69 Unilateral switch divider

quite a lot of complication and adjustment required. For no sawtooth generator can extend for more than a few semitones without coming to a halt or producing very false frequencies; new values for some parts of the circuit must then be inserted to continue synthesis. But all bistable frequency dividers yielding square waves respond equally to all injected frequencies without adjustment, hence they are called aperiodic.

Tone forming from square waves is not conducive to the highest accuracy, although a large number of most agreeable sounds can be produced thereby. For exact simulation, one should of course have square, sawtooth and sine; it is convenient to make a very useful synthetic sawtooth from a good square wave. The technique is called staircasing, and is used in a large number of modern organs. If we look at Fig. 72, under (A) can be seen a linear sawtooth. This is an idealized wave which has all the harmonics, both odd and even, in exactly the right proportions. But we need not be so exact as that. Since all the divider outputs are in step because they are locked to each other, then if oc-

taves are mixed together at the correct amplitudes for their position in the harmonic spectrum, the compound wave will look like (B). Clearly as one increases the number of sources the linearity becomes better, but this can only apply to the lower divider signals for one runs out of frequencies as the top is approached; but it is just at the lower pitches that accurate synthesis is most appreciated. The fundamental frequency is taken unaltered; the next octave upwards is reduced in level

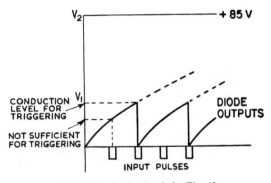

Fig. 70 Conduction levels for Fig. 69

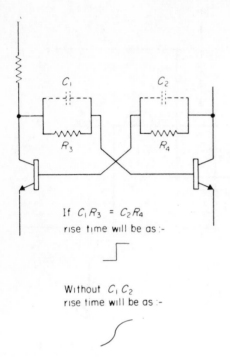

If $C_1 R_3 = C_2 R_4$
rise time will be as :-

Without $C_1 C_2$
rise time will be as :-

Fig. 71 Wave fronts of divider switching

busbars, over each octave, so that the total level is reduced, hence the mixer pre-amplifiers; in a straightforward summation of divider outputs, these amplifiers may not be required. It is evident, then, that a great deal of importance is attached to the presence of a linear sawtooth. All the same, some voices require a square wave and this can be produced from a sawtooth (if that is the generator system) as shown in Fig. 74. In this case we take a sawtooth wave one octave above the required fundamental, reverse its phase by means of a suitable circuit, reduce its amplitude by half, and re-combine it with the fundamental. In practice, the shape is not nearly as good as in the figure, but the important thing is that the even harmonics have gone and we are left with a wave which can be processed to give the 'hollow' tones of the clarinet, bassoon, gedackt and some other organ-pipe sounds. Such stops, if examined in a pipe organ, will be found to consist of stopped pipes—these can only sound an odd harmonic series.

by one half; the next by one half of the second and so on until either enough synthesis is obtained, or one has run out of wave forms. It must be quite clear that the effect of this linear slope is equivalent to adding even harmonics together, as can be seen from Fig. 26. In practical applications of the method, it is important that none of the lower frequencies leak back into the upper sawtooths. This can be adjusted by resistor networks suitably proportioned which connect all the sources together; or unwanted staircase outputs can be connected to earth by the key contacts to eliminate cross-talk altogether. This means a somewhat more complex contact arrangement. We can see, in the tone circuits of some commercial organs, further mixing of frequencies at the actual tone network inputs; in fact, staircasing could be done here. Intermediate effects like adding a higher frequency to that keyed, for the sake of extra brilliance, are also used.

The separate input frequencies must be added or summed in a suitable way, and Fig. 73 shows a commercial method. In this example there has been some equalization of level at the respective

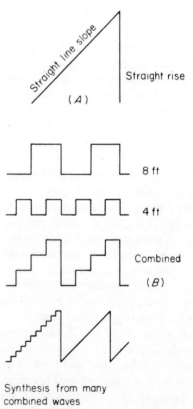

Straight rise

(A)

8 ft

4 ft

Combined

(B)

Synthesis from many
combined waves

Fig. 72 Process of staircasing

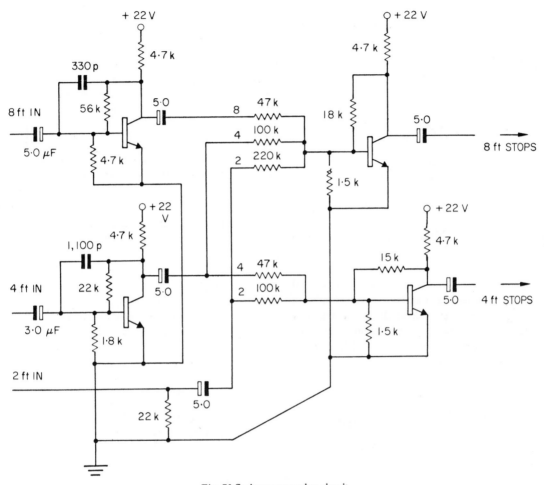

Fig. 73 Staircase summing circuit

To obtain the phase reversal for the higher saw-tooth, one can use the circuit invented by Winston Kock for the Baldwin Company some 25 years ago and shown in the complete tone filters on page 77. Today it is probable that a transistor device would be more acceptable, as in Figs. 74 and 75.

One simple way to obtain a square wave is, of course, to over-drive an amplifier so that it clips the upper and lower excursions of the applied wave form. This can only be done if one such amplifier can be inserted for each note. This can be seen on the part Conn organ circuit, page 131. Here we find a sine wave, a pulse and a square wave for every note, a very refined technique, which of course contributes to the tonal excellence of this make of organ.

In a conventional square-wave bistable, the switching is virtually instantaneous as in Fig. 71; but in the direct sawtooth divider, clearly this cannot happen and so it depends on a conduction level at which the diodes will trigger; the values of the RC nets to ensure this being set according to the line voltage used. The way it works is shown in Fig. 70.

There are many other circuits for frequency division, but those shown are reliable; we can add to them the blocking oscillator, and this is shown, revised for semiconductors, in Fig. 76. No physical characteristics have been mentioned since it is assumed that an experimenter would use discrete components as required; but today it is possible to buy encapsulated dividers in a very compact form,

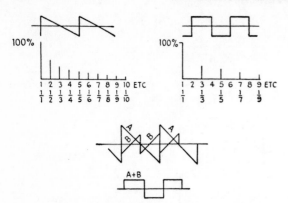

Fig. 74 Production of a square wave from two sawtooth waves

as for example, the Marconi–Elliott MA.60 dual three-stage divider. This contains, in a T.100 can (only 0·37 in. dia. × 0·18 in. high), two three-stage cascaded bistables, which can again be connected externally to make a six-stage divider; and of course there are other makes; all this enormously simplifies the wiring up of the dividers and the costs are becoming competitive with discrete elements, cf. the SAJ 110.

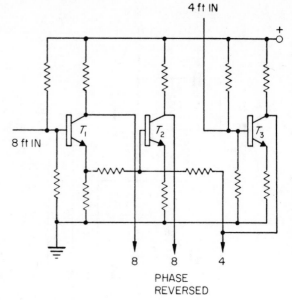

Fig. 75 Schober square wave circuit

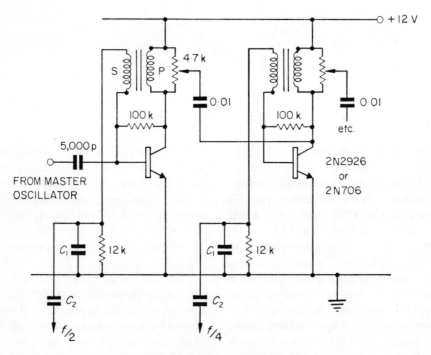

$C_2 = 2C_1$ for each successive division

Fig. 76 Blocking oscillator dividers

Frequency multiplication

Having given some space to frequency dividers, we now look at simple frequency multipliers. It may be asked, why not just use an oscillator for very high notes? The reason is that oscillators require time to build and have relatively costly parts; and further, if the notes required are above top C 2 ft (= 8372 Hz), then even the second harmonic is beyond the limit of audibility; therefore, a sine wave is quite adequate, and this is easily obtained from the same oscillator as is used for the top octave, as in Fig. 77. Here are two ways of generating this pitch. In the first case, a double-wave (or full-wave) rectifier is fed with the tone signal and gives out twice the number of input pulses. In the second

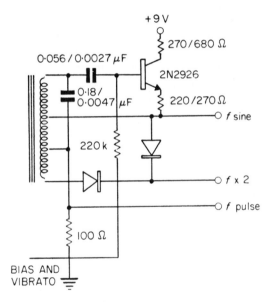

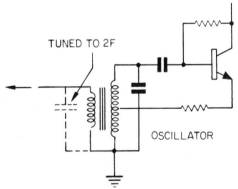

Fig. 77 Frequency doubling oscillators

case, the extra winding over the main coil is tuned to its second harmonic (which is the octave above the generated frequency), and the resultant signal is taken off from this winding. So we get two notes for the price of one, as it were—but, of course, there are few if any harmonics. Both these methods are used in commercial organs and accordions.

Single master oscillator systems

With the rapid developments in semiconductor fabrication methods, further experiments have resulted in the concept of an organ system in which all pitches are derived from just one master oscillator. If this is possible, clearly this can be an expensive and well stabilized unit; for example, a crystal circuit. Then any drift would be so small as to be of no account. The problem here, of course, is to find divisors other than two which will give the correct intervals of the equally tempered scale. This, as we know, is based on the frequency ratio of any two adjacent semitones being $1 : \sqrt[12]{2}$, which is an irrational number. The ratio of 196 and 185 equals this value to an accuracy of at least 10 parts per million, so would be adequate for a music generator. Gears having these ratios are used in the Hammond organ. However, unlike the mechanical Hammond, it is nearly impossible to multiply by these ratios electronically, although division is quite easy. Therefore any proposed system would use division. It must be emphasized at this point that the idea under discussion is only to obtain the master frequencies for the subsequent dividers.

We can take the Motorola dividers as an example. Any frequency divided by both 196 and 185 will produce two tones exactly one half tone apart, to an accuracy of 0·0001 per cent. The next number in the series is 208, which can be divided by 196, as can also the next number, 220. In this way, by continuing the process, 12 such numbers can be found which will give a reasonably accurate musical scale. The maximum error for any one note is + 4 cents, and we recall that 1 cent is 1 per cent of a half tone frequency, or 1200 cents to the octave. The error is small, but too great for an additive organ.

Therefore to improve the accuracy one must use larger divisors. The ultimate will be determined by the speed of the semiconductors envisaged, an example at 3·872 MHz giving a scale in which the maximum error is ±0·6 cent. This is now very accurate tuning, and on this basis, the table shows how the system averages the errors. To do this, a basic circuit is set up as in Fig. 78. This consists of a crystal oscillator, a bias source, a buffer stage and the driver; there is also a vibrato oscillator shown.

Table of Divisors, Digital Tone Generator. Oscillator Frequency 3·872 MHz

Note	Divisor	True Scale Frequency, Hz	Digital Frequency, Hz	Error, cents
C^8	925	4186·01	4186·0	0
B^7	980	3951·07	3951·1	0
$A\sharp^7$	1038	3729·31	3730·4	+ 0·5
A^7	1100	3520·00	3520·0	0
$G\sharp^7$	1165	3322·44	3323·5	+ 0·55
G^7	1235	3135·96	3135·3	− 0·3
$F\sharp^7$	1306	2959·96	2960·3	+ 0·1
F^7	1386	2793·83	2793·6	− 0·14
E^7	1468	2637·02	2637·0	0
$D\sharp^7$	1555	2489·02	2490·0	+ 0·5
D^7	1648	2349·32	2349·7	+ 0·2
$C\sharp^7$	1746	2217·46	2217·8	+ 0·2

When the crystal is in circuit by the switch S_1, the frequency is fixed; if it is removed, the frequency can be varied slightly by R_1. This enables transposition to other keys, or possible gliding tones.

So by using large enough divisors, one can gradually approach the required semitone intervals. Other approaches use different methods and different mathematics, but the results are the same; for in every case, the final accuracy depends only on how far the division is carried out.

One other way depends directly on the use of the division ratios 196 and 185, which means that only two dividing systems will be required to form the desired pitch progression (Fig. 79). But since the frequency intervals are not readily divisible in bistable circuits, use is made of a multivibrator system, for this can be tuned to any desired frequency and will lock in to this on a wave form of almost the same frequency being applied. Thus, from a master oscillator of fixed frequency, one signal branch is taken to a group of standard bistables each dividing by 2 (this is on the assumption that the frequency of the oscillator is based on

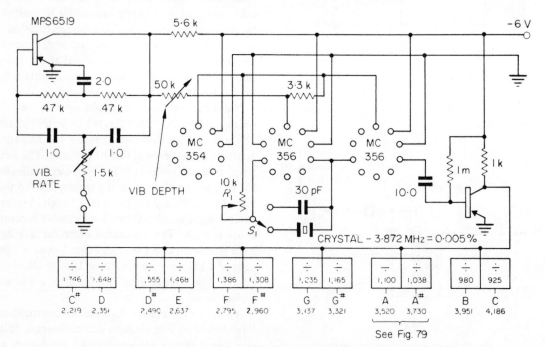

Fig. 78 Oscillator and divider system

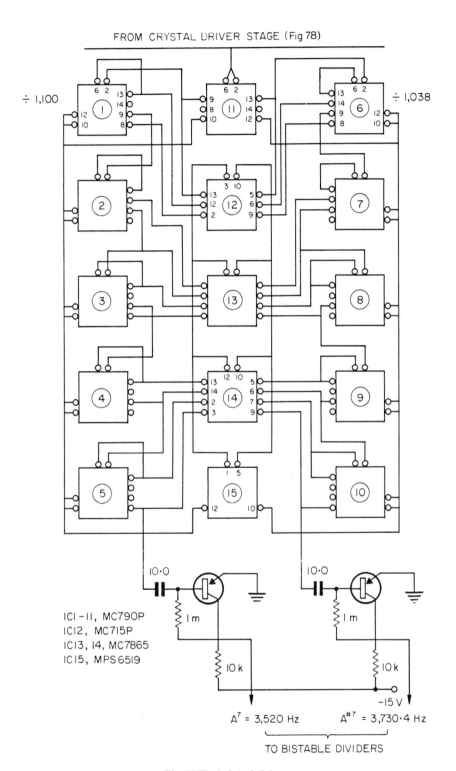

Fig. 79 Typical dual divisor

C); this will, of course, give all the C's required for the organ. The other oscillator branch goes to a multivibrator set to divide by 196. The signal output goes to a frequency comparator circuit, which ensures that the output will be exactly $f_{in}/196$. This corrected (if need be) signal now goes to a divide by 185 multivibrator, the output from which goes to a chain of normal divide by two bistables to give all the octaves of this frequency—which is now one semitone below that of the C circuit. The frequency comparator device acts on the ÷185 circuit also, so ensuring correct ratios equalling $f \div 0.9438$ per semitone interval.

All the semiconductor circuitry for these operations can be fabricated in a chip approximately 30×70 mm, and the normal bistables do not occupy any more space. The complexity of the complete circuit depends, as stated, on the number of required divisions; but this only applies to the bistables. These are calculated from the maximum frequency envisaged for tone forming; for example, if it is thought that 48 harmonics will be required for ultimate fidelity, then the master oscillator frequency must equal the 48th harmonic frequency of C; one would not, of course, expect to use 48 harmonics of the top C, no one could hear half of these; so one might take 48×261 or 12 528 Hz as a minimum; but probably this figure would be doubled in practice, to allow of higher frequencies for special effects, and if a full range of percussions, wind noise, etc. were required, the actual frequency would be nearer 500 kHz. Some commercial systems produce 18 octaves, of which at least 10 are usable tonally. A block diagram of the method is shown in Fig. 80.

The other important method is based on the rejection of a certain number of pulses out of a series of pulses. This number is so chosen that the number of output pulses will be $2^{-1/12}$ times the number of input pulses, in which case 12 circuits will give the normal tempered scale. With this system, the pulses at the outputs would be spaced irregularly, making the resultant tones sound rather harsh. This is got over by making the original frequency many times higher than the required frequencies, and then dividing these required frequencies by the same factor before using them. Thus, there is an input circuit and a

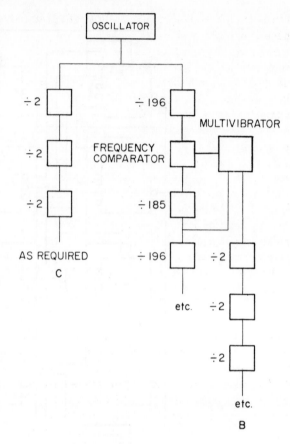

Fig. 80 Frequency derivation system

chain of dividers, the first group of which is used to smooth the wave form and the second group producing the tones for the organ.

If the input frequency is taken high enough, for example 4 MHz, then the first 10 dividers do the smoothing whilst the remaining are tone sources. Since bistables are so inexpensive, the extra complication is of little account. The tuning accuracy with this method is very high, and this is extremely important since the large number of frequencies available pre-supposes additive synthesis, where the accuracy cannot, in fact, be too great. The dividing circuits in the logic units reduce the frequency of the input signals by 30 929/32 768 and lead to an accuracy never worse than 47 parts in a million (related to the correct frequencies of the E.T. Scale). For instance, the theoretical beat frequency between d and a in the middle of the keyboard is 0·9944 Hz; in this system it is

0·9962 Hz, far better than could be realized by manual tuning.

An interesting point about the method is that by using two dividing circuits, one having the values just given and one with the value 0·957031, then, if these are combined in certain ways, it is possible to obtain different values for A♭ and G♯, so enabling a mean tone instrument to be set up, if so desired, or to be switchable to either scaling. And note that, with either system, by simply changing the frequency of the input pulse or master oscillator, transposition into any key can be carried out at the console by turning a knob. The mathematics of this last division system are considered too formidable to appear in this book, but they can be consulted in Appendix IX.

We can show an example of frequency conversion based on the expression of E.T. frequencies in a binary system, the master frequency being 10 in binary notation and the half master frequency being 1. All 12 notes within the octave must now be given by a binary number between 1 and 10. Of course, any scaling—mean tone, just intonation, Werckmeister's, etc.—can be so converted when the appropriate frequency intervals are known. A table of intervals for the equally tempered scale is appended. Observe that these figures are based on a master oscillator frequency for C, this enabling us to use a chain of simple bistables for this note sign. The number of binary digits required is determined by the accuracy to which this synthesis must match the frequencies required by the particular system of tuning. If we go for the closest we can reasonably get to perfect tuning on the E.T. system, then the error should not exceed 0·05 per cent = 1/2000 = an accuracy of 1/11 = 1/2048 for the binary frequencies and hence 11 digit binary numbers (and frequency dividers) are required.

In the actual circuitry, gates with OR and NOR characteristics, polarity inverting circuits and bistables are exclusively employed in this subtractive system; and we append an illustration of the synthesis of an F from the master oscillator running at C; from which it will be seen that while the early stages contribute to the smoothing of the pulse trains, the later stages are available for tone forming. Although some octaves must thus be discarded, these can all be far above audibility so that

Ratios of the 12 Notes of the Octave to the Frequency of the C

	decimal	*binary*
C	2·0000	10·0000000000
B	1·8878	1·1110001101
A♯	1·7818	1·1100100001
A	1·6818	1·1010111010
G♯	1·5874	1·1001011010
G	1·4983	1·0111111110
F♯	1·4142	1·0110101000
F	1·3348	1·0101010111
E	1·2599	1·0100001010
D♯	1·1892	1·0011000010
D	1·1225	1·0001111101
C♯	1·0595	1·0000111101
C	1·0000	1·0000000000

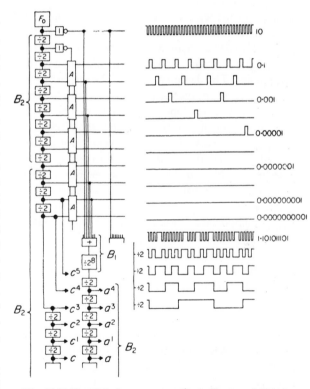

Fig. 81 Philips digital tone system. Block diagram of digital tone generation with integrated circuits A and B. The circuit operates by pulse subtraction. The production of the note A is shown by way of example; the subtraction takes place in a B_1 circuit and the pulse train obtained is divided by 28. Further division-by-two in a B_2 circuit gives the As for the various octaves of the instrument. Every note is produced in this way with the aid of two B circuits, with the exception of the various Cs, which are produced by direct division-by-two from the master oscillator

by the time the pulse wave forms become equally spaced, there are still 9 or 10 octaves available for tone forming—more than adequate for a very large organ. In passing it might be mentioned that this system, developed by Philips Gloelampenfabrieken requires only 1·6 volts to operate it (Fig. 81).

Oscillations can be produced by the movement of a conductor in a magnetic field, or the reverse. There are two practical ways of attaining this result. Fig. 82 shows a vibrating system in which a free reed of the harmonium type, actuated by wind, moves cyclically in front of one pole of a permanent magnet. The reed may be made of iron or have an iron insert in the vibrating end of the tongue. The permanent magnet is surrounded by a coil of wire, through which a steady flux flows. When the iron armature moves with the reed, the flux is varied in a manner corresponding with the excursion of the armature. The changing lines of force induce a changing voltage in the coil, which may be amplified. The damping effect of the magnet exercises a restraint on the reed tongue, which alters the harmonic development of the reed. The use of the end mode of vibration only almost entirely cuts out the excessive harmonic development of the reed. The net effect of these factors is to cause the induced voltage to have a smoother form. Thus the amplified signal gives predominance to the fundamental tone.

An important feature is that it is no longer necessary to rely on the size or power of the reed to produce acoustic energy. Thus lighter reeds, which will speak more rapidly, can be used. This is particularly noticeable in the bass, where the pitch note of, say, sixteen-foot reeds is never heard at all. The depth of tone obtained electrically is strikingly effective. At the same time there is a certain degree of transmission of physically generated harmonics

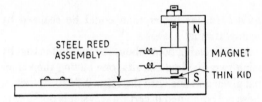

Fig. 83 Magnetic pickup for reed

through the metal of the reed, and although this can be reduced by making the end of the magnet an extremely sharp chisel-shaped point, there is some wave-form distortion for this reason.

It is most difficult to 'voice' steel reeds to produce imitative tones, so that, whilst it is possible to use brass reeds with iron inserts to generate a complex wave, if the whole tongue is made from steel, the use of this form of electromagnetic generator for simple wave forms is precluded by the greater hysteresis (see page 57) introduced by the steel. The electrical output is also very small, because only one pole of the magnet is being used. But by means of suitable electrical filters quite pure waves may be generated, provided that the reeds are in constant vibration.

In Fig. 82, the pickup is shown at the end of the reed. The frequency generated will then be twice that of the reed, since the pole passes the magnet twice in each complete cycle. To generate the natural frequency, a single-sided pickup is required. This is shown in Fig. 83. Note that there is a complete magnetic path in this arrangement, hence the efficiency is four times that of Fig. 82. If the magnet is too powerful, the reed tongue may tend to stick to it; 9 per cent cobalt steel is suitable.

Another form of magnetic generator is shown in Fig. 84, which represents diagrammatically the arrangement employed in the well-known Hammond organ (Chapter 7). It must be emphasized that in this chapter only the principles of operation are summarized, and constructional details are not

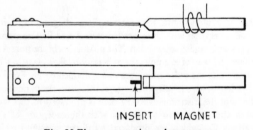

Fig. 82 Electromagnetic reed generator

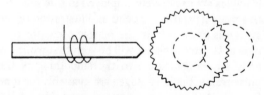

Fig. 84 Arrangement of Hammond tone wheel

given. It might be supposed that after the introduction of the commercial alternating current generator, the idea of producing musical sounds by some form of rotating machine would follow, since the resultant frequency is a function of the number of poles and the speed of rotation. This was indeed so, and the first generator employing a rotating electromagnetic mechanism was devised and made by Professor Thaddeus Cahill in 1897. The patent specifications relating to this instrument show that not only were the fundamental pitch frequencies produced but that Cahill completely anticipated the requirements for harmonic mixing. In those days amplification by means of valves was not possible, since the de Forest patents were not launched until 1907, and further development was abandoned.

Fig. 84 shows a toothed wheel of soft iron driven through suitable gearing by a constant-speed motor. In close proximity to the teeth is a permanent magnet with a chisel-shaped point at this end. On the magnet is placed a coil of wire. Rotation of the wheel produces an alternating voltage in the coil of a suitable frequency, which can be amplified. The strength of the signal can be altered by moving the magnet farther from or nearer to the wheel. There is one such wheel for each fundamental frequency, driven by means of a train of gears so proportioned as to increase the pitch of each successive wheel by the required interval of a semitone. The generator wheels have differing numbers of teeth and other distinguishing features, which are detailed in Chapter 7.

Owing largely to the compactness with which a generator of this type can be produced, and its stable mechanical characteristics, as well as its remarkable electrical simplicity and high signal-to-noise ratio, coupled with ease of production and maintenance, this form of generator is widely used.

It is interesting to examine the possible defects which characterize magnetic generators. Since there is a magnetic field of varying intensity acting on the iron armature, owing to the constantly varying position of the latter, the flux must change with the change in magnetic field. The effect of this on iron is shown in Fig. 85. It can be seen that the flux increases rather slowly with the magnetic field, gradually more rapidly, and eventually ceases to produce much effect. At this latter position the iron is said to be saturated.

Thus the change in flux in the iron is not linear

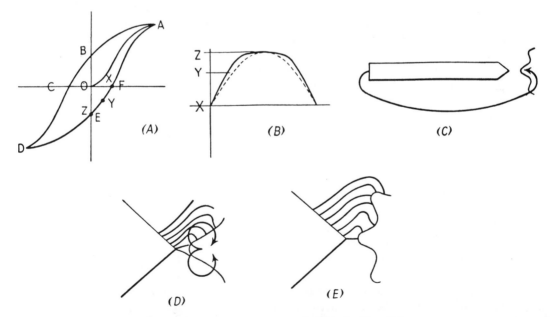

Fig. 85 Change of flux with magnetic field. A = Hysteresis loop; B = Effect on wave form; C = Effect of one end of magnet only; D = Eddy current effect; E = Fringing effect

in relation to the magnetizing force. This gives rise to another effect, known as hysteresis (from the Greek, 'lag behind'). Fig. 85 (*A*) shows a typical hysteresis loop. If the magnetizing force is applied at *O*, the flux will rise to *A* (point of saturation). If now the magnetism decreases, the flux will not return along *AO* but along *AB*. Thus it has not diminished, but is lagging behind. If the magnetizing force is now reversed and simultaneously increased, the curve *BCD* is traced out. Once again, if it is reduced, it gives rise to the curve *DE*; and so on until *A* is reached.

Successive changes reproduce the curve *ABCDEFA*, but *OA* is not traced out again.

The width of the loop at *BE* is dependent on the nature of the material, and is lowest for soft iron, this being the main reason for the use of this material in generators of the type used for music. The effect of the hysteresis loop on the wave form can be seen from (*B*). If we have a rotating device which mechanically traces out the profile of a sinusoidal wave, and it is associated with means for varying the strength of a magnetic field, we can assume the device to have a point which describes the wave form (curve *A*). If three points, *X*, *Y* and *Z* are taken on the hysteresis loop of the magnetic circuit, then at the appropriate moments when the tracing point passes through that portion of the loop the current in the device with the point must be modified by the non-linear rate of change in flux so as to displace the wave which would be generated by a linear rate of flux change (curve *A*) to the position of curve *B*.

The effect of this is to somewhat flatten the top of a wave resulting from the combination of *A* and *B* (which are shown exaggerated) and, as we know, the flat top must contain harmonics. There must therefore be some distortion. If we consider (*C*) it will be seen that if only one end of the magnet is used, the flux lines due to the other pole will be absorbed to some extent by the armature or screening box. This will somewhat affect the wave form. (*D*) shows the effects of eddy currents in the armature, which produce a field at right angles to the main magnetic field and modify it. The eddy current loss is proportional to the square of the frequency; it is also known that the eddy current loss is related to the grain or particle size of the iron, becoming less

as the grain is reduced in size; heat treatment of the discs can also be used to modify the magnetic properties greatly. (*E*) illustrates the effect of fringing due to adjacent teeth, causing a fresh distribution of flux.

All the foregoing effects are interlinked and greatly complicated by the fact that the relative positions of the armature and magnet are constantly changing. But the total amount of distortion is small and can be much reduced, though not entirely eliminated, by suitable electrical means.

In any generator loaded by a permanently energized magnetic system, there is a force acting to cause any wheel, when at rest, to assume a position so that a tooth is opposite the end of the magnet. This reacts on the gears when the system is rotating, and acting upon that force again is one due to the rate of change of the force from the driving motor acting upon the teeth of the gear wheels. That is because there is, or may develop, some back-lash in the teeth of the gear wheels. Ingenious methods have been devised to overcome this effect.

Another approach to the rotating magnetic generator is shown in Fig. 86. The Hammond arrangement is designed to produce sinusoidal wave shapes for additive mixing. At the same time, the gears driving this generator must conform to the intervals of the equally tempered scale (or very nearly so). A glance at the frequency table (Appendix I) shows how limited are the powers of synthesis from E.T. tone sources; only the even harmonics are really usable, all odd harmonics beyond the fifth producing considerable distortion. Clearly the

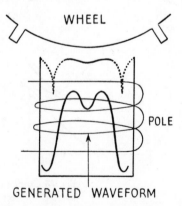

Fig. 86 Complex-wave-form rotary magnetic generator

synthesizing powers of such an instrument are very limited.

The generator of Fig. 86 used the wheels as pitch sources only, the wave form of the oscillations being obtained by shaping the pole piece in the desired manner. A generated wave consisting of fundamental and third harmonic is drawn on the pole piece required to produce this wave. Owing to fringing effects, it is no use deepening the clefts (*shown dotted*). An advantage of such a generator is that several different pole shapes can be radially disposed around any one wheel, thus enabling pre-formed tones to be extracted even if the pitch wheels are in equal-temperament relationship; for the harmonics from each wheel will then be in the correct ratio to the fundamental, so the biggest drawback to the additive instrument is removed.

In order to tune such generators exactly, each train of wheels for seven octaves is mounted on a non-magnetic spindle and rotated by a coned friction disc, as shown in Fig. 87. For seven octaves, the wheels would have 1, 2, 4, 8, 16, 32 and 64 teeth respectively.

The use of such a generator also simplifies the keying arrangements and allows stops to be added to a reasonable extent, which is not possible with the Hammond method (Fig. 84).

It seems such an obvious thing to use magnetic tapes pre-recorded with suitable wave forms as an organ generator, that it is, on the face of it, surprising that no such instrument is on the market. However, there is a special kind of magnetic tape musical instrument on which a very large number of effects is obtainable, including organ tone qualities. This is the Mellotron, and because of its complexity, the description of the device will be found under commercial organs in Chapter 7. Broadly speaking, the problems of wear, dust altering the head gaps, partial magnetization in time, noise, and the enormous mechanical difficulties all combine to make a true organ of conventional tonality almost prohibitive. Precision mechanical engineering is always costly and such an instrument could not compete with the transistor generator.

Electrostatic generators

Oscillation generators of this type fall into three groups—

1. Those using vibrating wires as the source, actuated by hammers.

2. Those using vibrating reeds, actuated by wind.

3. Those using rotating capacitors of variable capacitance, driven by a constant-speed motor.

The principle upon which these groups function is common to them all. It is a function of the capacitance change induced by relative movement of the parts.

Fig. 88 shows a circuit comprising a variable capacitance C, a resistor R between one element of the capacitance and a source of high voltage, and a grid resistor Rg associated with an amplifying valve. If the relative separation of the capacitor plates is varied, the capacitance changes and a corresponding voltage drop occurs in the high resistance R. The voltage variations are transmitted through Cg (which has a capacitance many times that of C) and so effect corresponding variations in the grid potential across Rg.

The resulting potential variations due to the change in C are proportional to the change in

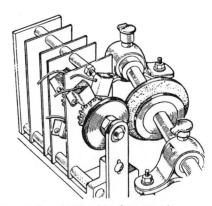

Fig. 87 Cone friction drive for magnetic generator

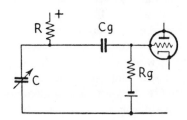

Fig. 88 Capacitance principle

capacitance of C divided by the total capacitance, provided the values of the resistances of R and Rg are sufficiently great to prevent any appreciable current from appearing in C. If current flows, the voltage variations will reduce in proportion, and the response will not be linear.

Since the capacitances involved are usually extremely small, the device is essentially a high-impedance one, and the grid lead should be kept short to avoid stray fields. The capacitance of the leads should also be small. This capacitance must be included in the total capacitance mentioned above, so that if the leads exercise much shunting the output will be reduced.

1. *Stretched wire generators.* At least two forms of electric piano have been developed employing such generators. The wires are polarized by means of a high-voltage source through a resistance. When the string is vibrated by means of the hammer action, changes in capacitance between the wires and small metal studs mounted above them are induced as explained, for one end of the studs is connected to the valve grid. These changes in capacitance follow the movement of the wire exactly, and in consequence the amplified voltage changes are a replica of the vibrating condition of the wire at that point. Further details of the exact construction are to be found in Chapter 7.

2. *Vibrating reed generators.* These function in exactly the same way and are connected in similar circuits, metal studs above the reed being coupled to the valve grid and the reed tongue and base suitably polarized (Chapters 7 and 8).

3. *Rotating variable capacitors.* The only real difference here from 1 and 2 above lies in the construction and drive. In consequence no detailed explanation will be given at the moment. One important feature is that since at least part of the generator is rotating, there must be a means of making constant contact with it. In some cases this is done with a brush, like a d.c. electric motor, in other cases the capacitance change is transferred through an associated capacitance, the relative spacings of which do not alter. A capacitor may rotate and still fulfil this condition which is the principle of the long-established Compton organs. Since it is difficult to explain the basic circuits without expanding them into a complete organ

system, the reader will find the rotating generator and charging system described in Chapter 7 under Compton.

The signal level from most types of electrostatic generator is very low and owing to the high potential difference between the electrodes, noise may be introduced if the insulation is not quite perfect. Very careful attention to the screening is necessary and it is most important to exclude damp. Physical or mechanical vibration has an adverse effect on capacitative generators, since if any of the elements can vibrate owing to an external force they may function as a microphone and introduce spurious signals. Mechanical rigidity in the assembly is probably more important in this group of oscillation generators than in any other type.

Photo-electric generators

Several instruments have been made using the principle of the varying conductivity of certain materials under the incidence of light. The variation in conductivity is caused by the emission of a more or less dense stream of electrons from the material and was, of course, the means by which sound films were reproduced until recently.

A structure with these properties is known as a photo-electric cell. One form consists, for our purpose, of an evacuated glass bulb in which are mounted two electrodes. One is a plate of metal on the surface of which is deposited some substance rich in photo-emissive properties, and the other is a wire structure to which the electrons are attracted. This is generally small in cross-section so as to allow as much light as possible to reach the plate.

Fig. 89 shows an elementary circuit in which the wire is the anode and the plate the cathode. If the cell is connected as shown, on applying a positive

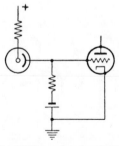

Fig. 89 Photo-electric principle

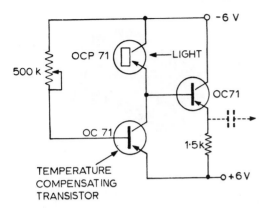

Fig. 90 Circuit for a photo-sensitive transistor generator

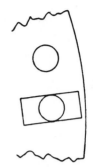

Fig. 91 Disc with round hole and square aperture

potential to the anode a stream of electrons will leave the cathode and travel over to the anode if light is allowed to fall on the cathode. The current will be proportional to the amount of light if the circuit constants are properly calculated for the type of cell in use. Increased sensitivity can be obtained if inert gas is introduced into the cell. With the introduction of photo-sensitive transistors, most of the difficulties encountered with conventional photo-cells have disappeared. Because of their small size, one can be used for each signal, and very small light intensities and operating voltages are required. A circuit for such a transistor is given in Fig. 90.

As a matter of fact, all transistors are to some extent photo-sensitive and light has therefore to be excluded by an opaque casing or coating. A portion of this is removed to make the cell light-sensitive. Other materials can be used to make cells responsive to light, notably cadmium sulphide or cadmium selenide. This kind of photo-cell exhibits a slight time lag which makes it unsuitable for photo-electric organs, but it is used to a considerable extent for volume, stop and keying controls as we shall see later on. By correct proportioning, the resistance change under the influence of light can be made to cover from several megohms to only a few ohms.

At the present time, all types of semiconductive cells suffer from a limited upper frequency response, which in the best case does not extend much beyond 5 kHz. The vacuum cell just described must therefore be used for frequencies above this.

This property of photo-emission may be used to generate either simple or complex waves by variations in construction. If we project a beam of light on to a photo-cell through holes cut in an opaque revolving disc, then if the holes are circular and spaced two diameters apart, running past a fixed rectangular hole one diameter wide, the variation of light on the cell will be approximately sinusoidal (Fig. 91). It is obvious that by properly choosing the number of holes and speed of rotation, a note of any pitch can be produced.

A further extension of this method is to use narrow slits instead of circular holes and to cause them to scan a mask of length equal to the spacing between the slits. If the mask has the wave form of some characteristic instrument engraved on it, a sound of that wave form will be heard on amplifying the output from the photo-cell (Fig. 92). A number of concentric rings of slits may appear on one disc of large diameter, the combined images of which can be focused on a common photo-cell by lenses or a parabolic mirror. If each mask has its own exciter lamp, these lamps may be controlled

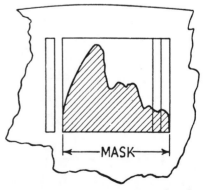

Fig. 92 Disc with rectangular slits and mask

by playing keys and the volume of the sound regulated by altering the brightness of the lamps. The apparatus for this very convenient method is, however, extremely difficult to construct, and in the form described it has not been found possible to reduce the frequency errors as between one row of slots and another to even the maximum departure of ± 0.05 per cent.

Another method is to record photographically a fundamental together with the appropriate harmonic series of wave forms, as in Fig. 93. Then, if a sufficiency of exciter lamps is provided, it becomes possible to use such a generator for additive synthesis, with little or no limit to the number of combinations usable at any one moment. An organ with four manuals, using this method, has actually been built.

In yet another arrangement, rotating glass discs carry photographically-reproduced wave forms which may be either simple or complex tones. In one instrument of this type the discs could actually be changed, so that it was possible to keep a number of different 'stops', as if they were gramophone records. The qualities of photographic emulsions are not particularly stable, especially under the influence of concentrated light, and some shrinkage of the emulsion has been noted, giving rise in time to distortion.

Recently some interest has been shown in a method by which pre-formed tone qualities are photographed on to a metal disc, which is subsequently etched away so that light can pass through the 'sound tracks'. Previously the thin

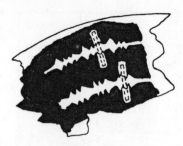

Fig. 94 Noise reduction system

metal foil has been bonded to a glass disc to hold it rigid. The standard arrangement of exciter lamp and photo-cell used for motion picture projectors is satisfactory, but to make the assembly of the 12 sets of discs, etc., more compact, the images from the slits are collected by a concave mirror and focused on a single central photo-cell.

An interesting point is that in any other photo-electric system, the light can pass through any aperture exposed, regardless of whether this contributes to the sound or not. This problem arose in the early days of sound film and gave rise to background noise, due to abrasions and imperfections of the film base. By electrical means, the light was later practically removed except at moments of modulation, thus ensuring a silent background. As an organ is a sustained-tone instrument, any ground noise can be very irritating. The reduction system is seen in Fig. 94. A double-sided track is recorded, and at times of no sound, only a minute slit appears. The herring-bone track is scanned by a horizontal slit, shown dotted.

One of the difficulties with any generating system is to obtain enough tone sources, in a comparatively simple device, to synthesize a large instrument. For example, one set of 8-ft pitch oscillators cannot be used over and over again for different tone qualities without some (if not all) of them becoming degraded. Of course, this is often done in the less expensive organs, with disastrous effects on large combinations of stops. All the individual tonal qualities disappear, and only a 'sound' is left.

A new form of generator overcomes those difficulties in a novel and convenient way. Fig. 95 shows a transparent cylinder, arranged for mounting on a driving spindle. The tube, made from

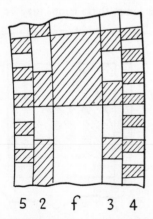

5 2 f 3 4

Fig. 93 Section of photo-electric disc for additive synthesis

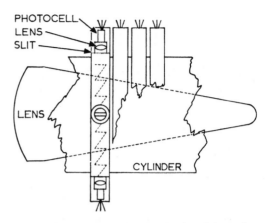

Fig. 96 Conical lens for even illumination of the tracks

Fig. 95 Diakon cylinder for mounting on driving spindle

Diakon, is sprayed with an opaque plastic layer, which will attach itself to the Diakon but will not cement itself thereto. The black layer is then engraved on a special machine with eight sawtooth tracks, as illustrated. The engraved strip is pulled off, leaving the sawtooth wave forms transparent and the rest opaque.

Eight non-metallic rings encircle the cylinder, each of which contains pairs of photo-transistors with short focus lenses, situated 180° apart. By this means, small errors in engraving or concentricity are cancelled out and the signal strength is increased. Even illumination of all the tracks is ensured by a conical plastic lens, as in Fig. 96.

Since each track has twice the number of waves of the previous one, eight octaves are available on any one tube. Each cylinder is driven, through pulleys, at the correct speeds to produce the intervals of the equally tempered scale. Thus twelve cylinders form the complete generator.

The advantages are—

1. By having enough photo-cells, one can have as many *quite independent* stops as desired.

2. Through the use of sawtooth-shaped waves, all the harmonics required to form any tone are contained in *each wave*, so that there is no robbing or degradation due to borrowing or addition.

Such a generator is not cheap to make, but is far less expensive than a comparable valve organ. As described, it is possible to have six 16 ft, twelve 8 ft, ten 4 ft and eight 2 ft separate sources and, of course, mutations as well. A very novel feature is that if the rings are mounted so that they can be rotated to and fro around the cylinders, a large number of different rates of vibrato can be obtained. Rings may be coupled by connecting rods so that groups can be simultaneously oscillated.*

The following general notes apply to all rotating photo-electric generators—

1. The aperture must be quite evenly illuminated.

2. The focused image must be sharp.

3. No shadow should appear on the photo-cell as the wheel passes the mask.

4. The photo-cell itself should be evenly illuminated over its whole surface; this is now easy if photo-transistors are used, or the ORP12 types.

It should be remembered that the rate at which the filament of an electric lamp heats up is usually of the order of thirty to seventy milliseconds; therefore direct keying of lamps is not a possibility if percussive or even very rapid attacks are called for in a photo-electric musical instrument. The same characteristic is of course an advantage in organ simulation, since the build-up times correspond quite closely to those of pipes.

* Patent applied for.

5 Tone Forming, Keying and Vibrato Circuits

Having obtained the wave forms required from some type of oscillator or frequency divider, they must now be processed to form acceptable sounds. There are two approaches to this problem, but both really entail similar techniques. Either the aim is to imitate (or simulate) known orchestral or organ tone colours; or, it is simply required to produce a number of agreeable musical sounds. There are two schools of thought here, reminding us somewhat of the conflict between the theatre and the church or concert pipe organ. These two opinions further divide into whether the resultant final tone should come from a number of sine waves suitably combined (as in some Hammond organs), or whether the sounds are better formed by treating a complex wave form to adjust the number of harmonics generated therein. At first sight the method of combining sine waves seems the most attractive, as clearly the resultant fidelity only depends (for a steady state) on the number and loudness of the relative sine sources. But unfortunately the difficulty here, until recently, lay in the simultaneous keying of all these sources; it is a mechanical problem, not easy to solve. However, to show what has to be done, we illustrate in Fig. 97 part of a Hammond organ circuit which shows a few tone (or sine wave) sources, the mixing and selecting drawbars using a tapped transformer for the various levels, and the keying busbars and contact system. The taps on the mixing transformer are so designed that each gives an equal increment of loudness and the pitches connected to the keys are: sub fundamental; sub 3rd; fundamental, 2nd, 3rd, 4th, 5th, 6th, 8th and in some cases, 10th and 12th. From mixtures of these sources, which are a close approximation to sine waves, a great many tone colours can be compounded, and at all times the exact composition of the voices is under the control of the player.

But one must take a closer look at the principles underlying electromagnetic generators to understand the problems.

In all circuits using this method the required generator signal voltage is developed across a coil of wire. This has many turns and is thus an inductance. The effect is increased by the iron core. At the same time the winding possesses resistance. The reactance of the coil is

$$2\pi f L$$

where f = frequency,
L = inductance.

The reactance and the resistance combine to give the impedance

$$\sqrt{(4\pi^2 f^2 L^2 + R^2)} \text{ ohms}$$

It can be seen that the frequency term enters into this equation. Now in transferring energy from one circuit possessing impedance to another of like nature, the maximum transfer can only be obtained if the impedances are matched. They may match 1 : 1, 1 : 50 or in any other ratio, but the optimum value can hold for only one frequency at one impedance ratio. Clearly then if we have a series of coils having different impedances at different frequencies, we shall not have a very effective energy transfer. For even if the individual coils are properly designed, should they be connected in varying numbers to a fixed impedance there must be a changing ratio of power transfer.

The only satisfactory means of mixing the output of inductive generators is by some means of inductive coupling, and this involves loss of signal strength if many such circuits are simultaneously connected. It is for this reason that it is not possible to add or combine 'stops' in instruments using inductive magnetic generators.

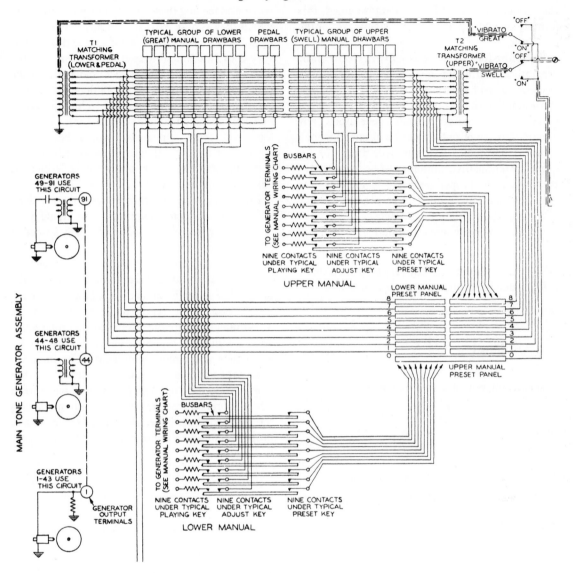

Fig. 97 Hammond mixing circuit

Now if the resistive component of the impedance is made high compared with the inductance, there will be a voltage drop resulting in a loss of signal strength. But the relative changes in energy due to mismatching of the inductive component will not be so marked. In consequence a deliberate mismatching, if not carried to excess, will help to reduce the difference in energy when varying numbers of generators are keyed.

More recent organs have found a way to overcome this rather serious limitation, and in the G-100 for example we find a method whereby the impedance is raised to figures which permit addition of ready-formed voices; in other words, the pre-set voices shown appear in the form of stop keys and not independent drawbars, therefore the player has no control over the voicing. Fig. 220 (Chapter 7) is very useful as indicating the correct proportions of the various sine waves for the sounds named; this formula would apply to any sine-wave organ generator.

Therefore for additive mixing with electrostatic generators, harmonic mixing is comparatively easily achieved by varying the polarizing voltage. If a suitable switch is made to apply the required potentials to the appropriate generators, any required degree of output can be obtained from a series of harmonics so combined. Since the required potential distribution must be logarithmic, to produce the proper increases in loudness the note key resistances must have a higher ohmic value than the regulating resistances.

For any one harmonic combination, if

N = number of note key resistances in parallel
R_1 = value of each note key resistance in ohms
R = value of regulating resistance in ohms

then the gain in decibels

$$= 20 \log_{10} \left(\frac{R_1}{R} + 1 \right) \times N \div \left(\frac{R_1}{R} + N \right)$$

The charging potential to the generator is

$$E = \frac{V_1 + V_2 + V_3}{N + \left(\dfrac{R_1}{R} \right)}$$

$V_1, V_2 \ldots$ = potentials of busbars

There are preferred resistance ratios to satisfy properly the requirements for correct increments in loudness. In general R is recommended to be $\frac{1}{3}$ to $\frac{1}{5}$ of the ohmic value of the note key resistances.

Owing to the relative ease with which straightforward control of d.c. potentials may be carried out, it is possible to exercise an overriding control on the above polarizing derivations by an adjustable resistance functioning as a swell pedal.

With the introduction of the integrated circuit and its ability to contain large numbers of semiconductors in a very small compass, and extending this to embrace digital techniques, it is possible to key as many wave components as required by converting their electrical properties as analysed acoustically into digital signals representing the increments of energy in a sound

wave, and feeding these into memory circuits from which they can be extracted in any way required by suitable gating elements. Of course this sounds very complicated and indeed it is, but in time the cost of the circuits will reduce and perhaps the complexity will reduce too; it all depends on how far digital, analogue and manual techniques are to be combined in one organ. Clearly for a simple instrument, these approaches would be far too costly; but for the ultimate where cost is of little account, examples so far produced underline the value of these techniques.

Fig. 98 shows an imaginary sound wave with an analysis on a selected point basis; the actual wave is divided up into several sections equally spaced in time, as many as might lead to the required fidelity. The amplitudes are plotted but if the increments of amplitude are plotted there is some saving in the detail. These might be shown digitally as in the figure, each digit representing an increase of amplitude; there are thus steps, not a gliding scale, and the number of digits used must be governed by economics and circuit complexity. The information in the figure is common to all pitches; in other words, it is only necessary to find a wave form which sounds correct, to use this for compounding the whole keyboard spectrum. The respective and proper bits (which are of course really equivalent

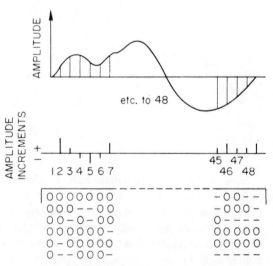

DIGITAL REPRESENTATION OF AMPLITUDE INCREMENTS

Fig. 98 Selected point analysis

to harmonics at selected amplitudes) are routed to a memory store, from which they are taken out by a gating system operated by a stop; therefore, there would be as many diodes (if it were a diode memory system) as there were required harmonics to form that particular tone colour. From the gates there could be attack and decay circuits and then a summing amplifier is required to add the information together before transferring from the digital to analogue converter which introduces the time scaling. It can be seen that by this somewhat complex arrangement it is possible to analyse, generate and store any particular wave shape with any required fidelity and amplitude limits, depending only on the permissible complexity of the circuitry; some memory devices might be unsuitable for music; the diode system of course must be recycled continuously but has the great advantage of cheapness and small bulk. In this example, ring counters are energized by the playing keys to maintain the diode memory circuits.

Another way to form pitches for subsequent tone forming and also using a binary system is to subtract the required frequencies from a large number—in other words, to reject a certain number of pulses from a series of pulses. In this particular system, a very high frequency is used for the single master oscillator and pulse trains are formed by halving this frequency (suitably reduced by division). These correspond successively with the binary numbers 0.1, 0.01, 0.001 etc., and provide the material for making up the binary numbers between 1 and 10 with the required accuracy (no deviation greater than 0.05 per cent, $= 1/2000 = 1/2^{11}$, hence 11 binary numbers). If the basic frequency 1 is note C, then to form A (as an example), the following pulse trains are added (cf Fig. 81, Chapter 4). This will be seen to correspond with the decimal ratio of A to C, viz. 1.6816. However, it has been found simpler to obtain this note by subtraction from the binary 10 of the primary frequency; the A just mentioned is equal to 1.1010111010 which is equal to $10 - 0.0101000110$. These elaborate techniques are only possible with the aid of micro-circuits and the several thousand transistors and diodes required are fabricated on incredibly small chips which, even when encapsulated, make the

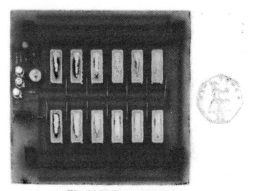

Fig. 99 Philips organ generator

whole system only $4 \times 4\frac{1}{2} = \frac{1}{2}$ in.—see Fig. 99.

Clearly these advanced methods are costly at present, but on the other hand the labour cost of assembly is much reduced; undoubtedly this will form a major technique for organs of the future.

Subtractive tone forming

It is easily seen that additive tone forming requires a very large number of tone sources; and it must be added, these have to be tuned to a very high accuracy, a very few parts in a million. This is why mechanically-driven or single oscillator systems have the advantage: they cannot get out of tune. But for the less expensive organs, and for the experimenter, much better results are obtained by removing certain harmonics (or possibly even accentuating them) from a complex wave form which has been generated either by an independent oscillator system or by frequency dividers. But, if we do this, then the circuits must give the result desired as the player has no control over the sound spectrum except by some auxiliary device such as a glide or wah-wah modifier. This again brings us to the consideration of whether we need to imitate existing known pipe organ sounds, or whether we are content with some pleasing sounds of a generally acceptable nature—perhaps flute-like or string-like effects, but not striving after especial fidelity; for after all, the majority of inexpensive domestic organs today fall into this category, whatever the makers may say!

We have seen from earlier chapters that in the case of additive synthesis, we have only to study the harmonic plot of any steady sound to be able to compound it from sine waves. To understand sub-tractive tone forming, we must see what the method involves. We shall only deal with square or sawtooth input wave forms, because it is only from these shapes that satisfaction can be obtained. Therefore, in each case there will be sufficient har-monics to synthesize many organ tones, and since it is harder to do this with known voices, we will see what must be done.

The whole principle of subtractive tone forming is based on the use of filters. Of course, these are rarely (if ever) the exactly calculated filters having sharp cut-off characteristics used in telecom-munications; but they are so described for want of a better word. If one looks at the formant bands for some well-known orchestral instruments (Fig. 11, Chapter 2), it is obvious at once that it is a kind of sliding action which is required of the filters, and this is very fortunate otherwise the cost and com-plexity of sharp-cutting and matched filters would price any organ off the market. Three main types exist: one to remove upper frequencies; one to do the reverse, remove low ones; and one to accen-tuate a broad or narrow band of frequencies. These different types may be active or passive; active filters incorporate a transistor or valve, passive ones merely have the network required for their purpose. All sounds having a flute-like nature require low-pass filters; the derivation of the name is evident, they pass low notes and remove high ones. Firstly we will show the basic networks for the various purposes, then specific examples which are known to yield good results. Look, then, at Fig. 100. This is a two-stage low-pass circuit of a type very commonly used today. The method works because the reactance of the shunt capacitors is made small compared with the series resistance of the filter and the impedance to which the output of the filter is fed. Under these conditions, a section

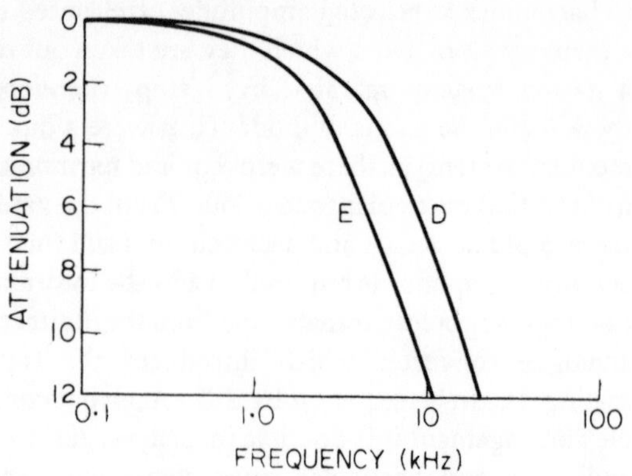

Fig. 101 Low-pass integrating filter.

	E			D	
$R = 50\,k\Omega$	$C = 1280\,p$		$R = 50\,k\Omega$	$C =$	640
$20\,k\Omega$	3200		$20\,k\Omega$		1600
$10\,k\Omega$	6400		$10\,k\Omega$		3200

Theoretical cut-off $f = 1/(2\pi RC)$

of RC filter reduces each frequency component of voltage applied to the input side according to the relation

$$\frac{\text{a.c. across capacitor}}{\text{a.c. across input of section}} = \frac{1}{2\pi fCR}$$

R being the series resistance and C the shunt capacitor. The number of filter sections determines the attenuation, whilst the 'shape' of the transmis-sion depends on the type of section used. The ac-tion of a single section is shown in Fig. 101, the capacitance bypassing the upper frequencies to earth. Obviously the action will be different for different frequencies if C and R are fixed. This can be seen from Fig. 102, which shows the effect of a single section with differing time constants $(=CR)$ on an input pulse of constant width, i.e. constant repetition frequency. The longer the time constant, the more effective will be the harmonic removal and the smaller will be the output be. Thus, any application of this kind of circuit should be re-calculated every octave at least, as that is a frequency ratio of 2 : 1. In extreme cases, such a filter might be used for every single note. The effect is best if the capacitors are not too large, better results being obtained if two or more sections are used in cascade.

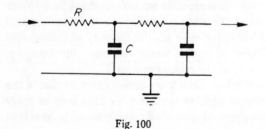

Fig. 100

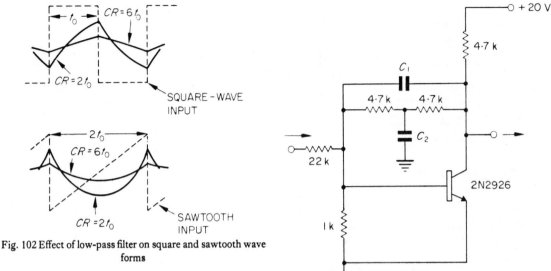

Fig. 102 Effect of low-pass filter on square and sawtooth wave forms

It will be realized that owing to the series resistance, the signal will be reduced in level regardless of the filtering action; therefore some organs use active filters, which incorporate a transistor to offset the loss; this kind of circuit can also be tuned more sharply, and examples are shown in Figs. 103 and 104. The bridged-T network acts as a frequency-selective feedback path and the turnover point can be adjusted by altering the value of C.

Fig. 103 Active low-pass filter

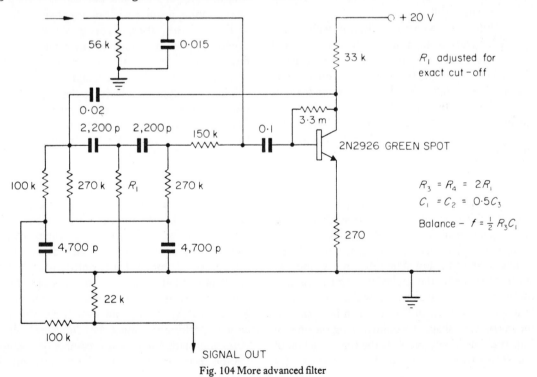

Fig. 104 More advanced filter

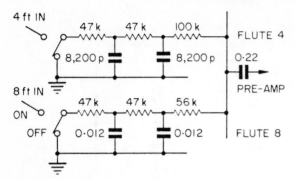

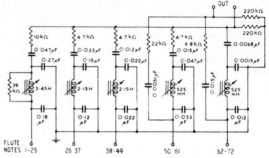

Fig. 105 Application of simple low-pass filters

Note the ingenious way in which the base biasing resistors are also made to function as part of the twin T filter. In practice, some extra circuit elements are often introduced for one reason or another, and we now show two methods of applying these elementary sections to actual organ circuits. Fig. 105 is a simple case, where one filter of two sections is made to cover four octaves. We show the differences in values for 4 ft and 8 ft pitches. In both cases, the constants are chosen to make the filtering most effective about the middle of the compass. For a simple instrument, this gives quite pleasing results.

Fig. 106 shows a complex filter, in which each octave is treated separately. Note that tuned chokes are used here; these have the property shown in the inset and therefore do not cut quite as much as the *RC* networks. The natural tendency of the chokes to resonate at some particular frequency is reduced by the series resistors and capacitors so as to flatten the curve. In some cases, such filters may be fed from more than one frequency source, i.e. we could feed in 8 ft pitch as the main frequency and superimpose a trace of 4 ft to add brilliance. Tibias, flutes and diapasons are formed from suitable disposition of low-pass filters—this also applies to higher pitched tones of the same families, e.g. piccolo, fifteenth, nazard, twelfth etc.

The effect of the low-pass filters must differ according to whether the applied wave form is a sawtooth or is square, since we know that the circuit is frequency sensitive; in Fig. 107 can be seen how the initial wave shape is modified along the lines of Fig. 102. The '*t*' referred to is the time constant of the *RC* network compared to the time constant (or

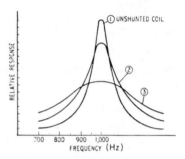

Fig. 106 Complex flute filter

length) of the applied pulse (we use the term pulse here meaning a single wave of any shape or form). In Fig. 107 the pulses, of course, are sawtooth or square; applied triangular waves would be modified by this filter but sine waves would only be attenuated or bypassed to ground.

The next filter to consider is the reverse of the low-pass one and is naturally termed a high-pass type; removing the low notes and passing the higher ones. We use this kind of circuit for only one purpose, the simulation of organ string tone. Such voices are relatively quiet and uniform in harmonic content. This may sound strange, but the fact is that if the fundamental or pitch sound is removed (or largely so), then the ear cannot discriminate between harmonics if there are very many of these. Now by keeping the level low, agreeable string-like sounds can be produced at any pitch; of course it is appreciated that pipe-organ string stops do not sound in the least like orchestral strings; but this is because the nuances of intonation possible by a human performer cannot be duplicated in instruments with fixed wind pressures or voltages; the spectrum for a fixed note of very short duration

ORIGINAL SQUARE WAVE

ORIGINAL SAWTOOTH WAVE

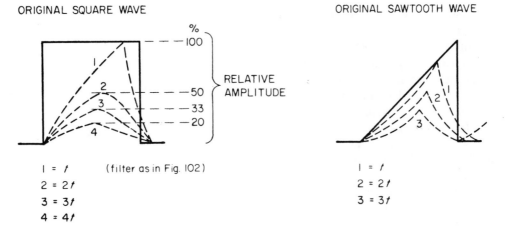

Fig. 107 Modifying wave forms

would be very similar but we cannot imitate the expressiveness. We might note here that a sawtooth wave has a rather string-like sound without any processing.

In a high-pass filter the capacitor comes first and is shunted to earth by a resistor. Because the capacitor cannot charge instantly and must discharge exponentially, the output wave form is a function of time and capacitance—

$$e_0 = E^{-t/RC}$$

RC should now be very short compared with the time taken for the input wave form to undergo an appreciable change. Since the capacitor must always be in series with the signal input, there will always be some effect—even when '*t*' = the period of the pulse. Quite an effective high-pass filter can be made, using the property of decreasing reactance of a capacitor with frequency, by just connecting a suitable capacitor in series with the signal and the pre-amplifiers. An example shows that a capacitor of $0.01\,\mu$F has a reactance of $160\,$kΩ at 100 Hz, but only $3.2\,$kΩ at 5 kHz. The bass cut resulting from a well-designed high-pass filter is given in Fig. 108 together with the circuit arrangement. The regulating resistor *R* may be omitted for high pitches. Sometimes a resonant filter is used instead of a high-pass one, and we now examine this kind of circuit, which is used for simulation of all kinds of reeds; and sometimes for the effect of certain stopped pipes and tibias.

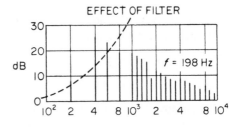

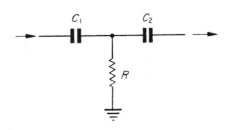

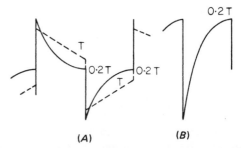

Fig. 108 Effect of high-pass filter on (*A*) square wave and (*B*) sawtooth wave

Resonant filters are required when the frequency bands have to be sharper and better defined than is possible with *RC* networks, which are characterized by a relatively slow and indefinite effect on small bands of frequencies; though the effect on a wide band is very marked. But we know from previous chapters that orchestral instruments often have formant bands which give them their distinctive sounds, and this is equally true of reed organ pipes. So the need for resonant circuits is quite real; they cause the required formant bands to stand out above the other frequencies present in the complex wave with which the filter is fed.

There are two kinds of resonant filter circuit, the required inductance may be in series with the capacitor, or it may be in parallel with it. Resonance occurs when the reactance of the coil equals that of the capacitor, and if the resistance of both elements is zero, this can only occur at one frequency—

$$f_r = \frac{1}{2\pi\sqrt{LC}}$$

In practice, of course, the coil has a finite resistance and this is a good thing otherwise the sharpness of resonance would be far too great to be of use on a complex wave. Fig. 109 (*A*) shows both series and parallel resonant circuits, the inherent resistance being shown dotted. Now we can see the effect of having some resistance, because if this is made adjustable, the resonant peak can be broadened and so made to simulate the formant band of almost any reed instrument. The effect from either form of circuit is roughly the same, except that the input to the series circuit should be of low impedance for maximum selectivity, whilst that for the parallel circuit should be of high impedance. Also, there is control over the actual prominence given to injected signals by varying the '*Q*' of the coil used—

$$Q = \frac{\omega L}{R} \quad (\omega = 2\Pi f)$$

This figure should be high, brought about of course by winding with a low resistance wire. Equally, the inductance should be large and the capacitance small for sharpness of resonance. But Fig. 109 (*B*) shows these effects lumped together, on the assumption that ωL is constant and R is varied to

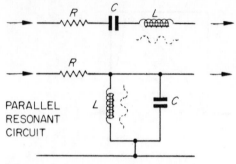

SERIES RESONANT CIRCUIT

PARALLEL RESONANT CIRCUIT

(*R* is a regulating or matching resistor)

(*A*)

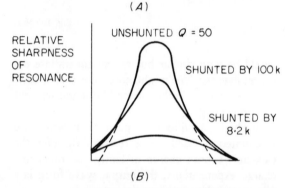

RELATIVE SHARPNESS OF RESONANCE

UNSHUNTED *Q* = 50

SHUNTED BY 100 k

SHUNTED BY 8·2 k

(*B*)

Fig. 109 Principle of resonant filters

reduce *Q*. A value of 50 is a very useful one and can be broadened by shunting with a resistor as required instead of degrading the coil. Of course, it is possible to use resonant circuits in series to obtain overlapping effects, or in other complex arrangements for special effects; but such circuits are usually confined to a specific organ for some particular reason and are not of general value. It might be added that, so far as possible, all inductances should be wound on closed cores of the ferrite pot type; this ensures a high '*Q*' and more important, prevents external field interference which can easily occur if the coils are wound on open laminated cores. This means that filter coils can be stacked close together in a tone forming box or tray, just behind the stops. There are different types of ferrite, but all have a winding formula of the type—

$$n = 65^* \sqrt{L \times 10^3}$$

which gives the number of turns for one millihenry. The value shown with an asterisk is obtainable from the makers, and we can recall that the inductance of any given winding is proportional to the square of the number of turns.

The reader would only be confused if an attempt was made to show all the commercial variants of this kind of circuit; such applications are not always straightforward, and often depend on other factors in the design of the organ. But tone forming is such an essential and vital part of a complete tonal specification that we illustrate several approaches by different manufacturers to virtually the same problem (Figs. 110–13). All these filters

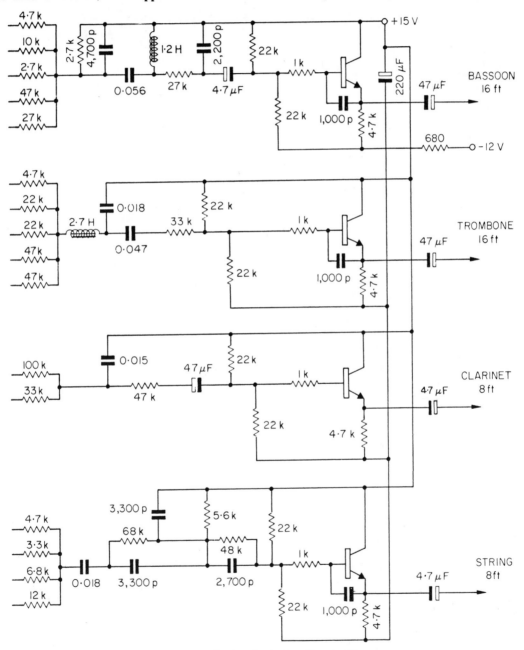

Fig. 110 Voicing circuits from Yamaha E5

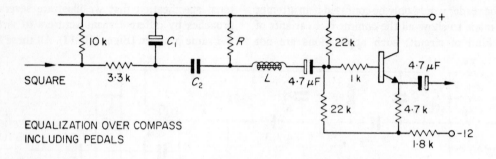

EQUALIZATION OVER COMPASS
INCLUDING PEDALS

OCTAVE	1	2	3	4	5	6	7	8	9	10
C_1	0·47	0·47	0·47	0·33	0·33	0·27	0·18	0·15	0·12	0·082
C_2	0·47	0·33	0·22	0·18	0·12	0·082	0·068	0·039	0·027	0·01
R	120 k	120 k	120 k	120 k	47 k	33 k	33 k	68 k	47 k	47 k
L	8·2H	6·8H	5·6H	3·9H	2·7H	1·8 H	1·2 H	1·0 H	470 mH	330 mH

DETAILS OF YAMAHA 8 ft FLUTE

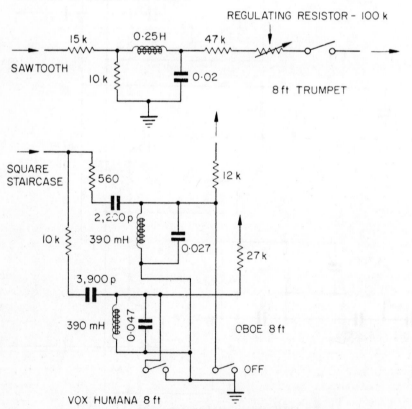

Fig. 111 Further examples of tone forming

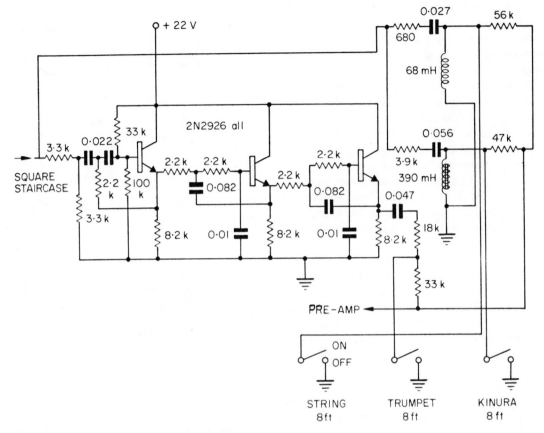

Fig. 112 Wurlitzer voicing circuits

work very well but only on the type of input wave form specified. Their effect will be much modified by varying input impedances and provision must always be made to prevent short-circuiting of the outputs. Note the different ways of cutting off the stops. It will be appreciated that other devices could be used instead of switches, notably photocells energized by a lamp when the stops are operated.

The total sound spectrum for a well-balanced organ of classical type should be as in Fig. 114. For domestic or entertainment instruments, no such graph is possible.

Now there are many other ways of modifying the initial wave form to produce envelopes suitable for tonal treatment. One method is to rectify a sine wave and apply it to resonant circuits. Another is to pass the wave through a non-linear conductor, such as silicon carbide; this can be polarized, that

is, have a d.c. voltage applied to it as well as the signal, when it distorts the input signal in various ways, some of which are useful as tonal wave forms (Fig. 115). But further control is possible by the method of keying the actual signal or, at least, the note circuit to produce an interval of the scale.

A quite recent technique is voltage control of filters, which confers a degree of flexibility to their pass bands; but the chief outlet for such applications is in synthesizers, and there would be no great advantage for keyboard musical instruments. For those interested their application is discussed at some length in *Electronic Music Production* by the same author and publisher as this book.

When we examine keying methods presently, diodes will come into the picture; therefore it is worth remembering that these are readily overloaded by a strong signal, and if this occurs, harmonics are generated, usually third and possibly other odd-numbered ones; therefore tones analogous to stopped pipes can be produced by over-driving a diode, of course with a sinusoidal input wave form.

The non-linear exponential characteristic of the base-emitter diode of a transistor can be put to good use as a diapason synthesizer. The principal advantage is that whilst many harmonics can be induced in suitable circuits (Fig. 116), their position in the frequency range is favourable for this voice because the higher terms fall off very quickly; so we are left with a dense band of lower-order partials as in Fig. 116. The amplitude, phase and impedance level of the base input circuit are selected to obtain the required harmonic content. The 100 k and 0·015 μF feedback circuit (Fig. 116) can be adjusted to control the amount of fundamental frequency. It will be realized that one such circuit as above is required for each note to be so treated, and this is perhaps more of experimental than practical value. It does underline that the distorting properties of diodes and transistors could be much further exploited.

These circuits all use transistors, but exactly the same networks can be employed with valves. We have not included any in this edition because there are now so few all-valve organs being built; many references to such circuits can be found in past issues of *Electronic Engineering* (see Appendix IX).

Having now obtained an insight into the way tone colours are formed, we have to consider how to bring the frequencies required to these networks; this problem is called keying and today can be performed in a great many ways; but again, some of these methods are related to a certain design or class of organ, and are not therefore suitable for the experimenter. Two approaches are possible. In the first, it is assumed that all the tone sources are independent oscillators which are out of circuit until a key is pressed to energize one or a group of these. This kind of organ is called a free-phase one, but since nearly all oscillators of whatever kind are in random phase relationship, it is far better to call them independent oscillator organs. This being the case, it is the supply line which has to be closed and in most cases this can be done by a

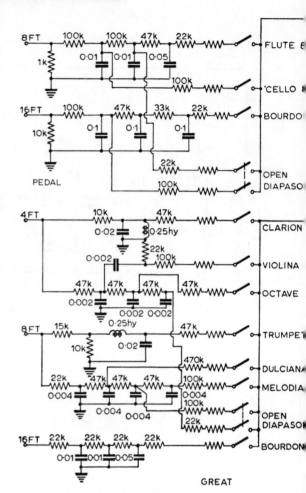

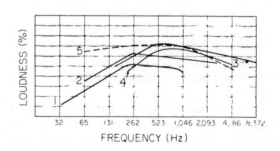

I	Double open diapason	16 ft
2	Open diapason	8 ft
3	Principal	4 ft
4	Fifteenth	2 ft
5	Trumpet	8 ft

Fig. 114 Balance for organ voices

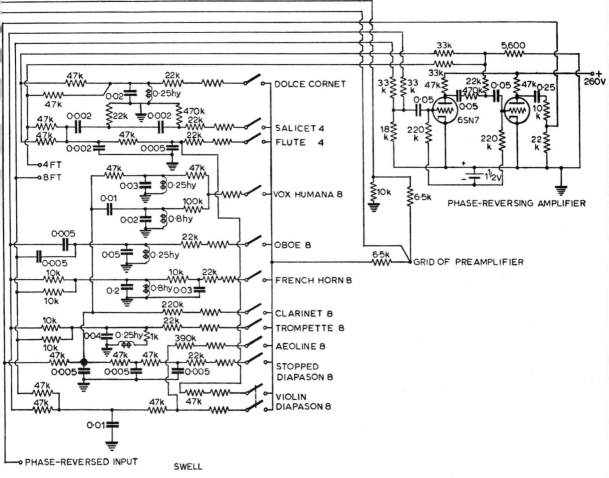

Fig. 113 Complete tone-forming circuits, Baldwin Model 5 organ

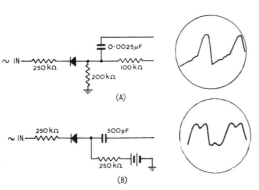

Fig. 115 Wave-form modifiers

simple contact of sufficient cross-section to carry the current. In any normal design this current will not exceed 2 mA per oscillator, often much less; the wire which has become almost a universal standard is hard silver. This contains 4 per cent copper, which makes it springy and the usual gauge is 0·016 in. We will not at the moment look at the mechanical aspects of construction but in any case, standard contact blocks can be bought with from 2 to 20 wires in each.

Both valves and transistors start oscillating very quickly, with the result that a click or some other objectionable transient can be heard at the start of the tone. This will be of very short duration and therefore of high frequency, and is quite easily

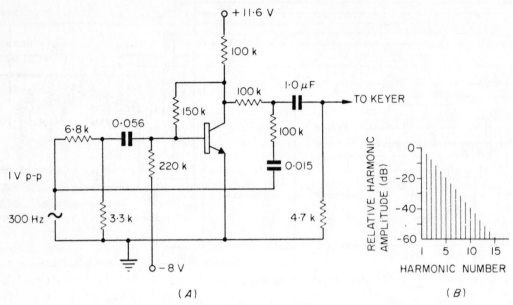

(A)   (B)

Fig. 116 Diapason synthesizer

removed by a simple bypass arrangement as in Fig. 117. This is a single low-pass filter of an uncritical kind. Some independent oscillators are used in a different way, for it will be appreciated that if we have one per note, then 61 will only provide unison or 8 ft pitch over the keyboard; and if we need higher or lower pitches not obtained by couplers, then extra ranks of oscillators tuned to these pitches must be provided. This makes the organ complicated and expensive, but if it is a pipe-simulating instrument, then this is by far the best way. To economize in units, however, some instruments only use one set of oscillators and run them continuously, diverting their tone outputs

on to busbars in such a way that the same oscillator is used for more than one pitch—in other words, the signal is keyed rather than the actual circuit supply. So one obtains the multiple pitch advantages of a divider system, whilst retaining the chorus effect from a series of separate oscillators. But if there was some transient in keying the line voltage, there will be a very objectionable one if the signal is keyed by breaking into it direct. This will be evident if we look at Fig. 118, which shows a sine wave cut into at different periods of time. It is only when crossing the zero line that noiseless keying would be possible, and the chances of this are almost out of the question. The steep wave

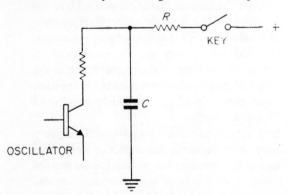

Fig. 117 Simple bypass filter

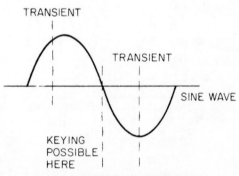

Fig. 118 Effect of keying sine wave

front shown produces a very loud click and must be removed by some system of delayed keying. Since this problem is exactly the same as encountered in keying the signal from frequency dividers, similar methods can be used for both cases.

There are organs in which the suppression of high notes is so great that the circuits can be keyed directly by precious metal contacts; since the unpleasant transients all reside in the upper frequencies, if there are none the worst that can happen is a kind of thump; but obviously the fidelity would be very poor. Then some instruments are direct keyed through conductive rubber sleeves or other elements, which are compressed by a keying wire and so become a kind of variable resistance. There is no doubt that this can be most effective. Philips supply such sleeves, part number 4822.325.800.68, and they are used in Philicorda organs. The advantage here is that quite ordinary bronze wires may be used for the switch fingers.

The Baldwin Company made the resistance switch famous; for many years all their organs were keyed by these elements, until technology brought along the conductive 'rubber'; for, of course, it is not rubber, which would quickly corrode any wire contact because of its sulphur content. Details of this unit are given in Chapter 8, with some variants. But broadly speaking the current trends in instrument design call for longer

delays with preferably some control over these times.

The most common is the use of diodes which are cut off until a conducting voltage is applied by a playing key. This is slowed down by the charging of a capacitor which is usually so connected that the tone signal decays slowly after the key is released; indeed, the delay is often under the player's control so that it may be extended to a state of sustain. All commercial organs today incorporate these circuits. It is essential to use diodes having very high back resistance and very low forward resistance, otherwise signal leakage will be prevalent or the signal may not be completely cut off; for in such cases, the signal is continuously applied to the diodes and only the bias voltage is controlled by the keys. We show one arrangement in Fig. 119, and some variants of this (Figs. 120–1) for the experimenter to try. The method can also be applied to valves as in Fig. 122, and when the generators run continuously another circuit shown in Fig. 123 is very useful. The advantages of the foregoing are that a number of pitch contacts on busbars located above each other can be closed by one key if required, and in some cases this is done so that a tuning or pitch contact can close just before the diode control contact closes; or in generators giving out more than one wave form per pitch some of the contacts can be used for

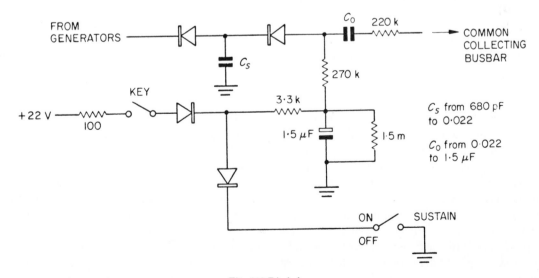

Fig. 119 Diode keyer

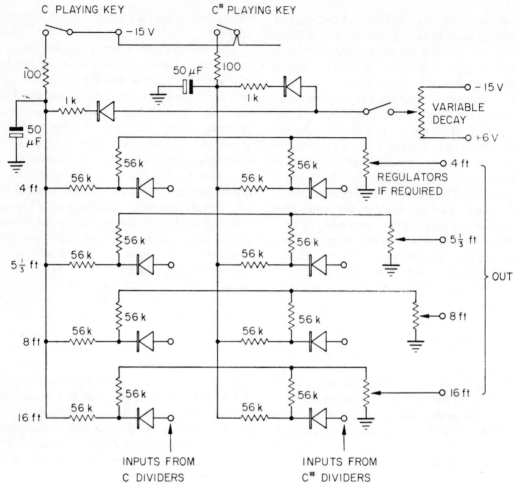

Fig. 120 Further diode keyers

one wave and perhaps routed to semiconductor keying, whilst other contacts can be used to control the second or third wave form directly; for we can say now that it is quite possible to cut into a sawtooth wave at any part of the cycle since the worst that can happen is that the whole slope is reduced by some small amount, see Fig. 124. There are already so many harmonics that any transient merely augments or diminishes some of the existing ones and so is not really apparent. This method is used in Conn and other organs. Another economy can be effected by keying only the upper two or three octaves with diode delay circuits; this is possible because the time constants for the lower frequency or pitch filters are so long that the transient is absorbed and so cannot be heard.

One rather unusual and ingenious delay circuit is shown in Fig. 125. This works the other way round to most such delays. Each oscillator is supplied with a keying voltage through a playing key, but this voltage is also applied to a control device consisting of a large capacitor, a diode and means for biasing this latter between −9 and +3 V. If −9 V is connected to the diode resistor, it can never conduct. The large capacitor can then only charge through the oscillator supply and this takes time. But if the diode voltage is reversed, the large capacitor will not only discharge through the oscillator but also through the diode and the 1000 ohms; so the decay time is made short. In-between settings of the diode potential result in intermediate times.

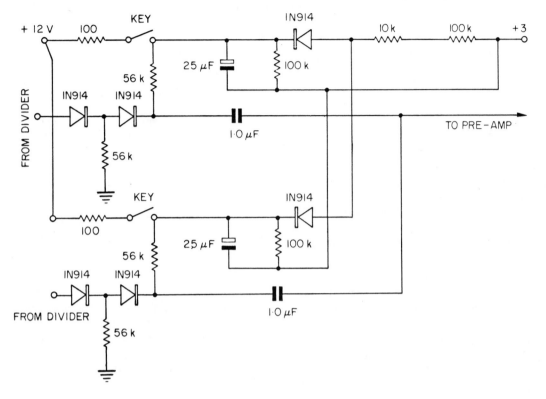

Fig. 121 Diode keying for pedal notes

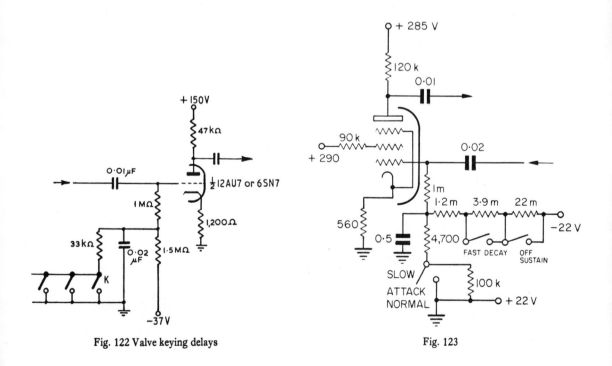

Fig. 122 Valve keying delays

Fig. 123

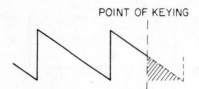

Fig. 124 Keying into sawtooth wave

We may note that the smallest interference of any kind is at once noticed in a sine or near sine wave signal. Therefore there must be no trace of transient when keying this type of wave form. The keyer shown in Fig. 126 shows how this is done. Note that it is the bias which is keyed; the signal is continuously applied to R_1. The transistor is cut off because of a bias approximately $+0.25$ V supplied to the base from a temperature-compensated supply. (This can be seen in the complete circuit diagram of this organ in Chapter 7.)

When a key is depressed, $+28$ V is applied to R_2 causing the $0.68\,\mu$F sustain capacitor to charge; this makes the base of the transistor conduct and the signal passes out along the collector line. As soon as the key is released, the base is once more cut off; the sustain capacitor discharges and the signal is blocked. However, the discharge is controlled by a switch; in the normal position (as shown) the capacitor would discharge rapidly through R_3 and diode D_1. In the sustain position, $+12$ V is applied to diode D_1. Now when the

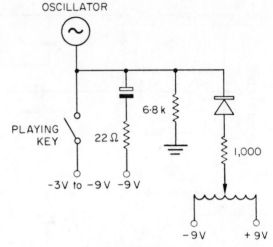

Fig. 125 Gulbrausen keyer

keying voltage is removed, C will discharge quickly through R_3 and the diode but only until the 12 V threshold level has been reached; after this the diode appears as an open circuit and further discharge of C is through R_3 and R_4 at a much slower rate.

In the long delay position the same action takes place, but this time $+20$ V is applied. Once again C discharges through R_3 and D to the 20 V level, after which it slowly discharges towards the base 'off' voltage through R_3 and R_4; so all we need is a voltage divider across the $+30$ V supply line for the full range.

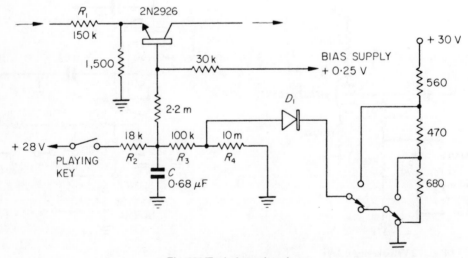

Fig. 126 Typical transistor keyer

Naturally there are other ways of using a transistor for keying. In the case just described the capacitor charged slowly when the key was depressed; it is possible to reverse the process, so that the capacitor is always full when the circuit is at rest. By this means, it can be discharged very quickly when the transistor is turned on but will recover during one half cycle of the square wave signal input. If the time constants are carefully chosen, the discharge/recovery times can be arranged to deliver a sawtooth wave to the output circuit; thus it can be a converter as well as a keyer. In this case, *CR* must be adjusted every few notes to give about the same amplitude of sawtooth; and the input wave form must be symmetrically square for all pitches (see Fig. 127).

The use of the tremulant or vibrato has assumed great importance in recent years. This is partly due to the limited number of tone colours on the simpler organs; partly because all electronic flutes are lifeless without vibrato; and partly because this effect is a part of natural sounds, none of which remain in the theoretical steady state for more than a few seconds—if at all. Vibrato implies a cyclic change in pitch, usually about 7 times a second; there may be some change in amplitude as well. Tremolo is a change in amplitude only, at about the same rate; sometimes both are available since the audible effect is not the same; but on the whole, vibrato is to be preferred.

With the stability possible in modern transistor oscillators it may prove difficult to modulate them in a simple manner, but we show a number of ways to do this. Some types of oscillator cannot be modulated in any of these ways, e.g. rotating wheel or vibrating reed generators; modulation must then be applied after the signals have been mixed and keyed, usually on the way to the amplifiers. Alternatively, the well-known Leslie loudspeaker systems can be used on any organ, giving an amplitude modulation directly and some slight Doppler effect on reflected waves from far walls etc. in the room; the combined effects are most acceptable. There are mechanical variants of Leslie's system, for example the Compton Rotofon (see Fig. 182, Chapter 7).

The earliest attempts at vibrato were probably those of Constant-Martin, who passed the organ

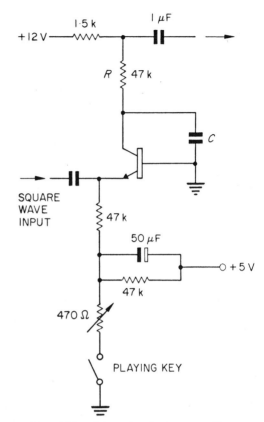

Fig. 127 Transistor sawtooth convertor and keyer

signals through what was virtually the field coil of a small electric motor; the armature coils were then connected by slip rings to the amplifiers etc. When the armature was rotated by another motor, the coupling varied as the air gap changed during rotation of the pole pieces, and so the signal rose and fell in strength. The efficiency was incredibly low-frequency current applied to the other winding; this current was obtained by a multivibrator. winding of a transformer being modulated by a low-frequency current applied to the other winding; this current was obtained by a multivibrator. Much more elaborate phase-shifting circuits were later evolved for treating the mixed signals after keying, but today simpler devices are used with greater effect.

Possibly the most useful modulator is one which acts on the tuning or tank circuit of an oscillator. This is susceptible to capacitance variations much more readily than it reacts to alteration in the base

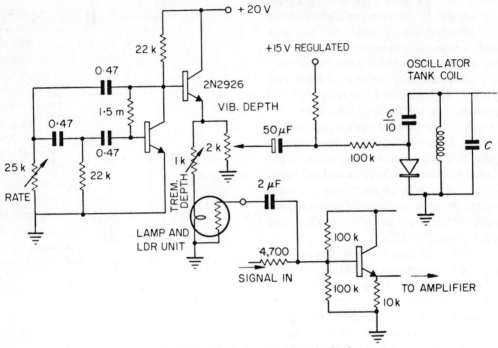

Fig. 128 Combined vibrato and tremolo circuit

bias voltage of the transistor. Fig. 128 shows a good circuit which has the advantage that the phase-shift oscillator also provides a variable resistance to ground which can be used as a tremolo circuit by varying the gain of an amplifier stage associated with the tone circuits. When the diode is biased so that it is only just conducting, and the a.c. vibrato signal is applied, the diode is alternately turned off and full on. This is equivalent to altering the value of the capacitor above; it is in fact a reactance modulator, and so the frequency of the tank circuit is slightly changed. Of course, the setting of the diode bias and the phase-shift oscillator must be connected before the tone oscillator is tuned.*

The Conn multivibrator modulator is shown in Fig. 129, and the action will be obvious. Yet another and simpler external modulator is given in Fig. 130, and this consists of a small inter-valve transformer and four photo-transistors. If the lamps are flashed alternately, the phase changes

smoothly across the transformer and there are no thumps, therefore no filters are required. The lamps are of course in the collectors of a multivibrator running at the customary speed of 6–7 Hz.

No book would be complete without a drawing of the most popular vibrato device, the Leslie Tremulant. Although invented as long ago as 1940, it was by no means the first rotating loudspeaker; for instance, British patent no. 404,937 of 1934 discloses the same thing by John Compton. But the other Leslie methods, in which the actual loudspeaker remains stationary whilst a rotating baffle alternately blanks off and admits the sound to the external air, is now the most generally adopted arrangement; it obviates difficulties with slip rings or rotating transformers etc. (mercury cups are even used).

Fig. 131 illustrates the mechanics. The back wave from the cone must be kept away from the front wave. Over the face of the cone is a shaped drum or bowl with a part of one side cut away. If this is rotated at a suitable speed, the sound is swept around in a very agreeable manner, creating

* Another reactance modulator can be seen in the Bambi organ, page 133.

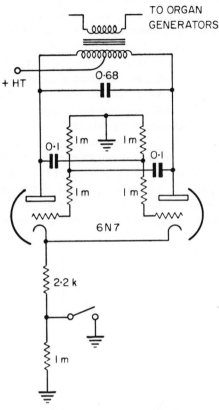

Fig. 129 Multivibrator modulator

an illusion of both frequency and amplitude modulation; though on examination by an oscilloscope the change in level is nearly all amplitude. The shape of the side of the cup has a great bearing on the effect of the tremulant, also on wind noise and the power required to drive the device. One advantage is that owing to the length of the sound waves at low frequencies, they leak round the sides of the rotor and are cut off; thus there is an automatic cancellation of the vibrato at low frequencies, e.g. on pedal notes, which is a musical advantage. The total depth is not very great, but is quite adequate for all but extreme effects.

Some further reference to experimental methods of vibrato or tremolo will be found in the last two chapters of this book.

This section is concluded with some references to reverberation circuits and devices. Everyone

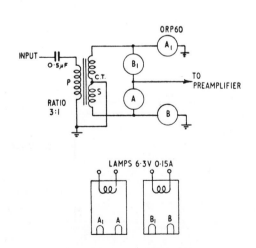

Fig. 130 Simple external modulator

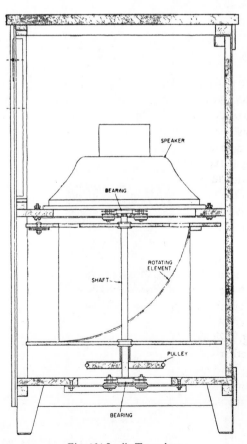

Fig. 131 Leslie Tremulant

knows that organ music sounds much better in a large hall, church or cathedral; indeed, it is said with some truth that the room makes the organ. But it is impossible for the domestic user to simulate these conditions unless he is very fortunate; let us say to start with that the bottom note of a 16 ft pitch pedal stop cannot develop unless the minimum length of the longest wall in a room is 27 ft; and there will be no reverberation unless the volume of the room exceeds 3000 cu. ft. So we must seek some compromise, and luckily the ear is very easily fooled. What is reverberation, and how does it improve the sound? In a normal building which is not cubic or round, the path lengths from a fixed sound source within the

building all vary in length to an observer also fixed in some other part of the room. Since sound travels at a finite rate, about 1100/1200 ft/sec at normal temperatures, the sound must take longer or shorter times to return to the observer if the building is rectangular or, more often, containing side apertures; sometimes the sound can circulate round such configurations for a long time, the reverberation time being said to be too great and means must be found to reduce it. All the time this is happening, energy is being lost from the initial sound waves: partly by absorption by walls and roof; partly by repeated reflection; partly just by sheer distance. The net result is that of Fig. 132. It is important to note that reverberation varies all

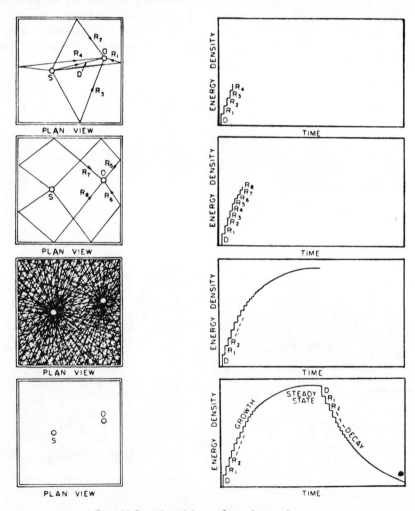

Fig. 132 Growth and decay of sound waves in a room

the time, with both frequency and power. It is these two factors which make it so difficult to imitate with any success in a reasonably simple and compact manner.

An echo chamber, which is simply a small room with hard walls, floor and roof, is a good solution, using a microphone and loudspeaker; but this is a luxury. A room with dimensions in the ratio of 2 : 3 : 4·5 and having a cubic capacity of 600 cu. ft, and an opening (for the sound to get out) of 15 sq. ft will have a reverberation time of one second. A disused chimney or staircase makes a good reverberator. However, the theory of transmission lines is the basis for most organ reverberation devices, relying as they do on one or more springs. The rate of propagation in metal ensures little or no loss if a signal is entered at one end, and if there is no compliance (elasticity) at the other end, nearly all will be reflected back again. This process may go on many times; each time a small proportion of the signal will pass to a rather stiff transducer at the far end and be removed.

Springs are used as a convenient way of getting the required length of wire to give the time delay; as the energy is gradually dissipated in the metal, the signal gets weaker and weaker. Unfortunately all springs have resonances and these are easily excited if the applied signal is too loud; but if it is weak, there may not be enough reverberation; so it is a compromise. Also, the rate of propagation in a spring of uniform diameter is the same for all frequencies, and this alone makes the effect unreal. The Baldwin Company discovered that if the spring is made in the form of a helix with tapering

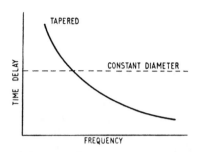

Fig. 133 Effect of tapered spring compared with that of a parallel one

diameters for some of its length, then clearly the turns will have a different mean length. There is a variation in time delay for different frequencies, as can be seen by Figs. 133 and 134, which compare the effect of a spiral spring of uniform diameter with the Baldwin tapered spring. The driving amplifier for this is shown below the curve, and is ingenious in that the impedance of the drive coil varies with frequency; for the higher ones the coil takes more current than the resistor, 2·2 k; whilst for lower frequencies, the current prefers to flow through the resistor. There is automatic frequency compensation, according reasonably with the acoustic analogy.

The more simple springs are standard in the majority of small organs today, and since the unpleasant effect of resonances in a single spring have been mentioned, we often find two or three (or in some Hammond units, five) of differing resonant frequencies all acting together as one unit. A compromise is thereby attained.

Since reverberation is an acoustic phenomenon,

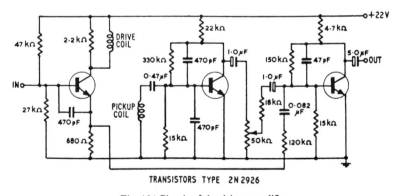

TRANSISTORS TYPE 2N2926

Fig. 134 Circuit of the driver amplifier

it is not surprising that RCA turned their minds to a solution involving an acoustic transmission line. At first sight this seems a simple idea, but the secret is in the material of the tube; for if any reader has tried to talk through a long metal tube, he cannot fail to have noticed that the natural resonance of the tube is superimposed on his voice and colours it. Fig. 135 shows the block diagram of the signal path. We might note here that this feedback system is in common use with magnetic tape reverberation units, none of which, however, are featured in organs.

Basically the device consists of a tube of much greater length than the longest wavelength to be transmitted. At intervals, specially designed ribbon microphones are inserted into the tube. These are energized by the signal injected into one end of the tube, but progressively delayed by the physical separation of the ribbons. The initial and subsequent signals are mixed in amplifiers having feedback loops which produce a complex decay pattern in the system. The delayed signals are mixed with the original signal and appear at the same loudspeaker.

The tube is 100 ft long and 1 in. diameter. The ribbons, which are very narrow so as not to interfere with the acoustic energy, are spaced at intervals of 25, 55 and 75 ft from the driver end of the tube; the other end is damped with tufts of felt. The acoustic delays due to this geometry are 23, 50 and 69 msec. The outputs of the three microphones are mixed so that for each circuit of the sound there are three components unequally spaced with respect to time, to provide a measure

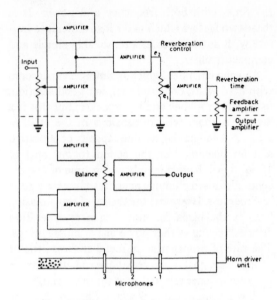

Fig. 135 Electro-acoustic reverberation device

of randomness in the components of the reverberant sound.

In Fig. 135, if the reverberation control be disconnected and a voltage e_1 is applied to the input amplifier of the delay unit, the output voltage will be e_2. The reverberation time, in seconds, will be

$$T = \frac{0 \cdot 207}{\log (e_2/e_1)}$$

The potentiometer provides ratios of e_1 to e_2 giving reverberation times of from 0 to 4·0 sec. The frequency response of the system is from 50 Hz to 10 Hz.

6 Amplifiers, Loudspeakers and Power Supply Units

We know from Chapter 4 that the signals resulting from any type of electronic organ are of the same order as those from radio or gramophone records. They have to be amplified to be of any value. This chapter is divided between valve and transistor apparatus, because high-power transistors are still expensive, the power supplies for them require regulating, and there is always a problem with heat removal which does not exist with valve amplifiers. Moreover, many experimenters are not too happy with semiconductors and, finally, a very large number of valve organs are still in use and certainly valve amplifiers are likely to be with us for some time yet. So we have tried to cater for both schools of thought.

Not so long ago it was quite something if an amplifier of any power was found to be distortionless over the whole range of frequencies; yet at the same time, entirely distortionless amplifiers have been in use for some 40 years in broadcasting equipment; so it must be concluded that transistors were the main culprits, and this was so. Today, however, it is difficult to find an amplifier which distorts, but transistor circuits are still very touchy about input impedances and overloading. It will not be necessary to give space to reasons for distortion which was a feature of previous editions.

The first thing to be noted is the difference in power requirements for programme music and for organs. This occurs because radio and records etc. have an average power which is not steady but rises and falls in a random manner; whereas in reproducing from organs, the sound power is much steadier and more approaches a sine wave drive. The power for programme music is shown dotted whilst that for organ music is given as a series of full lines in Fig. 136. It is easy to see that for safety, one must allow twice the power as compared with radio or record reproduction. Even then, if purchasing a transistor power amplifier, it is as well to check with the makers in the matter of sustained pedal notes, though generally sine wave drive does not become dangerous until well above the pedal range of frequencies.

As far as actual power is concerned, if we take the acoustic power of a large reed organ as 5 watts, and the efficiency of a typical loudspeaker as 5 per cent, then it would be as well to allow 20 watts and possibly a little more if the room is very heavily damped; but then an organ can never sound well in such a room, whatever you do. Examination of many domestic installations shows that, in general, there is far too great an amplifier power provided by the makers. Noise does not make tone. The first amplifier we look at was designed for the Post Office and has some outstanding properties including a very simple output transformer—it can be wound by hand. Fig. 137 gives most of the information. Power supplies required are 100 mA at 300 V d.c. and 2·5 A at 6·3 V a.c. Note the excellent response shown under the circuit—and this includes the output transformer. Perhaps the

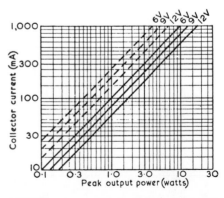

Fig. 136 Different power requirements for programme music and organs

89

reader may be unable to lay his hands on a suitable power supply unit, so one is shown in Fig. 138. There is no need for any stabilization, but it is desirable to fit the interference suppression capacitors across the primary of the mains transformer. Twisting the a.c. leads to the heaters will reduce pickup from these to adjacent equipment. Be sure to use the maker's recommended

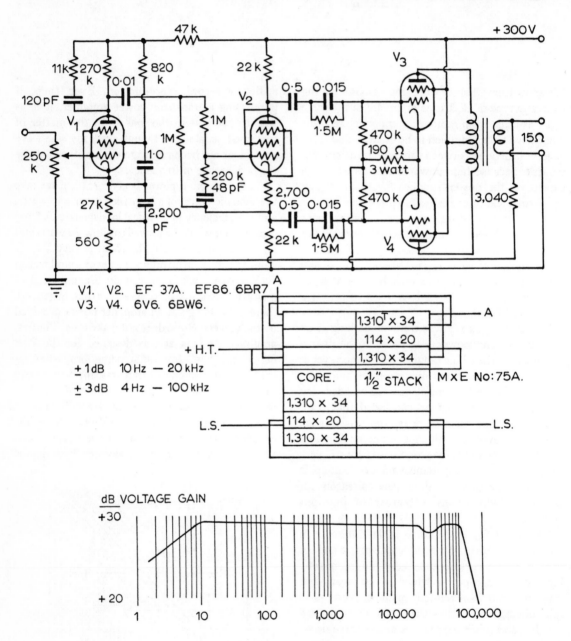

Fig. 137 Amplifier designed for the Post Office

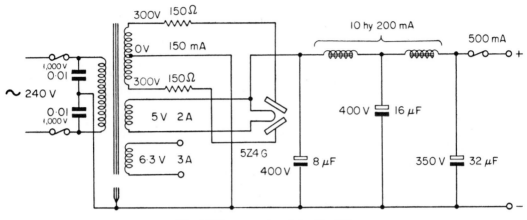

Fig. 138 Power supply unit for Fig. 137

limiting resistors in series with each anode of the rectifier valve; if in doubt, this is—

$$R_a = R_s + n^2 R_p$$

where R_s = resistance of half secondary

R_p = resistance of total primary winding

n = ratio of number of turns on half secondary to number of turns on whole primary.

In general, these values lie between 100 and 200 ohms, a little higher with cheap transformers. Filtering should be good if pre-amplifiers are also to be fed from the same power supply, and this means thorough decoupling (see page 35). Finally we show a stabilized power supply unit (Fig. 139), perhaps for oscillators etc.; it will not give more than about 100 mA at 185 V; of course the supply of 350 V should be well smoothed, but just as with

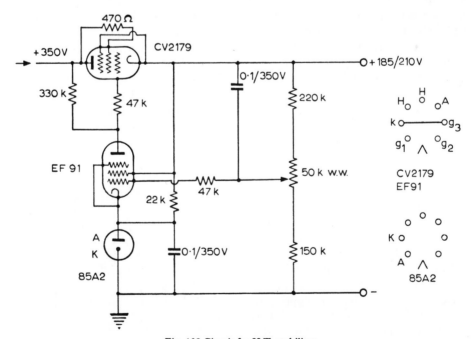

Fig. 139 Circuit for H.T. stabilizer

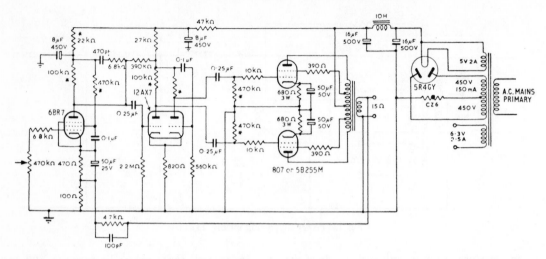

Fig. 140 30 W amplifier ($\pm 0 \cdot 2$ dB, 25 Hz to 20 kHz. *Indicates high stability ± 2 per cent)

transistor power supplies, a good deal of ripple reduction takes place in this circuit. Now that so many small- and low-voltage parts are on the market, one must be very careful if using valves to ensure that components will stand the working voltages, and this applies especially to electrolytic capacitors, which may deteriorate quite severely with long periods of disuse. A somewhat more powerful valve amplifier is shown now, for those who wish to use many loudspeakers etc. The power unit is an integral part of the diagram which needs no explanation (Fig. 140).

Perhaps a quick look at valve pre-amplifiers would be useful. Because of the high input impedance and the remarkable isolation of one element from another in a valve, one can do almost anything with a valve pre-amplifier. But their very properties call for screening to a much greater extent than with transistors since they are prone to hum pickup. The question of gain control is also a rather vexed one as high voltages make small scratching noises etc., from volume controls, very evident. One can use capacitive control as in Fig. 141, which shows a generally useful pre-amplifier. If this is used from the stabilized supply just described, no trouble will be experienced. The main supply to Fig. 140 can also power the amplifier in Fig. 141.

One convenience of valve circuits is that mixing is easily effected without using any active elements. If we have, say, two organ generator outputs, these can be taken to a transformer as shown in Fig. 142, which is bass-compensated—that is, the treble is reduced quicker than the bass as the volume is reduced; it compensates to some extent for the deficiencies of the hearing curve. The small transformer shown may have 5000 turns of 44 swg enamel copper wire on a $\frac{3}{4}$ in. square Mumetal stack—that is, the centre limb is $\frac{3}{4} \times \frac{3}{4}$ in. But it must be enclosed in a tinplate box and leads entering and leaving must be screened; the box is earthed. The 100 k pots shown as volume controls

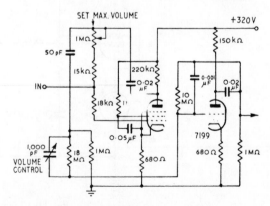

Fig. 141 Capacitor volume control

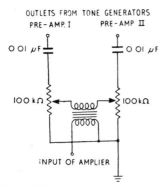

Fig. 142 Mixing circuit for two signals

could be replaced by a proper stud control system, having a wiper arm and a circle of studs connected to a logarithmic network of resistances. These would have values as follows: next to earth, 100 ohms; then progressing up the chain, 330, 620, 1000, 1300, 1600, 2000, 2400, 2700, 3100, 3300, 3900, 4200, 4700, 5200, 5600, 5900, 6400, 7000, 7700, 8500, 8900, 9400, 10 000 ohms. The upper end connects to the signal source, the wiper to the amplifier grid. The smallest resistors one can get will do for this unit, which should last a lifetime. Of course, many current organs use photo-cells in one way or another for volume control, and these can be applied in several ways (see Fig. 143).

Cadmium selenide is slightly quicker in response than the more common cadmium sulphide. If one uses a 6·3 V lamp, very much under-run (and therefore very close to the cell), it can be operated directly from the raw a.c., since the filament will then have too much thermal inertia to follow the 50 Hz ripple on the mains and there will be no hum pickup. One can either control the filament brightness by a rheostat, or cause a shutter to intercept the light to control the cell. This latter has the advantage that the shutter can be shaped to conform with any law required.

Turning now to transistor amplifiers, we only really encounter problems with audio amplification when the output current is high and, as a result, heat is generated. Since the active parts of a transistor are buried inside its case, the temperature can rise quickly and destructively unless the heat engendered can be removed rapidly. There is no warning, the action can be very quick and destroy the transistor in microseconds; they have little overload capabilities, unlike valves which are hard to destroy by overloading and, indeed, good ones can run with red-hot anodes—some are designed to do so. We therefore only touch on two matters: the stabilization of the base biasing and the removal of heat from the output stages. A good deal of attention will be given to power supply units as, because of the much lower impedance of all transistor devices commonly used in musical instruments (except for rhythmic units and certain special purposes), they are prone to cross-coupling

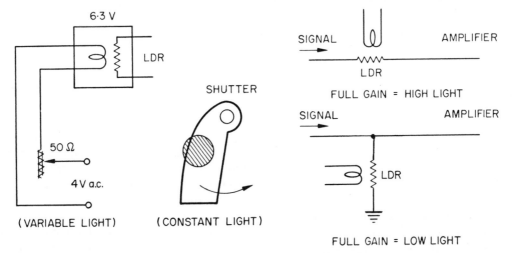

Fig. 143 Various ways of using photo-cell controls

and mutual interference in many ways—especially with the many common circuits necessary for an organ.

The importance of using a potential divider to supply the base of a pre- or small-signal amplifier is not so important now that silicon is almost universal as a material for small-signal transistors; leakages and the effects of temperature are almost a thing of the past. However, for germanium users, one should attempt to make the emitter resistor (which introduces d.c. negative feedback) high and the base resistance (which is equal to $R_1 + R_2$ in parallel), low. Values shown in Fig. 144 ensure reliable operation. The usual concept is to make the collector voltage V_{ce} approximately half of the supply voltage V_{cc}. This is achieved when—

$$R_b = h_{FE}R_c$$

where h_{FE} is the d.c. current gain of the transistor. Of course, one unfortunately finds that owing to the rather wide gain spreads of unselected transistors, a compromise is necessary; so an average value of h_{FE} is taken from the maker's literature on the particular transistor used; for example,

$$h_{FE} = \sqrt{h_{FE}(\text{max.}) \times h_{FE}(\text{min.})}$$

$$= \sqrt{50 \times 300}$$

$= 122 \cdot 5$. This is for a well-known type.

The collector load R_c depends on the supply voltage and the required amplification of the stage. Typical values lie from $4 \cdot 7 \text{ k}\Omega$ to $47 \text{ k}\Omega$. In Fig. 145 we see a similar silicon n-p-n stage and this is a very useful general-purpose amplifier. Note that here there is a different way of biasing the base. In this circuit the upper end of the base resistor is taken to the collector and not direct to the supply line. Therefore the base current depends on the

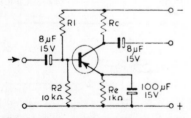

Fig. 144 Typical *RC*-coupled amplifier stage using OC71 or similar type. Supply voltage = 6 V; collector current = 1 mA; $R1 = 39 \text{ k}\Omega$; $RC = 2 \cdot 2 \text{ k}\Omega$; $I_{out}/I_{in} = 23$

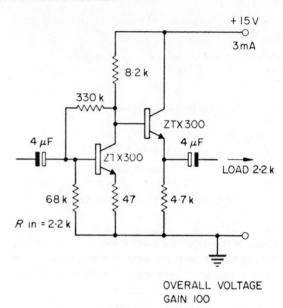

OVERALL VOLTAGE GAIN 100

Fig. 145 Variation of Fig. 144, using n-p-n transistors

collector voltage and the circuit is more or less self-adjusting for any variations in gain between one transistor and another. If a higher gain transistor is used, then for a given set of conditions the collector current would increase and so reduce the collector-emitter current; but if this happened then the base current would reduce and this would offset the tendency for the collector current to increase. In actual fact, changing the gain by a factor of as much as 10 would only give a variation of about ± 5 V in an assumed collector-emitter voltage of 10; and *pro rata*. There are many types of small signal amplifiers shown in service manuals for various electronic organs, but one must always remember that some of the component values shown have been chosen to work with parts of the circuit coming either before or after those in which we are interested; and the values will be different if the output is to be taken from the collector (when the gain of the circuit will be realized), or from the emitter (when the gain cannot exceed 1). The latter arrangement is convenient if there are very long leads involved.

Unlike amplifiers for record or tape playing, there is no necessity for any form of tone controls since we can adjust any organ generators to give the desired response; and this is a very useful way of matching them to a particular loudspeaker. However, because of the many experiments which readers carry out, a wide-range tone-control circuit giving up to 15 dB treble or bass boost is shown in Fig. 146. The circuit does not give any gain, but a low noise transistor should be used if possible.

In the matter of heat removal from power transistors, it is the heavy current output units which require great care, otherwise they will be instantly destroyed—and may cause much damage to associated parts such as transformers, capacitors and loudspeakers. The critical factor is the junction temperature and the maximum permissible value of this for any particular transistor can always be obtained from the manufacturer. However, we will expand a little on the problem of heat sinks. These should be mounted vertically so that air can pass freely over the transistor, for if horizontal, e.g. the use of an amplifier chassis, then heat transfer may be reduced by as much as 60 per cent. It is not always realized that the use of a correct heat dissipating device can make up to twenty times the useful power available from a transistor and, furthermore, increase its life enormously. To ensure a good transfer of the heat engendered in

action, the base of the transistor should be lightly coated with a silicone grease. The most effective heat sinks have a finned aluminium shape and can with advantage be blackened.

The following calculations are reproduced by courtesy of Ferranti Ltd and are included because of the importance of the subject.

When the transistor is mounted on a heat sink, the thermal resistance θ between the case and free air must be less than

$$\frac{T_c - T_a}{P_{tot}} \tag{1}$$

where P_{tot} = total mean dissipation of the transistor in watts

T_a = the maximum air temperature in degrees Centigrade

T_c = the rated case temperature in degrees Centigrade.

Alternatively

$$T_c = T_j - \theta_j P_{tot} \tag{2}$$

which together with (1) gives

$$\theta = \frac{T_j - T_a}{P_{tot}} - \theta_j \tag{3}$$

where T_j = maximum permissible junction temperature

θ_j = the thermal resistance between junction and case.

The thermal resistance θ for heat sinks consisting of different areas of vertically mounted square sheets of matt black copper or aluminium with natural air convection is

$$\theta = \frac{22}{L} \tag{4}$$

where L = length in inches of one side of the square plate.

Fig. 147 gives values for a range of conditions applicable to a well-known make of finned heat sink. It is sometimes necessary to insulate the transistor case electrically from the metal sink, in which case a thin mica washer is required. This

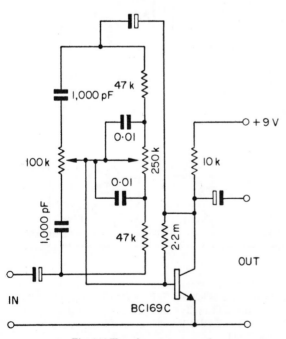

Fig. 146 Transistor tone control

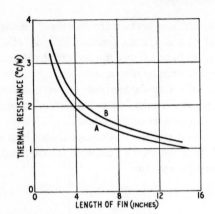

Fig. 147 Thermal resistance of extruded heat sink supplied by
Marston Excelsior Ltd. A—range 11D plain finish; B—range
10D plain finish

where θ_s = thermal resistance of washer
    p = thermal resistivity of washer (50–80
       for mica)
    d_s = thickness of washer in cm
    A_s = surface area of one side of washer,
       square cm.

In the present state of the art, most manufacturers use their own design of main or power amplifier. These are matched to the particular circuits used, which vary much more in the case of transistor organs than with valves. It is therefore more difficult to show representative circuits, but so far as efficiency is concerned, the amplifier illustrated in Fig. 148 has a performance superior to almost anything else available when used with the power supply unit shown in Fig. 149.

The author is indebted to Ferranti Ltd for supplying the circuit information, but it is now available to any interested reader as type AMP100; a 15 W version is also available. What is more important, specially matched sets of silicon

reduces the cooling according to the following formula

$$\theta_s = \frac{p d_s}{A_s} \qquad (5)$$

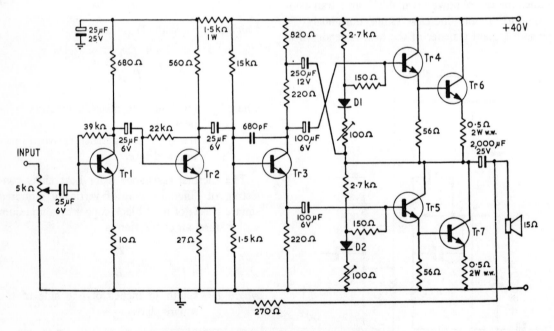

Fig. 148 Ferranti 7 watt amplifier. All resistors except those
marked are 0·5 W type. Ferranti transistors as follows: Tr1
and Tr2 = Type ZTR1; Tr3 = Type ZTR6; Tr4 and
Tr5 = Type ZTR4; Tr6 and Tr7 = Type ZTR3; D1 and
D2 = Ferranti type ZDR1

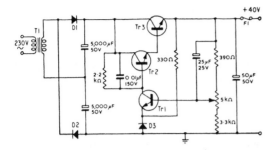

Fig. 149 Power supply unit for Fig. 148. All resistors of 0·5 W type. Ferranti transistors and diodes: Tr1 = Type ZTR1; Tr2 = Type ZTR4; Tr3 = Type ZTR3; D1 and D2 = Type ZDR3; D3 = Type ZKR2; T1 = Douglas transformer type MT3AT, primary 0–230 V, secondary 0–20 V; F1 = Belling Lee fast-acting fuse 1 A type L1510

transistors are also available in sets from Ferranti Ltd.

The maximum power of 7 W is suitable for most domestic applications and the frequency response is within 1 dB right down to 20 Hz, more than adequate for the pedal department. Another noteworthy feature is that the total harmonic distortion is extremely small up to 10 kHz, which again is adequate for any organ; typically it is about 0·3 to 0·4 per cent, and is shown in Fig. 150.

Since the circuit is designed to have a small quiescent current, it follows that there must be large swings as the power is raised, and to hold the regulation of the +40 V line steady, a stabilized power unit is provided; this also ensures a very low a.c. ripple, which of course is extremely disturbing on organ music.

Tr6 and Tr7 of Fig. 148 must each be mounted on a heat sink 4 in. × 4 in. of $\frac{1}{16}$ in. aluminium and

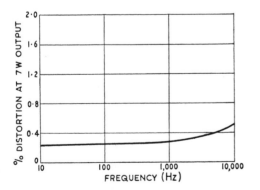

Fig. 150 Full load distortion curve for Fig. 148

these must also be insulated from the chassis. In the power unit, Fig. 149, transistors Tr2 and Tr3 have a common collector connection and should be on a 4 × 4 in. sink as above, also well insulated from the chassis. The diode D3 may be bolted to the chassis. It is of great importance that the earthing should be of low resistance, preferably a short 16 swg copper wire; the amplifier must not be on the same chassis as the power supply unit. Do not connect an earth to the input but where shown in the figure.

Many amplifiers have been described in the technical press from time to time, but there are special requirements for the reproduction of organ music and the transformerless circuit above is eminently suitable, and illustrates in a convincing manner how the distortion normally associated with Class B or AB amplification has been overcome.

Because of the heavy standing current drain and the low efficiency of Class A amplifiers with transistors, this kind of circuit has been developed to a high efficiency with a current drain in proportion to the signal strength. For instance, in the amplifier just described, the standing current is about 10/20 mA per side whilst at full drive, this rises to 300 mA. The economy resulting from this is evident and of course the danger of thermal runaway is reduced to small proportions. So we see that it is only the output stage which really causes anxiety.

The use of Class B output circuits enables one to make economical use of a push–pull drive, which not only increases the available power but reduces distortion. The efficiency is high, a typical output stage delivering some five times the collector dissipation of a single transistor. However, there would be a severe penalty to pay if the circuit was really operating in Class B; in fact, it is Class AB. Let us look at this for a moment, because the distortion sometimes arising from this configuration is not always understood. In true Class B, the transistor is biased at cut-off and emitter current flows for one-half cycle only on each side. The collector circuit adds the two half waves to the load. If we look at Fig. 151, because of the initial curvature of the input characteristic, the collector current will be zero until the input drive exceeds the knee of the characteristic. The collector current thus flows for

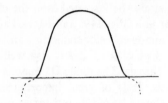

Fig. 151 Cross-over distortion

less than 180° and the load current shows a 'notch' whenever it crosses the zero axis. At low signal level this causes much distortion, giving in fact the reverse attribute to what is generally experienced, namely that as the signal power is decreased the distortion becomes worse.

The 'notch' is practically eliminated by biasing to a point close to the knee of the characteristic. By careful adjustment the notch may be virtually smoothed out. With such a bias, the mode must be AB, because it will be found that a d.c. collector current flows in the absence of a signal.

All transistor power amplifiers and most organ generators benefit from some form of stabilized d.c. supply. Not only can the required voltage and current be held very constant, but the output impedance of such supplies can be very low and this aids decoupling and ripple suppression. It will have been noted that supply voltages vary greatly for different circuits all doing apparently the same thing; but this is usually dictated by some other requirement of a complete circuit system. Regulators or stabilizers can give constant outputs of from about 5 per cent to over 1000 : 1. For a great many purposes quite elementary circuits suffice and especially if the current to be taken is small. For instance, a simple Zener diode stabilizer is given in Fig. 152 for a current of 750 mA at 15 V. Looking first at Fig. 48, Chapter 4, the so-called Zener voltage of the diode is that of the stabilized voltage required and the series resistor is selected to this end. XY is the voltage drop required of this resistor and YZ is the voltage drop across the diode

(− 6 V in this example). If the resistor brings the current to the point I_0 on the Zener 'curve', then a load line can be drawn as in the figure. If now the supply voltage should increase, the load line will move downwards to I_m (since the current in the diode must also increase); but the change in voltage between the conditions I_0 and I_m is almost nil, though clearly this depends on the slope resistance, easily obtained from the makers' data sheets. We must make quite sure that under the worst conditions, i.e. at I_m, the diode is not overloaded. Reverting to Fig. 152, the stabilization for an input voltage change of ±10 per cent is better than ±2 per cent, and the regulation from no load to full load is better than 3 per cent. There would be some ripple still on the output of such a simple circuit, easily removed by another filter section. A quick method for calculating the series resistor for a typical Zener diode is shown in Fig. 153. Here we must decide on the diode current, add this to the load current, and fix an input voltage, V_1. Knowing the diode current and its designed voltage, then

$$R = \frac{V_1 - \text{diode voltage}}{\text{load current} + \text{diode current}}$$

For instance, if the input voltage is to be 48 (it should always be at least twice the diode voltage for this kind of circuit), the load current is known to be 145 mA, and the diode current at its best mean regulating point is 100 mA, then

$$R = \frac{V_1 - 22}{245 \text{ mA}}$$

$$= \frac{48 - 22}{145 \text{ mA}}$$

$$= \frac{26 \times 1000}{245} \text{ (since the current is in mA)}$$

$$= 115 \text{ ohms approx.}$$

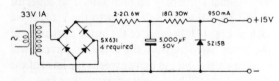

Fig. 152 Practical Zener stabilizer

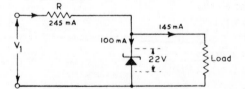

Fig. 153 Zener diode circuit calculation

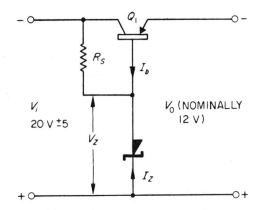

Fig. 154 Zener diode as constant reference voltage system

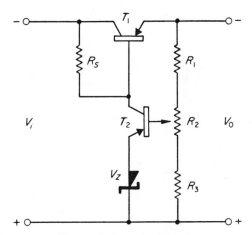

Fig. 155 Refinement of Fig. 154

The wattage for the resistor would then be 12.

The Zener diode can be more profitably employed as a constant reference voltage system controlling a power transistor. In this way, large currents can be made to flow in the load, without the loss associated with the simple Zener system. In Fig. 154 the resistor passes enough current to bias the diode to its Zener region. The base current of the transistor will then be held constant for any reasonable change in output current which, since the transistor can provide considerable current gain, may reach a figure much higher than the simple diode regulator. This circuit gives a regulated voltage of 6 for a supply voltage of 12, at up to 500 mA. One must be very careful never to short-circuit the output of this kind of circuit, a fast-acting fuse of 500 mA in the − lead is a wise precaution.

Now this is the basis of all regulators used today; but time has brought many refinements. Firstly, in this circuit as the current load increases the voltage across C_1 falls, due to the internal resistance of the rectifiers, and the Zener voltage would vary slightly. To overcome the fall in output (V_0) due to this change, an amplifier can be added to correct it. In Fig. 155, a Zener diode is connected to the emitter of the transistor T_2 and the base is connected to a proportion of the output voltage, approximately the value of V_z, which can be much smaller than V_0. If now V_0 falls due to an increase of load, the V_{be} of T_2 is slightly decreased, causing the collector voltage to increase because its emitter voltage is held constant by the Zener diode.

And because the base of the series transistor T_1 is connected to the collector of T_2, the base voltage rises and, therefore, so does the emitter voltage, tending to cancel the original change. In this application the Zener voltage would be reduced from 12 to perhaps 6 V and T_2 would then have 6 V between collector and emitter. The potential dividers R_1, R_2 and R_3 will have resistance values such that the potential at the base of T_2 is approximately 6 V. R_2 allows the output voltage to be set exactly. Another approach is to supply the diode from an independent rectifier as shown in Fig. 156. Note that this circuit is more sophisticated in that there is an additional control stage. The Zener supply comes through a high resistance source and is therefore almost independent of variations in the load current.

The other point we mentioned was the possible destruction of the series transistor by short-circuits on the output line. This can be guarded against by a high-speed triggering switch as shown in Fig. 157. The theory of this circuit is rather complex, but it is a very safe device which has to be re-set by switching off and on again in the event of a fault. Even so, the circuit will still trip if the fault still exists. The point at which it trips is set by RV_2. A lamp can be fitted where shown to indicate when the circuit has tripped. There is, however, a very small current still flowing through the series transistor; this cannot cause any damage.

If one has a suitable transformer and rectifier for low-voltage work, an even better regulator can

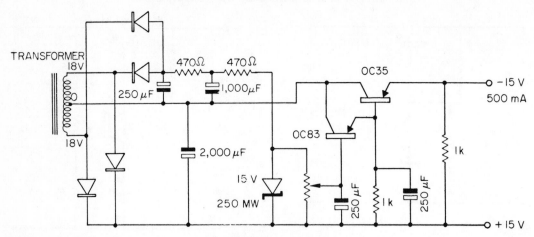

Fig. 156 Power supply unit

easily be assembled as in Fig. 158, and the points to which the trip circuit is connected are shown and lettered. But of course there are many variants of comparison circuits relying primarily on a Zener diode as a reference source. We show a couple for other voltages and currents in Figs 159 and 160. Power amplifiers often require higher voltages whilst organ generators usually depend on low voltages; the Philips system already mentioned only needs 1·6 V at 800 mA—less than 2 watts! Finally, the humble 12 V car battery has its uses as an emergency supply, and some portable organs have been designed to work from one; but it should always be shunted by about 1500 μF to reduce the internal impedance, which varies with the state of charge and especially with the changes in specific gravity.

Two things must be particularly remembered with transistor circuits; decoupling must be very thorough because of the naturally low impedances involved; and especial care must be taken over earthing or grounding. For instance, the mains earth must not be directly connected to the signal earth. This latter should be in the form of a busbar to which all earthed points of the circuit are connected, then the busbar is in its turn connected at one point only to the main earth. In this way, the chassis cannot carry circulating currents from the signal source, which often lead to hum pickup, noise and cross-talk.

If the reader owns a Variac, it is good practice when experimenting with transistor amplifiers to

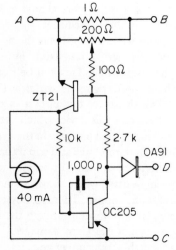

Fig. 157 Trip circuit

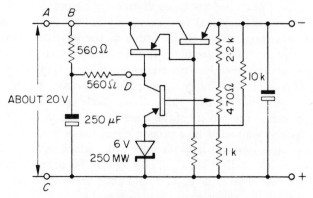

Fig. 158 More exact regulation unit

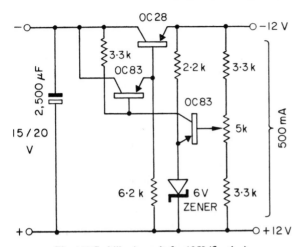

Fig. 159 Stabilized supply for 12 V (floating)

start with a low mains voltage and bring it gradually up to normal whilst adjusting the circuit. Naturally this will make the low voltage to the amplifier increase in proportion so it is a real safeguard when using high-power circuits.

In spite of all the data engineered into good organ or other music generators, it is the loudspeaking system used which will determine the success or otherwise of the overall scheme. So it is quite useless to think that any old loudspeakers, which sound all right on radio, will radiate the spectrum which has been carefully thought out for the organ tonal system. An organ can only be compared with another if the designed loudspeaker complement is used. And in designing a musical instrument as critical as an organ, the loudspeaker(s) form as integral a part as the tone generators. But first, what of the actual device itself? With the exception of one or two very costly (and bulky) installations, pressure horns are not used for medium or low notes. The reason is simple: a horn to develop pedal notes properly would be about 80 ft long with a square mouth 8 or 10 ft across. The use of a low-frequency horn implies great power, more than free cones could handle, and this does not come within our province. Of course, the efficiency is phenomenally high, some cinema horns achieve over 50 per cent; but a few watts one way or another is not going to bother us. Let us rather see what the cone can or cannot do. Any loudspeaker of normal construc-

tion consists of a cone-shaped diaphragm carrying a tubular coil at its apex, and supported around the base by a compliant mounting so that it can move freely to and fro. Since the coil must be immersed in a powerful magnetic field, it must be centred in the gap of the magnet and this is done by a restraining device attached to the coil tube; such a restraint must only be lateral, as the coil has to be free to move in and out to its limit. All these requirements are physical and easily met, but as soon as we apply a signal to the coil and cause it to move, the cone (which in nearly every case is also the diaphragm coupling the outer air to the vibrating element) behaves in some way depending on the interlinking of many factors. Firstly, the action of the magnetic field on the coil current produces a force which drives the cone outwards or inwards. This force is proportional to BlI where B = the flux density, l = the length of wire in the speech coil, I = the current.

However, it is not such a simple conversion system as appears from the above. The coil and cone possess mass, and there is the fluid mass of the air in contact with the cone. The centring device acts as a kind of spring and these factors result in a mechanical impedance which has to be overcome. The coil passing through the magnetic lines of force induces a back e.m.f. in the coil, which causes a voltage drop equivalent to adding another impedance to the speech coil circuit. The velocity of the speech coil vibrations are propor-

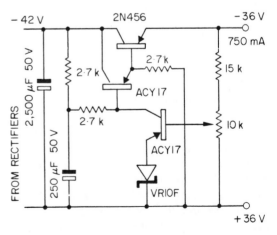

Fig. 160 Stabilized supply for 35 V

tional to the driving force divided by the mechanical impedance, whereas the amount of sound energy radiated is proportional to the square of the velocity multiplied by the radiation component of the resistance. This variation in velocity with frequency is usually met by making the fundamental resonance of the cone plus coil near to the lowest frequency to be reproduced.

At low frequencies, depending on the mass of the cone, this may act almost as a solid piston of the cone diameter. A complicated formula due to Rayleigh gives all the information required for designing such cone units—although it was written many years before there was such a thing as a loudspeaker. The top limit for piston action would be around 500 Hz but, since the larger the cone, the better the bass response, a 15 or 18 in. unit may cease to so act at perhaps 200 Hz. Thus we may say that for pedal notes approaching sine waves, and of 16 ft pitch, excellent reproduction is possible from a suitably mounted large cone unit at domestic volumes.

The radiated power is, however, inversely proportional to the frequency above this 'piston' point; but all this is for pure tones, and they do not exist except possibly for the very lowest pedal sounds which need not have any character. As the frequency becomes higher, waves tend to approach the source more and more closely; we mean by this that radiation comes more and more from the coil itself. Hence the well-known focusing effect for high notes. The upper range of reproducible frequencies is therefore fixed by the mass of the speech coil and not by the cone, as is often thought. Clearly one should have more than one unit to deal with the pitch range encountered in organs; for apart from the frequency dispersion, there is the matter of intermodulation. If we apply a sine signal of 40 Hz to a suitable loudspeaker, and one of (say) 4300 Hz at the same time, then other frequencies appear in the cone which are products or derivatives of the two injected frequencies; at any volume, a most objectionable spurious pitch is heard. Indeed, measurements carried out by the Bell Laboratories show that organ intermodulation is very prevalent; some tests give distortion figures of as high as 50 per cent. So one should always separate treble and bass into a minimum of

two channels. This does not necessarily mean that two amplifiers are required, though this is certainly the proper solution; but the frequency spectrum can be split by a cross-over network so that low sounds go to the large unit, and higher ones to a small loudspeaker. Fig. 161 shows a typical circuit and the appropriate values below. Some prefer to cross over at 500 Hz, in which case all these values should be doubled. Note that the resistance of the coils must be less than that of the speech coils or the damping will be adversely affected. There are many, many loudspeakers to choose from and one should not buy cheap ones for the sake of cheapness; they rarely give good results. But if we assume that the question of units has been settled, how are they to be mounted to give of their best? Regardless of the size of the units, we must face the fact that as the air-pressure waves are radiated from both sides of the cone, they will be 180° out of phase. At some frequency, therefore, they will meet at the edge of the cone and cancel out; the unit must be mounted on a baffle of some kind to prevent this. The baffle must not be capable of resonating at any frequency, therefore the construction must be heavy; 1 in. timber is suggested, but thinner material can be used if cross-braced with dowelling at various points inside; here we are assuming that the baffle will be

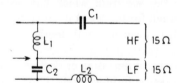

Fig. 161 Frequency-separating network

The constants can be computed from

$$L_1 = \frac{L}{\sqrt{2}} \quad L_2 = \sqrt{2L} \quad C_1 = \sqrt{2C} \quad C_2 = \frac{C}{\sqrt{2}}$$

For an attenuation of 12 dB per octave, cross-over frequency 1000 Hz,

	L	L_1	L_2	C	C_1	C_2
For 15 Ω coil	2400	1700	3400	11	15·6	7·75
For 3 Ω coil	480	340	680	53	75	37·5

folded round into box form, as the flat baffle is very large. The size is determined by the lowest frequency required to be heard; one-quarter wavelength is sufficient delay; to operate at 30 Hz, therefore, the dimensions of a plane baffle would be

$$\lambda \times 0{\cdot}25 \qquad \text{where } \lambda = \frac{V}{F}$$

V = velocity of sound in air (taken at 1056 ft/sec)

F = frequency (Hz)

λ = wavelength in feet.

Thus $\quad \lambda = \dfrac{1056}{30} = 35{\cdot}2$

and $\quad 35{\cdot}2 \times 0{\cdot}25 = 8{\cdot}8$

giving a baffle of 8 ft 6 in. square, approximately.

A very satisfactory approach is to fold the baffle into a box having a vent at the bottom as in Fig. 162. The internal tube can be used to tune the system to some low note which the cone might be rather weak on, or it can be abolished and the interior of the box lined with several layers of felt, each slightly separated from each other; for instance, glued over plastic egg boxes as separators. The width, 2 ft 6 in., appears large but we are interested in realism more than power and every effort should be made to exclude loudspeakers from the actual console; they cannot sound right to the player at any time.

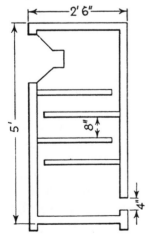

Fig. 162 Reflex cabinet for loudspeaker

Striking low-frequency realism is obtained from acoustic chambers utilizing the corner of a room wall to extend the effective length of the chamber. The form of the enclosure is now a triangle, its effectiveness being reduced if the floors and wall are not smooth and hard and quite clear of obstructions for at least 6 ft in front of the enclosure. The bass acoustic efficiency is many times that of a box standing out in the room, therefore less input power is required and although the cabinet must be about 9 cu. ft, it is a convenient part of the room in which to have it. As a guide to calculating the volume of a triangular cabinet, take an example in numerical form. Assume the base of the triangle to have two sides, meeting in the corner, each 21 in. long, and it is 30 in. across the face; then the area will be—

$$2s = 21 + 21 + 30 = 72$$

Therefore $\quad s = 36$

Now

$$\Delta = \sqrt{s(s-a)(s-b)(s-c)}$$
$$\Delta = \sqrt{36(36-21)(36-21)(36-30)}$$
$$= 6\sqrt{15 \times 15 \times 6}$$
$$= 90\sqrt{6} \text{ in. square}$$

The required volume is then height in inches × base area (from above). Naturally we are only discussing bass requirements; indeed it is only the bass which poses any problems. Much smaller cabinets will serve the manuals but one point must be noted: if several loudspeakers are used together, all the speech coils must go in or out in phase—otherwise there may be cancellation of some of the signals. It is easy to try this; take a 1·5-V cell and quickly touch each speech coil in turn; for the same polarity of the cell, you can see the cone dart out or in; make sure the leads are so connected that they all go the same way.

For small domestic situations, a very compact unit capable of excellent performance is the column speaker system using the Wharfedale units with aluminium speech coil. They take up very little room on the floor and are easily moved about. A typical unit has the dimensions of 18 in. × 12 in. × 4 ft high and the 8 in. loudspeaker unit will easily handle the whole of the manual stops of a good organ—though, of course, one such column on each manual would be ideal. The extreme bass from the column units is very soft and lifelike, but tends to be weak by comparison with the treble; this again underlines the importance of having separate bass and treble channels, for here the output of the bass amplifiers can be raised to equal that of the treble unit, giving a result far in advance of anything possible with one loudspeaker only. Today miniature cabinets are in common use; special loudspeakers with very flexible surrounds permit of a good bass response in spite of the stiffness imposed by total enclosure. An effective formula for the size of cabinet required is—

$$V = 2500\,R$$

where R is the radius of loudspeaker cone in inches; volume is in cubic inches. The volume of the actual loudspeaker itself in cubic inches must be deducted from the above, or indeed from any enclosure calculations.

We see now that there is little control of any cone resonances by air pressure and only a small amount by acoustic damping, so that the electrical damping system in the Onkyo loudspeaker (Fig. 163) is interesting, since there is an auxiliary coil fitted to the main system which can be used in a feedback circuit to suppress resonances along the lines of the devices invented by the late A. D. Blumlein in 1930 (British patent 350,998). The loudspeaker has been regarded in this chapter as for use in the home; it is not in our province to discuss public-address or other high-power methods, but today there are many ways of connecting amplifiers to give distortionless reproduction at a loudness unthinkable 30 years ago. One would not expect anything like the full frequency response from an organ under these conditions, where there is no reflected sound and every opportunity for dissipation in the open air.

The organ designer has a strong position so far as reproduction is concerned; with records or radio, only a limited amount of control is possible over the bass, treble and general balance. With an organ, the whole spectrum can be orientated with

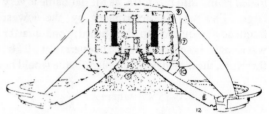

Fig. 163 Onkyo loudspeaker. (1) = Magnet; (2) = Voice coil; (3) = Feedback magnet; (4) = Feedback coil; (5) = Dust cap; (6) = Yoke; (7) = Damper; (8) = Cone; (9) = Field cover; (10) = Voice coil terminal; (11) = Feedback terminal; (12) = Gasket

the loudspeakers to give any 'curve' required. And by the way, should the price of a large loudspeaker solely for bass be dismaying, the problem can be resolved by using 9 or 10 smaller units placed close together on a common baffle. This was first used in the Hammond H-40 cabinet, where 9 × 10 in. units were stacked as close as possible on a baffle forming the front of the cabinet. Later models have two separate loudspeakers placed under the top of the cabinet, speaking upwards for the manuals; the group of 9 units was solely for the pedal department and it was one of the most effective units ever made. Speakers facing upwards are useful to reduce any key clicks or hiss from amplifiers etc. without affecting the sound otherwise; the Wharfedale unit is of this type.

Electrostatic speakers are most lifelike for reproduction of speech and most radio or record purposes; alas, they find little application to organs or the like, since the diaphragms are incapable of moving sufficiently for the kind of frequency range necessary. This is something inseparable from the principle of operation, and is much to be regretted, for they are free from all resonances and have the great advantage that every part of the large diaphragm moves in phase, thus creating a realistic sound field; for, as must be obvious, if we are simulating even a small pipe organ, the sound does not emanate from a point source but is spread out following the pipe layout. Therefore, anything tending to give the same audible effect must add to the realism.

7 Commercial Electronic Instruments

In previous editions it has been possible to show examples of all the well-known organs and similar sound sources. The main reason for this was that comparatively few of these instruments were generally available for the public to examine. Today we are faced with a positive glut of all kinds of music and effects apparatus and these are all in showrooms and studios in many countries. At one time, respective makers' instruments could be at once identified either tonally or structurally, but now designs follow each other so quickly that there is a scramble to avail themselves of the advances in technology.

There are a few instances where this has led to a real improvement in some properties of the organs, either tonally or on the effects side. But on the whole, there is a strong flavour of 'keeping up with the Jones', that is, being the first with a new device or facility. The specifications of many domestic organs make interesting reading, for the emphasis is on the rhythm, sustain, wah-wah, glide effects and little is heard of the tonal content! It would seem that anyone can make a flute, but few can compare with our rhythm boxes!

Well, tastes change and there have always been many kinds of music. No sides can be taken in a book of this kind but in this chapter are described a few instruments which are either of outstanding technical or historic interest, employ new techniques, or are suitable for the experimenter to make himself, though this aspect is perhaps better catered for in the next chapter. Some of the most intriguing devices were the simple melodic keyboards like the Solovox, Clavioline, Univox etc. Hammond used a number of inductances in his Solovox, but it appeared that equally good results were obtained with tuned multivibrators, the only disadvantage being the selection of the resistors in the pitch keying chain; for these had to follow a logarithmic law and this meant that the range of notes was limited, although by adding frequency dividers this was greatly extended. Values ranging from a few hundred to many thousands of ohms had to be carefully set for each note of the compass.

Today it is possible to use voltage-controlled oscillators which have two great advantages: the frequency is directly related to the voltage increments, therefore equal frequency steps mean equal resistors in the keying chain; and because d.c. is being keyed instead of the signal, the generator etc. could be some distance from the keyboard with no risk of hum or cross-talk pickup, and no screened wires. A simple VCO is shown in Fig. 164. This produces an excellent square wave which, of course, can be modified by subsequent tone circuits; and the pitch range is five octaves, far greater than any of the above previous keyboards, though again, dividers could be used to extend this. This circuit is very easily modulated with vibrato, and the circuit for this is on the left of the figure; vibrato can be made so deep that the tone frequency is swung several semitones away, thus opening the field for many new effects. Such circuits form the basis of synthesizers. This one is made by Taylor Electronic Music, Chester, and is one of a range.

Since the technique of obtaining a steady change in voltage by means of a rotary potentiometer or other device is well developed, there is no reason why this VCO should not be used as a stepless instrument—continuous gliding tones are easily obtained—or odd intervals of the scale. In fact, it is similar in some way to the ingenious instrument called the Trautonium.

The Trautonium

At the period of invention of this instrument, neon tubes had reached a considerable state of perfec-

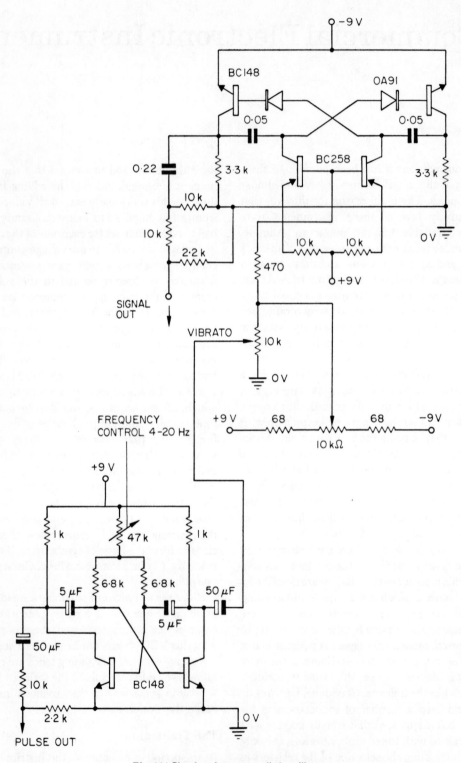

Fig. 164 Simple voltage-controlled oscillator

tion in Germany, and a number of investigators had adopted them in preference to vacuum valves for oscillation generators. Apart from the greater circuit simplicity, the wave form is always rich in harmonics, and thus the sound is readily modified to give musical tonalities which are not, perhaps, the same as those of conventional instruments, but which are quite pleasing. With this object in view, a simple single keyboard instrument was evolved in which one neon tube was coupled with a resistor and tuning capacitor so as to oscillate continuously.

This performed very satisfactorily but since such a tube must work into a very high impedance as any appreciable load will alter the action of the circuit, the modern instrument makes use of a gas triode (Fig. 165). This is more stable, easier to control, and can deliver appreciable power.

The variable resistor marked 'manual' in Fig. 165, together with capacitor C, adjusts the frequency range as required over about three octaves. To facilitate playing, the manual resistor is in flexible form, so proportioned that the frequency of oscillation is proportional to the length of strip in use. Dummy keys are mounted above the strip to indicate the approximate position of the main intervals, but it will be realized that the frequency can be made *continuously variable* and thus gliding tones may be played. Manipulation of the 'keyboard' simply consists of pressing the tubular

cover enclosing the resistance contact strip at the point selected to produce the correct pitch note.

The generator oscillates instantly; to control the attack or rate of build-up for the sound, an auxiliary resistance element is placed below the manual resistor and is so contrived that pressure on the playing strip also compresses the attack resistor, so causing the note to sound. Thus various modes of attack are possible, depending on the rate at which contact is made, and the pressure exerted at that time.

In simple models, there are formant circuits of an elementary nature, from which sounds approximating to reed (Fig. 166 (A)), string (Fig. 166 (B)) and flute tones (Fig. 166 (C)) can be obtained. The sounds are somewhat arbitrary, but the extreme simplicity of the device led to its wide adoption in schools abroad, where many pupils could practice simultaneously by wearing headphones, without interference. The circuit shown was used for this purpose, but by further amplification the usefulness was extended.

More recent models have grown up somewhat, and are fitted with two keyboards. The considerable length of wire required to develop enough resistance for variation of the grid bias over a range of three octaves made the physical intervals too large to be comfortably manipulated on the model described above. By winding the wire round a drum it has been possible to bring the intervals

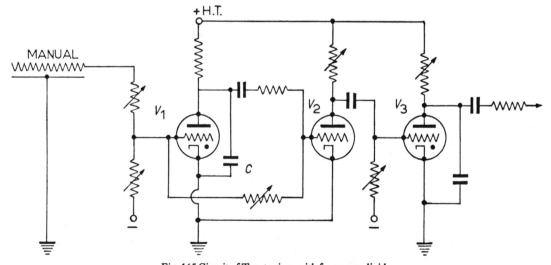

Fig. 165 Circuit of Trautonium with frequency divider

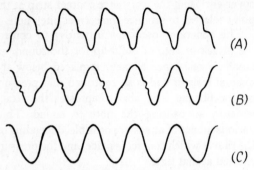

Fig. 166 Wave forms from Trautonium

closer. Keys indicate the main tones of the octave. Each manual remains melodic only, but is provided with its own independent thyratron oscillator. Greatly contrasting tonal effects are possible by playing one note on each manual simultaneously, and a further development is the provision of sub-octave generators with a much wider range of harmonics and resonant filters.

The attack and volume are primarily controlled by a liquid resistance contained in a flexible tube beneath the metal strip which contacts the spiral resistor as required to form a note. The main level control is a foot pedal.

This instrument is interesting as making no attempt to present ready-made or imitative tone colours, but providing instead a selection of harmonic filters so that a specific effect can be built up. In the hands of a skilled player this is unquestionably the right approach, but the Trautonium is not designed as a domestic instrument and as such would probably not be acceptable without normal keys and at least partly pre-set tone colours.

The Theremin

The simplest, and also the first, solo instrument was that of Leon Theremin (British patent 244,133). This has re-appeared from time to time in various forms, but a recent revision attributed to R. A. Moog is shown in Fig. 167.

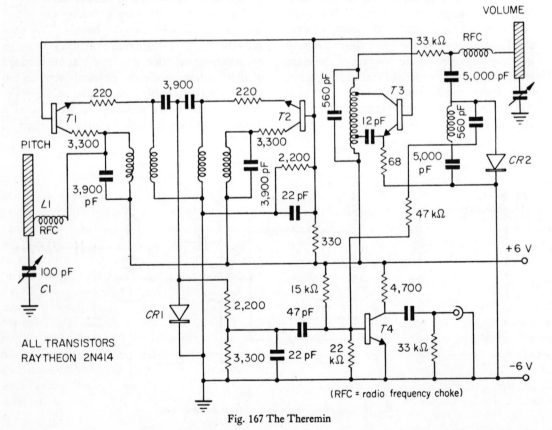

Fig. 167 The Theremin

Theremin's invention allows a performer to vary the pitch and the loudness of a note produced by the apparatus in any manner, because the pitch is altered by moving one hand nearer to a capacitive element which alters the tuning, whilst variations in loudness are produced by the other hand approaching a metal plate; a further modification by Martin Taubman consisted of a foot switch to stop and start a note at any instant; for otherwise notes glide from one pitch to another.

The basic arrangement is that of a beat-frequency oscillator, where one high-frequency oscillator works at a fixed value whilst the other is variable; the resultant beat lies in the audible range and is the signal. In the present circuit, one oscillator runs at about 150 kHz whilst the other one is tuned to this frequency but has the modifier consisting of $L1$ and $C1$ coupled to the metal rod marked 'pitch'. The effect of bringing the body near to the rod is to de-tune $L1$ and $C1$, so effectively re-tuning the first oscillator. The resultant beat is passed through the rectifier $CR1$ and so the signal at the base of $T4$ only requires modifying in loudness; this is done by bringing the other hand near to the plate marked 'volume', which re-tunes the oscillator of $T3$; as the impedance of $L4$-$C13$ increases, the r.f. voltage produced by $T3$ also increases. This is rectified by $CR2$ and applied to the base of $T4$ as a control bias; in other words, the gain is varied as this voltage varies. The wave form is rich in harmonics and whilst it is very difficult to 'play', certainly many effects are realizable which are almost impossible to obtain in any other way.

Solo devices on which only one note at a time can be played are not now so popular, but we can see in the Electravox a compact and simplified approach to the conventional method of generating organ tones.

The Hohner Electravox

There are several electronic accordions on the market, and surely the name which first comes to mind is that of Hohner AG. In previous editions we described the Multimonika; now the introduction of transistors has enabled some new effects to be incorporated into the Electravox. The circuit essentials are reproduced in Fig. 168.

In common with most musical instruments covering a number of octaves, the top 12 notes are derived from tuned LC oscillators, the remainder from bistable frequency dividers; these, however, are each followed by a sawtooth converter stage. The signal controls are divided between buttons for the bass (and bass chords) and the customary keyboard for the rest of the compass. Both bass and treble pass to percussion circuits, vibrato being applied from a phase-shift oscillator on the way. The percussion amplifiers are quite novel. The rapid start to the note is the natural rise time of the sawtooth converter, and on pressing a key or button this signal is made to pull in a reed relay by the amplifier shown; the effect of this contact closing is to stop the transistor feeding the small lamp, which goes out slowly. This affects a photo-transistor of the OC60 type, and as this forms part of a voltage divider, the ratio of this corresponds with the brilliance of the lamp, and so the tone changes in volume (or decays) as the illumination changes. Considerable latitude in the time constants etc. is allowed by means of rotary pots under the control of the player. It should be noted that this system must re-set after each note, so continuous or legato playing does not cause the effect; notes must be staccato or detached.

Post-amplifiers and the usual stop-circuits giving a range of reed, flute and string tones are present, the main amplifiers being separate according to the power required and the number of loudspeakers in use.

The Novachord

This is a single keyboard instrument on which chords may be played, and is capable of producing both percussion and sustained tones with a wide range of attack and decay characteristics. The keyboard has seventy-two keys, six octaves as against the normal piano compass of eighty-five or eighty-eight notes and the standard organ keyboard of five octaves. The controls are mounted as shown in Fig. 169, and in addition there are sustaining pedals and a volume-control pedal. The instrument operates on a similar principle to the Solovox, using a series of twelve master oscillators of fixed frequency for the top twelve semitones, and a series of frequency dividers for all the lower notes. Double triode valves are used in the

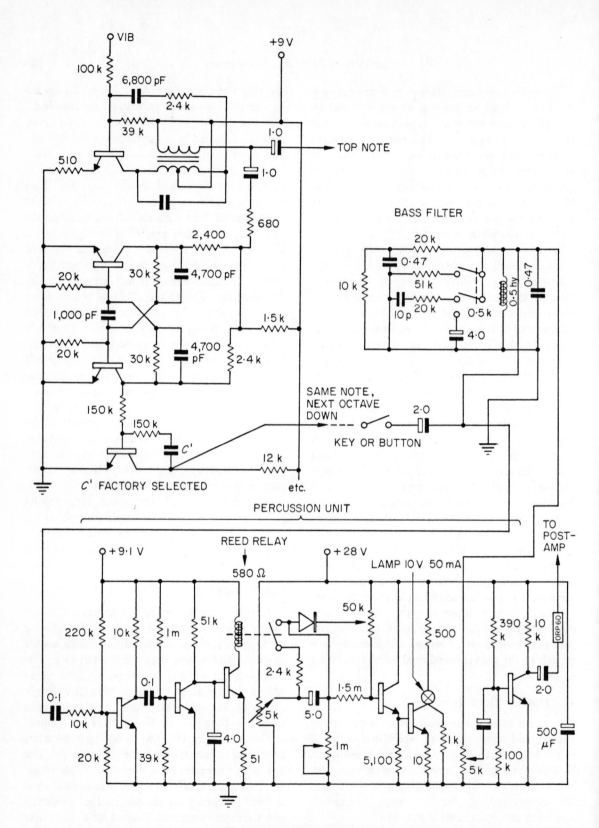

Fig. 168 Part circuit of Electravox

oscillators, the upper section being connected in a conventional tuned circuit which can be adjusted for pitch, whilst the lower section forms the vibrato device; a vibrating reed alters the grid bias of this section, altering the gain in a periodic manner.

The complete circuit for one note in all the pitch ranges is shown in Fig. 170. The frequency

dividers are different from those just described. Each one is a non-linear amplifier operating as follows. The steady anode current of the valve causes a drop across the 1 MΩ bias resistor ($RN6$) of 198 V. This opposes the -192 V fixed bias supply and there is thus 6-V bias on the valve. When a signal arrives from a preceding source, it is a sharp-pointed wave and the grid is made to go

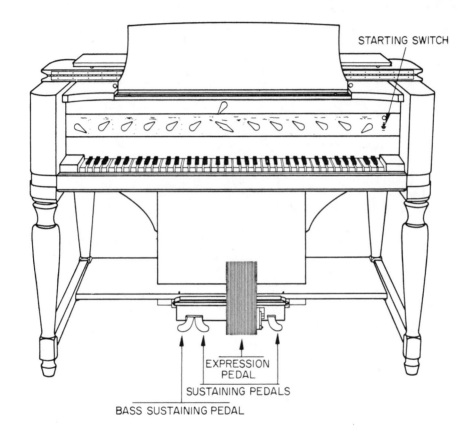

STARTING SWITCH

EXPRESSION
PEDAL

SUSTAINING PEDALS

BASS SUSTAINING PEDAL

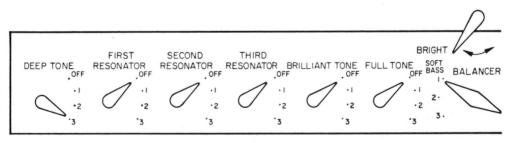

TONE CONTROLS

Fig. 169 Novachord

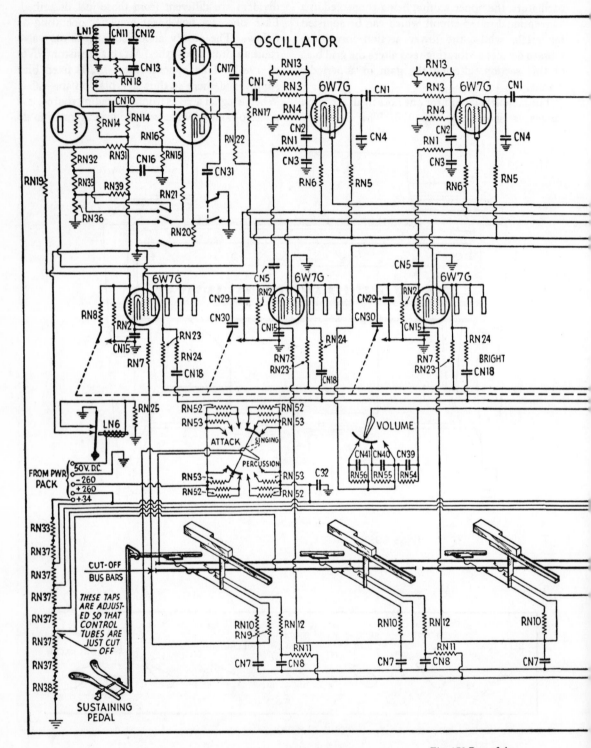

Fig. 170 Part of the

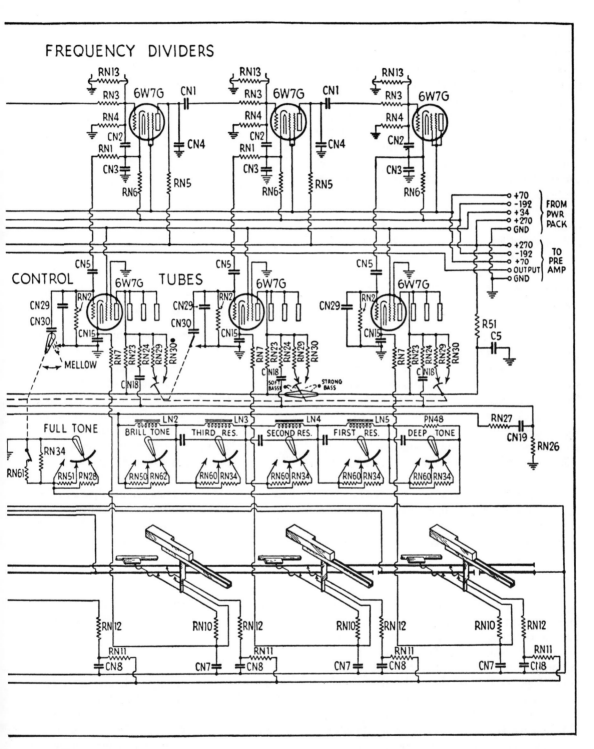

Novachord circuit

positive very rapidly. The resulting flow of anode current increases the drop across the 1 MΩ resistor and also makes the cathode go suddenly positive. Since this excursion is extremely rapid, it causes the grid to remain positive even after the initial wave has passed, because it passes through CN2. Thus whenever a pulse arrives, the resultant state of the valve is such that both anode and cathode potentials are almost equal, and no anode current flows. CN3 is therefore also charged to a corresponding value.

The signal having passed, the grid and cathode begin to float down towards earth potential. The grid potential leakage rate is fixed by the leakage through RN4 and RN13 into CN2 and CN3 in series. The cathode potential drops at the rate of leakage of RN6 into CN3. The time constants of these circuits are fixed so that the grid rate is greater than the cathode rate, so that when the second input cycle arrives and raises the grid potential it still does not rise above the cathode potential and the valve still remains cut off. The time constants are such, however, that the third input cycle finds the voltage so low that another cycle of operations can be started. Thus if the RC constants are correct, division by two takes place; if they are incorrect, division by some other number may take place or the circuit may not divide at all.

The frequency dividers operate continuously, but no signal is heard because interposed between the dividers and the amplifiers are control valves, one for each divider; that is, one for each note. These control valves are normally over-biased so that they are cut off. On depressing a playing key, various contacts are operated to which different potentials may be applied to produce many effects. It has already been pointed out that if the harmonic content of a mixed wave remains constant, but the time/amplitude curve is varied, entirely different effects are heard. This property is widely exploited in the Novachord. Should the busbar A have a high potential relative to that of C, the note will start with a steep transient front and be percussive in character. If A is at low potential and C at high potential, the note starts low and builds up to a high level. If A and C are at the same potential, the note has constant amplitude and will be sustained. Many intermediate settings of these

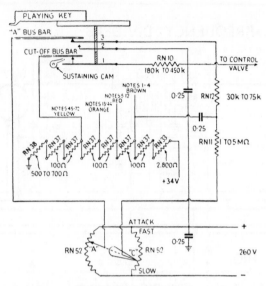

Fig. 171 Playing-key circuit

relative potentials are possible by means of the controls in the figures. Since the capacitors in these charging circuits are all discharged through resistors at known rates, then if the resistors are disconnected the rate is determined by the leakage in the valve and capacitor. This is very slow, and the sustaining pedal performs this operation, thus simulating the corresponding pedal on a piano. The way this is done is shown in Fig. 171.

The other controls which affect the harmonic development of the note as against the rate of attack and decay are conveniently combinable. This feature, in conjunction with the several different rates of vibrato simultaneously obtainable, produces many interesting effects. There is a highly stabilized power-supply unit feeding the 144 valves in the instrument, which are associated with the fourteen controls to perform the above functions. Most regrettably the Novachord is no longer in production.

The Philicorda

Although the principles of the divider organ have been described, and circuit excerpts from various makes shown, no complete organ has been examined in this book. The Philicorda is a simple organ of ingenious design and having voicing circuits admirable for domestic use. We therefore take a good look at how it works.

Primarily it is a two-manual organ with four octaves of playing keys each, but not offset as is common today. There are 13 or 25 pedal keys and 16 manual stops, 2 pedal stops, percussion and reverberation controls. All tone circuits are on a common expression pedal. A useful feature is a set of balance controls, so that the relative volume of either manual or the pedals can be adjusted as desired. The key switches under the manuals have bronze wires with conductive sleeves thereon. The ingenious percussion circuit is described on page 166, but as it is external to the organ it could of course be used with almost any tone generator system.

The tone signals originate in 12 Hartley oscillators of the series tuned type. These are sinusoidal, so would not trigger dividers; therefore a shaping stage follows, as in Fig. 172. During the positive cycles of the applied sine-wave voltage, TS2 is turned on, and during the negative half cycles, diode GR1 is turned on. Since the knee voltages of the transistor and diode are virtually equal, the output of this circuit will be a symmetrical square wave which is then, by the voltage divider and capacitor shown, applied to the first bistable divider. The signal is also removed via capacitor C122 for the top notes of the keyboard; in this way the wave form is the same as for the lower octaves from the dividers.

The BF195 silicon transistors allow a very simple circuit to be used for the dividers, which function as follows. When the supply voltage is switched on, both transistors will become conductive. But there are always random influences at

work, e.g. noise, which speedily upset the symmetry. Assume that the current through TS25 decreases slower than the current through TS26; the voltage drop across R196 will become smaller than that across R198. The collector voltage of TS25 will now increase, making the base of TS26 more positive. This increasing current causes a larger drop across R198; so the collector voltage of TS26 will become greater and, as a result, the base of TS25 will become negative, soon cutting off this transistor. At the same time, the current through TS26 increases so much that the voltage drop across R198 and R195 almost reaches the value of the supply. At this moment the circuit assumes a stable condition but, of course, is subject to an applied control signal. As the negative pulse from the oscillator shaper reaches the junction of R196 and R195, it affects the base of TS26 via R196 and R197, so that the collector current of this transistor decreases. The voltage at point B increases and so the voltage on the base of TS25 will also increase. When this transistor is turned on, its collect voltage will decrease again making the base of TS26 more negative and, due to the avalanche effect, the multivibrator will turn over to its second stable condition. TS25 is then fully conductive, whilst TS26 is turned off. Thus the circuit will change over after every subsequent negative pulse, switching alternately in such a way that the output wave form is square. From C the signal is sent to the key switches via equalizing resistors, but the

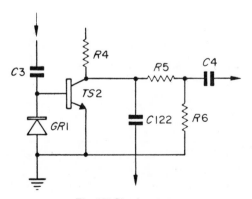

Fig. 172 Shaping stage

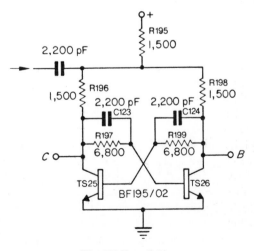

Fig. 173 Next divider

same wave form is present at *B*, only 180° out of phase with *C*; this voltage is used to drive the next divider, which again divides the frequency by two. Fig. 173 illustrates the above, with component values.

Now all organs of this kind require a vibrato oscillator. In this instance, as in most others, there is a 3-section phase-shift oscillator, resulting in a sine wave which is fed to the oscillator bases through resistors as shown; the rate is adjustable from 5–8 Hz (see Fig. 174).

All the signal outputs from the various dividers are brought to some audible level which does not accentuate either treble or bass by means of shunting resistors as indicated; the values for these will of course vary with the degree of equalization deemed necessary. This is a much better way to regulate the divider outputs than splitting the busbars as has commonly been done in the past.

From the busbars, the signals are collected at a number of pre-amplifiers as shown in Fig. 175, which shows the whole tone-forming circuitry of this organ. Observe the mixed wave forms for some of the solo stops. The lowest octave is taken to a multivibrator, where the signals are divided down again to form the 16 ft tones for the pedal section; one multi suffices here, as it is assumed that only one note at a time will be played; the pedal-switch connections take care of this.

Following a post-amplifier, the signals pass to two valve main amplifiers feeding high-impedance loudspeakers; there are two channels, each with two loudspeakers. Reverberation from a spring unit can be applied by a switch. The amplifier circuit is interesting, see Fig. 176.

Largely due to the wise provision of 2-ft registers, the whole of this organ appears to be suffused with life and there is a complete absence of the muffled effect so often observed. This transistorized model replaces the previous gas-tube instruments which were in production for so many years.

Harmonics GR84 organ

This very simple instrument has many novel features. Designed essentially for 'pop' groups, it consists of a single 49-note manual and no pedal section. Practically the whole organ external to the dividers uses 2N5172 transistors, a great convenience for servicing. Because there are no pedals, a latching bass system is applied to the lowest 13 notes. This controls the lowest note played and features sustain and cancel diodes. A bridged-T filter smooths the output wave form to give an agreeable tone. These circuits are shown in Fig. 177.

Frequency division is carried out by six Marconi-Elliott MA60 units. These small

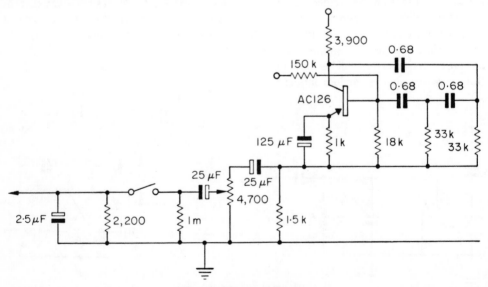

Fig. 174 Vibrato oscillator

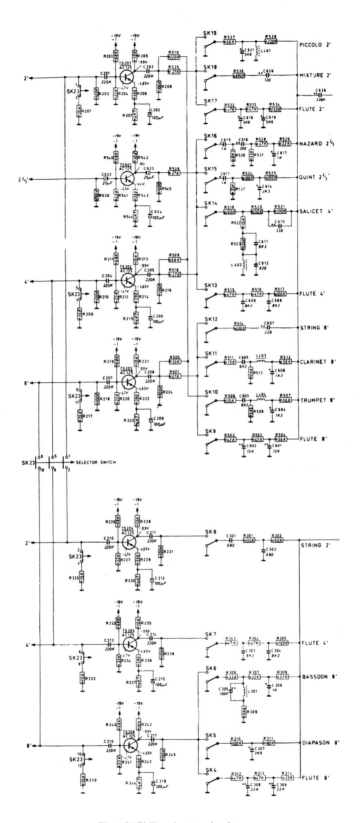

Fig. 175 Philicorda tone circuits

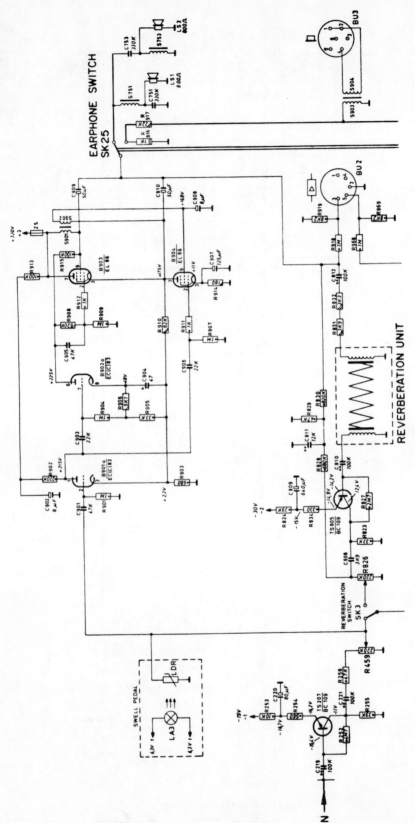

Fig. 176 One main amplifier

integrated circuits are housed in a TO18 can, each comprising six bistables and suitable isolating equipment, arranged in two cascaded groups of three. The connections are given in Fig. 178.

The use of 'wah-wah' or similar frequency-shifting circuits generally requires an inductance for the tuned circuit. In this case, control over the pass band is effected by the 10-k potentiometer shown, which for one complete rotation changes the filter characteristics twice (see Fig. 179).

Another way of producing this kind of effect can be seen in the circuitry of the Hammond 'Piper', page 153.

An entertainment feature much in demand is the glide or continuous frequency shift over a limited range. The usual method is to change the value of the bias voltage on the oscillator bases (as in the application of vibrato), but at a rate controlled either by the player or by a timing circuit. This latter method is used in the GR84 organ, as shown

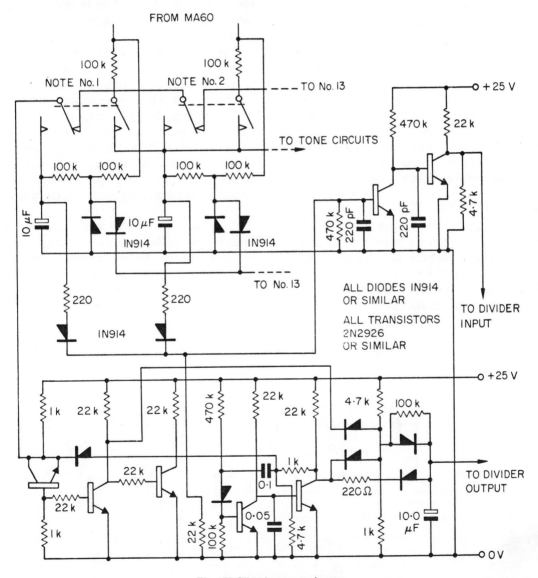

Fig. 177 GR84 bass control system

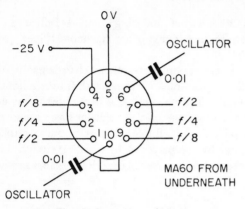

Fig. 178 Connections of MA60

here is due to O. Vierling. The appearance and scale is that of a normal grand piano, with the addition of several controls rather like the Novachord.

There are two basic intentions behind such a design; firstly, the possibility of varying not only the harmonic content of the string but also the attack and decay; and secondly, the quite considerable improvement in the lower registers when electrical pickups are used. This chapter merely describes some of the instruments designed to produce electrical music; in Chapter 8 some further consideration is given to this question of fortifying otherwise adequate tonal characteristics.

Basically the Electrochord has the same number and arrangement of strings as a piano. The hammer-and-touch mechanism is also the same. Each set of strings is provided with a series of electrostatic pickup plates in proximity thereto. There are a great many harmonics generated in each string, and these have different amplitudes and phases. Thus many pickups are arranged so that all or any of the overtones may be employed. A simplified diagram of the method is given in Fig. 181.

The pickups are of such an area that in every case this is smaller than the wavelength of the required harmonic. But if it is desired to eliminate certain harmonics the pickups may be much larger. These pickups are connected to a capacitor amplifier such as has already been described in

in Fig. 180. This illustration also includes the vibrato oscillator and one of the ingenious tone oscillators. The interdependence of the glide and vibrato circuits can thus be seen. Voltages of +25, −25 and −10 V are supplied from the unregulated power unit, and the transistorized power amplifier has a socket for an external loudspeaker in place of that built into the organ, if desired.

The Electrochord

This is an instrument of a type in which electrical conversion of physically produced vibrations is used. In short, it is a piano of such a design that the sound is heard electrically, i.e. through loudspeakers. There have been several such instruments produced, and the one to be described

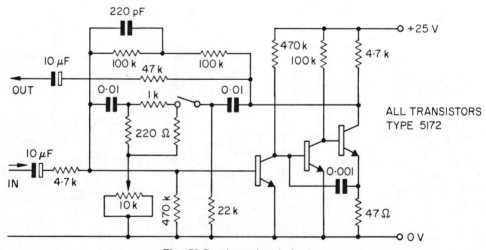

Fig. 179 Growl or wah-wah circuit

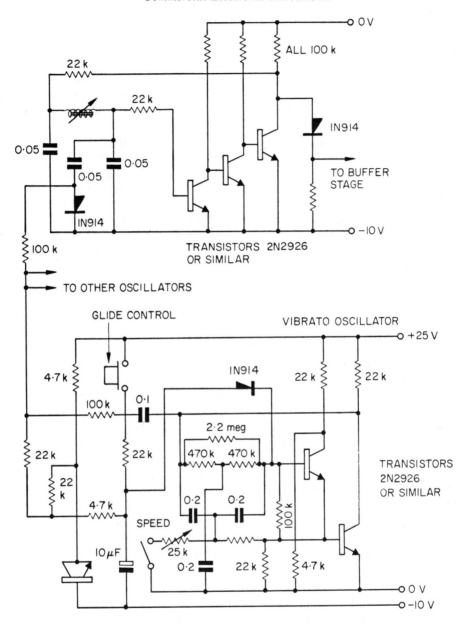

Fig. 180 Tone oscillator, glide and vibrato circuits

Chapter 4, and also to tone-control circuits which again are rather similar to those of the Novachord. Some tonal control is thus possible, indeed this instrument can be made to sound thin like a xylophone or extremely rich, more like an organ.

These tonal variations are not due to the electrical circuits alone; the most important characteristic of a piano is the transient starting tone. No amount of pickup ingenuity will produce this from the strings because it is a function of the combined effect of the damping due to the soundboard and the effect of the bridge which connects the strings to this soundboard. Thus additional pickups under the bridge are necessary, and to obtain a sufficiently rapid tonal decay, there must be something to absorb the energy from the strings

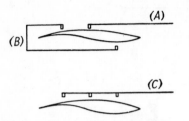

Fig. 181 Pickup arrangement. (A) = Odd tones; (B) = Even tones; (C) = Pure tones

after they have been set in motion. In this particular instrument, there is a smaller type of sound-board which has special damping constants.

There are time-delay networks of the *RC* type in the d.c. polarizing circuits to the strings, so that a very slow build-up of tone is possible; in this way, quite organ-like tones can be produced; but whilst it is very difficult to define exactly what constitutes good piano tone, the general effect of this instrument with the most percussive setting is rather richer and more mellow than the ordinary piano; that is, when harmonically set up to reproduce exact piano tone.

The Allen Company

The American Allen Company is noteworthy for its careful attention to detail, advanced circuitry, and the fact that any customer's wishes can be incorporated into an organ.

In common with a number of others, the new Allens use a single master-oscillator system but not only this; most elaborate storage, gating and other circuits are incorporated in the digital system employed. One might describe it as an additive system carried to the limit. Clearly, in this way extremely accurate synthesis of any tone envelope is possible, together with any form of attack, hold and decay. The details of the organ are too complex for this book, and we would refer readers US Patent no. 3,515,792 which describes the principle used in great detail. However, since the tonal results are clinically accurate, there are some who prefer the random imperfections which give the interest to so many of the arts, and since the Allen classic instruments are to be found in very many installations and, moreover, can be built by an amateur, some details of this well-developed organ circuit are appended. Today the organs are all

transistorized, thus enabling the makers to mount the many generators inside the console—for this is an independent oscillator system. In this instrument we find the only successful application of simulated wind noise, giving life and realism to such pipe sounds as require it. The basic approach has been to supply the oscillators, not with steady d.c., but with rectified white noise, in some cases superimposed on d.c. filtered in a suitable manner. Although the noise imparts great realism to voices like the open diapason, it is perhaps at the upper end of the compass that it is most useful, because otherwise very high-pitched oscillator sounds tend to scream; their artificial purity does not synthesize pipe voices such as mixtures very successfully. But with the admixture of controlled noise, these effects become realistic.

In Fig. 182 is illustrated the basic method of tone generation. Toroidal coils have no external field, therefore may be placed close together without screening. Since the oscillators are sinusoidal, they are not working very hard and this further reduces interference. The time constants for these organs are very carefully worked out, so that the generators speak at the same rate as pipes. All oscillators are basically sine wave and reeds and strings are formed from this wave form by rectification and other treatments. Note the use of a tuned choke in the flute circuits; this peaks at the tuned frequency and so, when brought down to its proper level again, any other frequencies which might have been present are now so attenuated that they will be inaudible. In this circuit, there is provision for shunting more or less of the noise input to earth by means of the resistor shown dotted; it can thus be equalized over the compass. Six octaves of oscillators are connected to one pre-amplifier, the remaining two octaves having their own pre-amps. All controls affecting tone quality or loudness are operated by light-dependent resistors, thus being noiseless and very long-lived. Below the flute oscillators can be seen the diapason, which is similar but the subsequent wave-form treatment is more complex, being broken up into frequency bands. The reeds are formed from the flute oscillators by rectification and the arrangement for this is also given in the figure. The constants for all parts of this circuit are

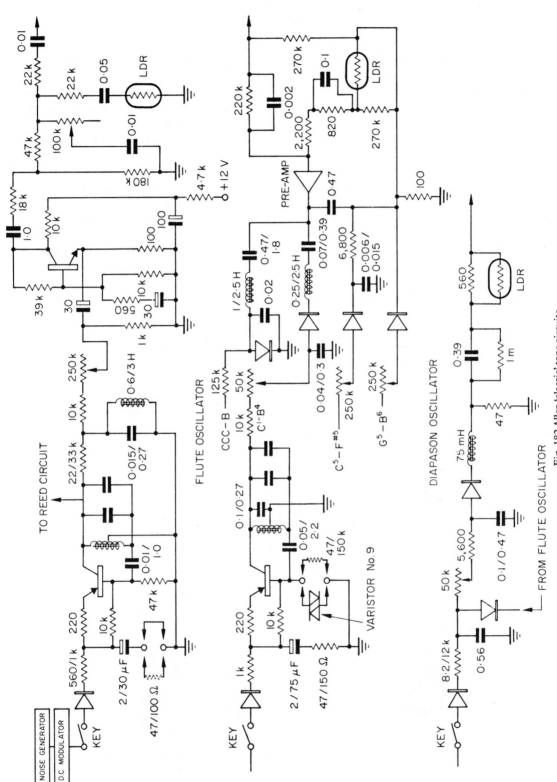

Fig. 182 Allen 'classic' tone circuits

very carefully chosen, resulting in extreme realism. It will be clear that such a complex generator system must call for several tone channels, and in fact each generator has a complete amplifying system of adequate power. Apart from the rotating loudspeakers described below, there would be 4 × 15 in., 16 × 6 in. and 2 × 3 in. non-rotating speakers for the diapason rank and 1 × 12 in., 1 × 8 in. and 2 × 3 in. units serve the reeds—except the pedal, of course. All the main amplifier gain controls are photo-cell operated, the LDRs being covered by a single shutter connected to the swell pedal. Chiff and sustain circuits are available on some models and of course there are the small entertainment organs incorporating piano and rhythm effects, also having independent generators. The interesting feature of the piano system is the so-called 'flying hammer', a simple weight-loaded flat spring mounted at the rear of the playing key. When the key is depressed, the spring jumps up and hits a contact rail; it is then

arrested by a damper bar. But if the damper is withdrawn, the weight allows the hammer spring to make a number of contacts in succession, so that reiteration is provided without any circuitry at all! Further, as the contact is made so quickly, the effect is more piano-like than if produced by some form of electronic circuit; but a point which is often overlooked is that the action of the hammers is somewhat random, greatly depending on how the key is struck; so that this alone improves the simulation of piano action.

Reverting to the loudspeaker system used with many Allen organs, this is shown in Fig. 183. As can be seen, two large and two smaller units are mounted on a large disc which is almost an airtight fit in an aperture in a box of baffle dimensions. A variable-speed motor drives the loudspeakers round and so produces a true Doppler effect; that is, both a frequency and an amplitude modulation of the organ signals. Whilst rotating transformers and other methods are used in some organs to

Fig. 183 Rotating loudspeaker assembly

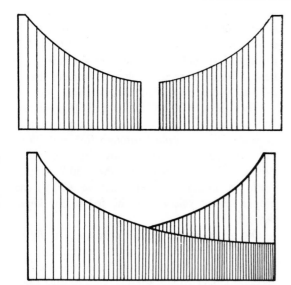

Fig. 184 Typical arrangement of organ pipes on windchest

couple the sound circuits to the speaker voice coils, Allen use silver-carbon brushes bearing on silver rings. It will be obvious that, driven at high speed, a tremulant effect is produced; at a much slower speed, a celeste results and if rotated very slowly indeed, there is a kind of spread of sound effect (only noticeable at some distance) which is meant to imitate the way in which the sound darts about between the pipes of an organ; for pipes are always arranged in one of the two ways shown in Fig. 184 to give the maximum spread of sound. The earliest Allen organs used a single loudspeaker rotating on an elliptical axis, but the gyro is more effective; where a tremulant is not called for, as on the great or pedal sections of a large organ, other static loudspeaker units would be used. It is interesting to note that on some models, as many as 16 loudspeakers are used on the diapason channel alone. The 'computer' organ is too complex to describe.

C. G. Conn Ltd

At one time, each different manufacturer had a distinctive and separate product which was readily identifiable with his name. Today, there is such a multiplicity of models that where the more 'popular' types are concerned, it is impossible to keep count. However, a few makers have resolutely set their face against the tonally-degrading practices now so freely adopted, so that mention of their name at once suggests the best methods and a proper tonal approach. The Conn Company has always insisted on the classical approach to organ-tone generation, namely the use of independent oscillators for every note. In this way, the tuning is never mathematically locked as in all divider organs, and true chorus effects are obtained as in a pipe organ. Even in the smallest Conn organs, this method of tone generation is used, and the oscillators are in fact all very similar so that circuitry for one type represents the whole range, except for percussion, delays and special keying effects which vary with the intended duty of the organ.

All organs are complex and even with the comprehensive diagrams it is impossible to show all the connections. The parts of greatest interest in Conn organs are the oscillators, transistor keying, tone forming and some of the power supplies. There are also rhythm circuits on some models, but as there are similar circuits elsewhere in the book these will not be reproduced. Since the inception of this organ in 1947, little has changed in the wave-form-producing part beyond the conversion to transistors from valves. Perhaps the most important alteration is the introduction of signal keying, which means that all the oscillators are operating all the time. This reduces the total number of oscillators required and allows the use of percussion and sustain in a simple manner, and the reader is urged to compare the various ways in which these effects are obtained in different organs.

In previous models, rotating busbars were used under the flute and other sine-wave tone sources. The mechanical complication resulting involved precision setting of the rotating units and other complications. In the more recent types, direct keying of the signal busbars by transistors acting as switches performs the same function with fixed busbars; greater compactness, reliability and less expense. The arrangement is shown in Fig. 185 and is based on the use of the appropriate stop tab for the pitch to be keyed. When a key is pressed, +45 V d.c. is applied to the junction of $R55$, $D8$ and $D9$. This latter diode has its cathode clamped by the common bus shown. If the busbar is at earth

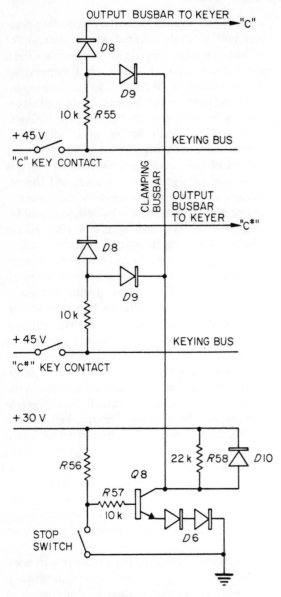

Fig. 185 Conn bus circuit

switch to either clamp the bus to earth or to some keying potential. If the stop switch is 'off', Q8 is conducting since its base is connected to +30 V through R57 and R56. With Q8 saturated, the busbar is held near zero volts and none of the 61 D8's allow current to flow on to a keyer.

When the stop is 'on', the base of Q8 is earthed and this holds it off. Now when a key switch is closed, +45 V is applied through R55 and D9 to the clamping busbar which allows its potential to rise until D10 conducts into the +30 V supply. With the busbar now clamped at +30 V, the proper keying voltage will be fed to the keyer through D8.

The actual keyers (which only apply to flutes etc.) are now modified to allow of sustained or non-sustained notes being played. Since the busbars need no longer rotate, these keyers receive their keying voltages from the diode couplers of Fig. 186 rather than directly from the keyboards. Keying voltage applied at A results in sustain, whilst voltage applied at B results in non-sustain.

The transistor Q10 is held off by a stabilized base bias of about +0.15 V; hence there is not enough forward bias for current flow. Depressing a great key sends a high positive voltage to charge sustain capacitor C18, via R68. As C18 charges, so the base of Q10 becomes more positive and is biased on, allowing the note to sound. When the key is released, C18 discharges until the keyer transistor is once again blocked. However, the rate of discharge of C18 can be regulated by passing through the diode D17 to earth, or through R69 and the diode, or through R69 and R70; each gives different lengths of decay.

Consider now the application of +30 V to point B. Passing through D12, D15, R67 and R64 to the base of Q10, this is again forward biased and allows the note to sound. R67 and C17 decide the attack rate, and when the key is released a normal or non-sustained decay; diode D16 now prevents any charging of the sustain capacitor C18. We assume the point C to be earthed so that any voltage appearing at B, D12 and D15 will simply be grounded at the lower end of R66. But if the switch connecting C to earth be opened, then keying voltage at B will charge C18 through D12, D14 and R68.

potential then the D8, D9 and R55 junction will also be at earth and no voltage will pass through D8 to a keyer. If the busbar is at +30 V, the keyer will be turned on (through D8) and a note will sound.

But for any one stop all the 61 D9 diode cathodes are tied to the busbar, which connects them to the controlling transistor Q8, which is acting as a

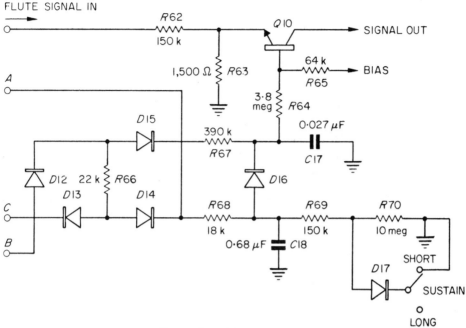

Fig. 186 Part of Conn keyer circuit

Sustain will now operate as before. The object of the two different circuits is so that one manual can be connected to point *A* and another to point *B*; thus one can have sustain on one keyboard but not on another.

It is usual on large organs to have some form of 'chiff' or similar circuit to simulate the starting tone of certain stopped pipes. The arrangement for doing this on the Conn 830 is shown in Fig. 187. Analysis of organ pipes shows that the chiff is always an odd harmonic, usually the 3rd or 5th. In this case the 3rd is used, thus for 8 ft pitch one would feed $2\frac{2}{3}$ ft into the chiff circuit. Since this effect is very transient and only persists whilst the pipe is getting under way, as it were, a discharge circuit must be used. When keying voltage is applied, a surge of current flows through *R*72, *R*74, *C*20 and *R*75. The voltage appearing across *R*75 will bias the diode on, allowing a $2\frac{2}{3}$ ft signal to pass through *R*76, *D*20 and *C*21 to the flute filter circuits. As *C*20 charges, the voltage across *R*75 drops below diode conduction level and the $2\frac{2}{3}$ ft signal is cut off; thus there is a momentary burst of this harmonic superimposed on the steady 8 ft tone.

Since this harmonic must be present to achieve the chiff, it is made use of to slightly colour the tibia voices. If a positive voltage is applied at *E*, current flows through *R*72, *R*73 and *R*78. This will bias *D*21 on, allowing the low-level harmonic tone to pass through *R*77, *D*21 and *C*22 to the flute filter input. But unlike the chiff, this tone will be heard so long as a playing key is held down (on tibia only).

In Fig. 188 we show a composite sketch of one oscillator, which delivers a sine wave and a pulse output; the arrangements of the signal busbars which are connected with playing keys when one of the latter is depressed; and the transistor keyer, which applies only to the flute or tibia circuits and incorporates delay circuits. Also shown (Fig. 190) is the power supply for the keyer, since it is a critical part of the circuit.

Note that the pulse signals are direct-keyed without any special delay such as, for example, a diode. Because the form of the wave is spikey, there are many high harmonics present; in this case, the few small extra spikes introduced by the keying transient are of little account and when passed through the respective tone networks

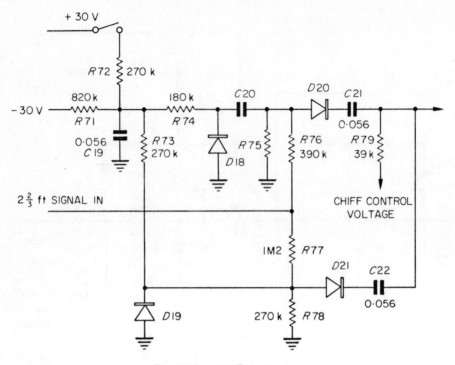

Fig. 187 Conn 'chiff' circuit

become inaudible; therefore, plain gold wires suffice for keying all the strings and reeds of the organ. Equally, since the signals are cut off by the transistor keyer until it is activated by depressing a key manually, silver contacts suffice because if these introduce a transient (which is most pleasant on flute and similar tone colours), it would not be heard because of the charging time of the delay capacitor. Indeed, were the operating voltage not so low, one could use the crudest of signal contacts here, like bronze or even brass.

The oscillators do not present any special

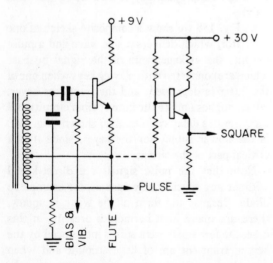

Fig. 188 Composite sketch of oscillator

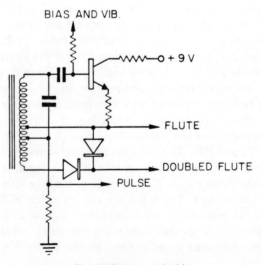

Fig. 189 Frequency doubler

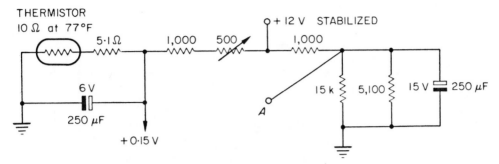

Fig. 190 Power supply for keyer

features except the frequency doublers for the top octaves (see Fig. 189). One ingenious arrangement is the detuning of certain oscillators to enhance the chorus effect, by altering the base bias; some are then tuned sharp, others slightly flat. Beats are thus engendered, which fill out the effect, especially on string and similar voices. All transistors in this generator, up to the power amplifiers, are 2N2926.

In some of the later organs, there are square wave-forming circuits as well as the other wave forms, and diapason inverting amplifiers. We accordingly show, in Figs. 191–5, some of these circuits together with some representative tone-

forming circuits. It can be seen that to obtain the requisite fidelity, more than one wave form is sometimes called for in the one filter. A number of pre-amplifiers are used, really as isolators, but most signals are combined after forming for the post-amplifiers. These circuits are from the type 830 three-manual Classic organ. Since tone-forming circuits shown for other makes of organ are not by any means the same, the reader must conclude that these differences are accounted for by the outlook of the maker and the type of input wave form to the respective filters. For even in the case of pipes, there is no agreement as to the precise geometry of a particular pipe for a

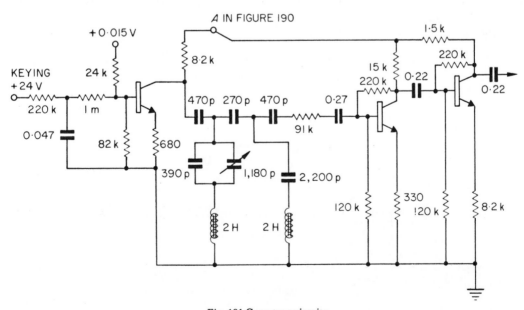

Fig. 191 Conn tone circuits

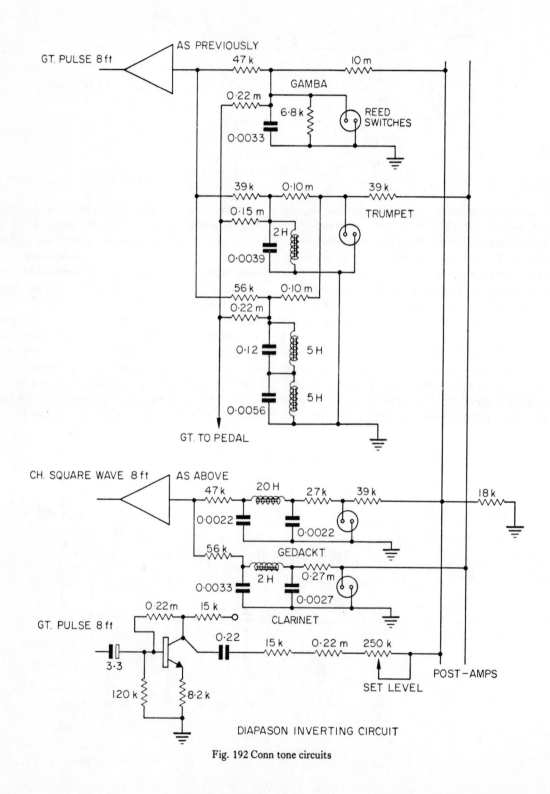

Fig. 192 Conn tone circuits

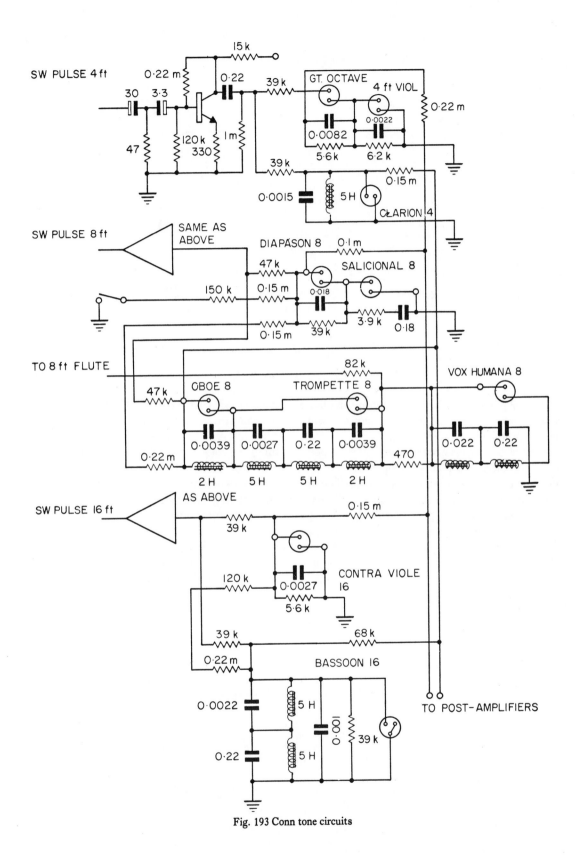

Fig. 193 Conn tone circuits

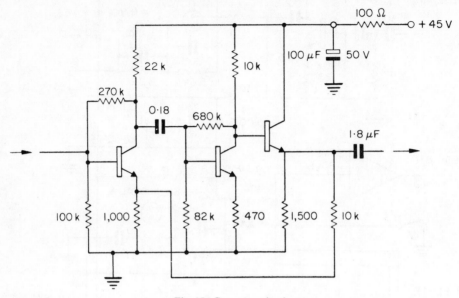

Fig. 194 Conn tone circuits

particular purpose, each maker altering the basic proportions to suit the balance, power, wind pressures and acoustics involved.

Most of the organs examined are far from portable, but there are plenty of openings for one which is easily carried about; and if this is combined with the ability to run it from a car battery, all kinds of uses must present themselves. The simple Bambi organ shown in Figs. 196–8 follows the conventional arrangement of 12 master oscillators and a chain of frequency dividers; but it is very interesting in that no tone forming as normally

understood is used; instead all the pitches are taken to what are virtually drawbars of a simple kind, and only two wave forms are available. One can mix tone colours at will from the various pitches and this endows the little organ with more versatility than would at first be apparent. Note the anti-robbing resistors at the playing keys, the light-dependent resistor as a volume control and the reactance stage for introducing the vibrato voltage; this is a refinement not nearly as much used as it should be, for it provides true frequency modulation of the oscillators.

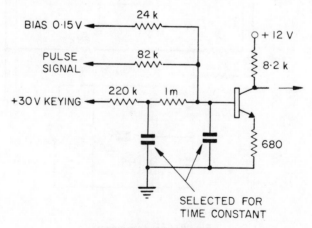

Fig. 195 Conn tone circuits

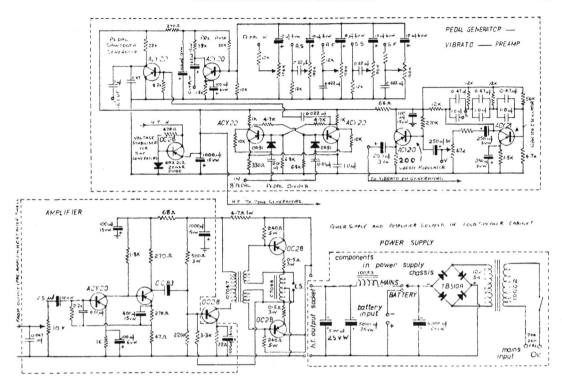

Fig. 196 The Bambi organ

The Compton organ

Rotating electrostatic generators are used here, the tone-forming circuits and the keying circuits being all in the d.c. polarizing lines. Thus there is the considerable advantage that the signal circuits are not interrupted. The method has already been outlined in Chapter 4, but certain points of design call for special comment.

One method of forming the electrodes consists of coating the discs or stators with a film of metal, about 0·002 in. thick. On a special engraving machine, a fine groove is cut corresponding to the required wave form and forms a complete circle. Either a circle or similar wave form is then cut adjacent to the first, resulting in an annular ring of metal of undulating width. The whole surface of the disc is thus divided into a number of rings, some of which are the wave forms proper and others the earthed margins separating them. The number of complete waves in the various rings

determines the pitch of the notes. Each ring is connected to the appropriate polarizing circuits by means of pins passing through the stator plate, to which leads may be soldered.

In some recent models, the tracks are formed by an etched circuit technique instead of mechanical engraving, which leads to better adhesion of the metal and much finer detail; it is also far cheaper, for the discs are printed by photographic means from a master negative and this means there cannot be any variation between one copy and another.

The actual form of the engraved waves varies; in some cases they may be pure sine waves; other rings have a completely integrated series of even harmonics, still others the same but odd harmonics; some may have a series of, perhaps, third and fifth harmonics; whilst still others can have fully preformed waves, e.g. an open diapason tone. See Fig. 199.

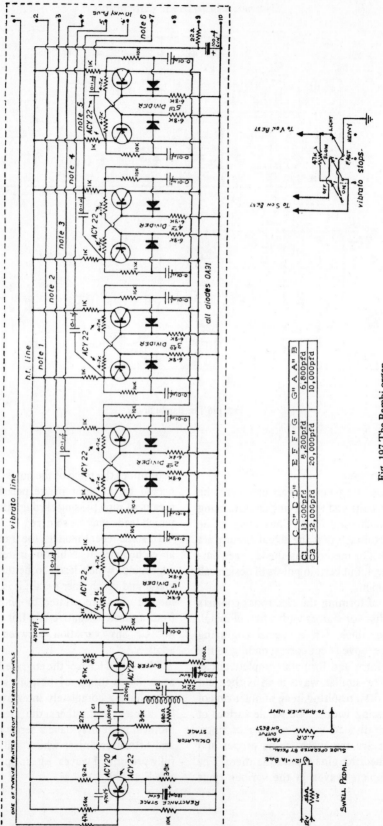

Fig. 197 The Bambi organ

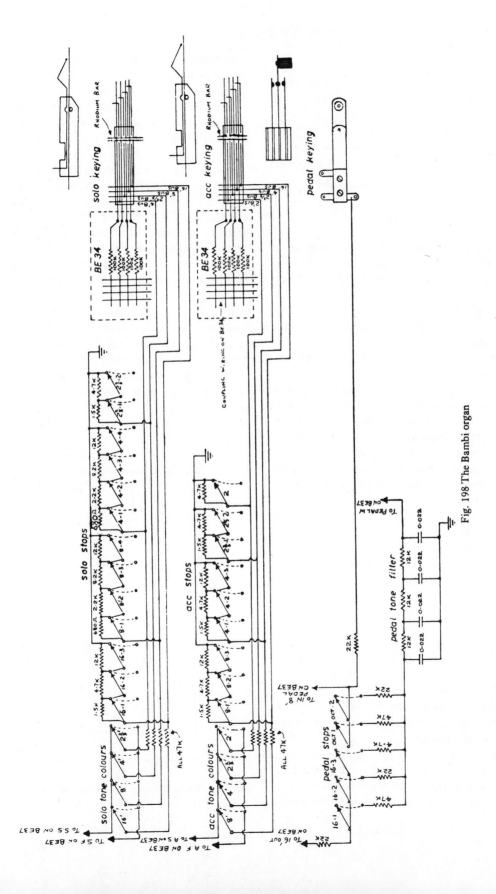

Fig. 198 The Bambi organ

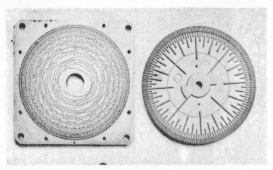

Fig. 199 Disc

The rotating member takes the form of a number of conductive radial lines arranged like a spider's web, except that the number of lines relates to the number of waves on the stator. The degree of pickup accuracy is determined by the width of the lines, and any spurious harmonic development which may have crept into the engraving process can be cancelled out by increasing the width of the scanning lines.

The rotor may be a metallized Bakelite moulding, or a metal die-casting of such a mass that it will be quite free from any tendency to flex. This is connected to an amplifier by means of a brush or, in some cases, by a capacitative pickup.

In the case of a single ring electrode, it will be seen that the capacitance between it and the rotor will be greatest when the radial lines of the rotor coincide with the widest parts of the curve, and least when they coincide with the narrow parts. The capacitance therefore varies in a continuous and cyclic manner as the rotor rotates.

If there is no polarizing potential applied to the rings, no a.c. potential can exist even if the rotor is moving; but if a potential is applied, an a.c. potential will be developed corresponding to the variations in capacitance which, of course, means that this potential will be an exact replica of the engraved wave form, assuming constant separation of the electrode assembly.

Fig. 200 (A) shows one electrode A with a polarizing circuit connected to it; this is the stator. The rotor is connected to an amplifier. The capacitor C by-passes any a.c. component which may try to return through the d.c. polarizing network, and together with R forms a time-delay circuit so that the build-up of the charge on A may

be controlled; it also serves to reduce objectionable transients which would appear if the polarizing voltage were suddenly applied.

When the key G is open, the resistor E keeps the electrode at earth potential. Capacitor F also modifies the time constant of the circuit, especially the delay; there may also be additional external circuits to produce special time/amplitude effects.

When key G is closed, current from the d.c. supply H charges F, C and A. D may, for instance, be 1 MΩ and C 0.001 μF; F may be 0.01 μF but for very long time-delays it may be 1 μF, depending on the leakage rate of E. Fig. 200(B) shows the equivalent electrical circuit where Z is a zero-impedance generator, Y is the stator-to-rotor capacitance of one speaking note and X is the shunt capacitance of all the other chargeable electrodes together with that of all the earthed areas separating the various rings. The input impedance of the amplifier is indicated by R.

There is an important point in design here; the wave form of the earthed rings is the inverse of the wave form proper. From grid to earth, therefore, the capacitance is constant at all times irrespective

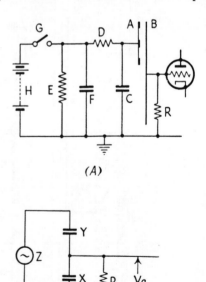

(A)

(B)

Fig. 200 Basic circuits. $A =$ Compton basic circuit; $B =$ Equivalent electrical basic circuit

of whether a signal ring is in use or not. Thus each earthed ring acts as a differential capacitance to the ring to which it is adjacent. If an electrode were, for instance, standing proud with no earthed rings, the grid-to-earth capacitance would vary as the sum of all the other wave-form capacitances, resulting in modulation. For instance, if a high note were sounding (small capacitance), then the comparatively large changes in shunt load due to a bass note (large capacitance) would modulate the high note.

There are other methods of connecting such generators, but in general they result in loss of signal strength, frequency discrimination and noise.

In playing an organ of this circuit type by normal methods, many frequencies will coincide when played from different notes on the same or other keyboards simultaneously. For instance, a second harmonic coincides exactly with the fundamental pitch of one octave higher. It is therefore necessary to provide an electrical network which will allow the same ring electrode to be polarized from many different contacts without interaction with each other, and at the same time to ensure that when two or more are operated together, the tonal increments will follow a correct law.

Fig. 201 shows the circuit for this purpose, the electrode arrangement being as just described. The contacts at each point of the keyboard at which the particular note is required are shown at *G* and each can make contact with a busbar *M*. According to the setting of the stops, these busbars may be at any potential from zero to about 400 V. At each contact point there are two resistors, *K* and *L*, usually of equal value and of the order of two megohms.

Under these conditions, if two busbars are at equal voltage so that depression of either contact would sound the note at the same strength, the

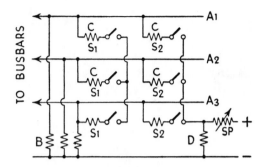

Fig. 202 Basic stop circuit

note should increase by three decibels when both contacts are closed together. If four contacts are simultaneously closed, the voltage will roughly be double, resulting in an increase of six decibels. This ability to compensate for keying additional notes in a common generator system is extremely valuable and overcomes one of the principal disadvantages of such systems.

The tone colours are formed by adjustment of the relative potentials on the various rings. The busbars are common to all keys on any manual and each is associated with one tonal quality. Suppose that only one bar is raised in potential; then the keys will only apply voltages to rings appropriate to that harmonic, all the remainder of the bars being at zero potential. Each stop is arranged to raise any combination of bars to any potential, and it is by this means that the tonal qualities of the instrument are set up.

Fig. 202 shows the stop circuit in essence. Each busbar is connected to the main h.t. supply through resistors *B* via the leads *A*1, *A*2, *A*3 etc. Each stop controls as many contacts as are necessary for the harmonic development of that particular tone colour. The figure shows two stops, *S*1 and *S*2. Between each contact and the h.t. source are resistors *C*; the values of these resistors are so chosen that the busbars are raised to the correct relative values when the stop is operated.

Volume control is effected by means of the variable resistor *SP*, operated by the swell pedal; this is part of a potential divider, *SP/D*, connected across the main h.t. supply line. There is a tremulant which produces frequency modulation by oscillating the stators which are mounted in ball bearings for this purpose.

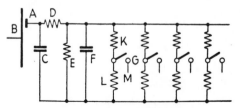

Fig. 201 Polarizing equalizing circuit

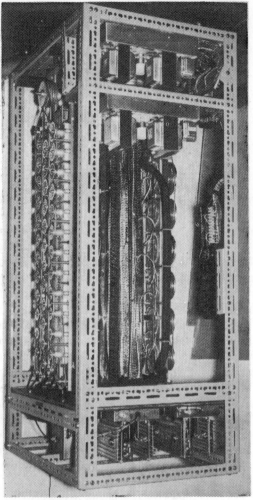

Fig. 203 Electrone showing motor control panel

Although the harmonic derivation system is similar to that of the Hammond, and additive synthesis is used, stops of conventional type are used and the tone colours are fully pre-formed; they can be added to any desired extent. This is because the circuits are high impedance, therefore robbing does not readily take place. Many sizes of Compton organ are made, from single to four manuals; the generator shown is for a three-manual model. For the reasons above, we do not give any specification; most organ tones are available on request.

Experiments carried out over some years resulted in a simpler organ using miniature discs engraved with sine waves only. In this way, the same kind of harmonic derivation can be used as in Hammond organs, and quite simple multiple contacts behind the keys and directly actuated by them will suffice. This has a further advantage in that the regulating or voicing resistors for each

Fig. 203 shows the complete system, and the generators in their die-cast screening cases can be seen behind the pulleys, which are of the required diameters to produce semitone intervals; they are driven by means of an endless flat belt from the motor at the foot of the cabinet. The comparatively large number of complete wave forms required (twenty to thirty) are accommodated by using a stator on each side of each rotor.

The boxes in Fig. 204 contain the playing key relays, stop switches and polarizing resistors. There are a great number of these, but as there is little current flowing in electrostatic generators they can be of extremely small size.

Fig. 204 Electrone showing keying relays

Fig. 205 Compton organ with sine-wave generators

note are hung from the busbar system by springs so that one can be unhooked and another substituted if required. All the same, some quite comprehensive organs have been built up using only one of these generators, with their ten available harmonics (Fig. 205).

With such a small generator, everything is contained in the console except for the loudspeakers, whereas all the larger organs have magnetic relays which are too bulky to allow of this; but, since the keying is all d.c., the generator cabinets can be remote.

Compton organs have always been made with consoles of the highest grade; indicating stop keys or drawstops, pistons etc. Most have double-touch cancelling, and recently a rotating loudspeaker

system very similar to that of Allen has been used with larger organs; the loudspeakers on this might be four 8-in. units and one 18-in. unit. All organs have split-channel amplifiers, that is, treble and bass are independently amplified and have separate speakers. Compton electrostatic organs are made by J. J. Makin Ltd, Rochdale, Lancs.

There have been other variants of electrostatic frequency conversion, and we show briefly one ingenious application which comes from Spain—the Harmoniphon. Although basically similar to the Compton generators, some stators have additional rings with pitches one-fifth above the fundamentals, so that by mixing these with other rings, synthetic frequencies are formed. In this way, seven discs can be made to do the work of twelve with no

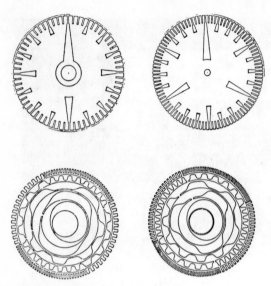

Fig. 206 Harmoniphon generators

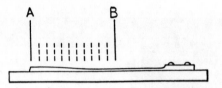

Fig. 207 Range of pickup screws

loss of fidelity but a great saving in cost; the unit is also much quieter. Fig. 206 shows typical generator discs.

Wurlitzer organs

Like most of the 'moderns', this company designs its organs around one single master oscillator running at 1 MHz and a series of integrated circuits divided by two bistables, though the term flip-flop seems a common way to describe them. But although some aspects of these organs will be shown, it must be appreciated that they become more and more complex and as the effects circuits multiply, so it is harder and harder to reproduce the circuits in the space available. Therefore, since many of the attack, decay and rhythm circuits are very similar to others described in these pages, we only give certain design features which contribute something special to the sound or produce a new effect.

But first of all some attention will be given to the original electronics of Hoschke (1934) which Wurlitzer purchased from the Everett Piano Co. and which made their name in the electronic organ field. The reason for this is that simulation of the church instrument, including attack and decay,

follow automatically from the use of free reeds. What Hoschke did was to mount free reeds, as in an American organ or harmonium, in such a way that if a pickup screw was brought near to the upper vibrating surface of the reed, and the reed base polarized, a variable capacitor was set up and a signal at the frequency of the reed became available. Now this is the interesting thing: whereas the sound from the reed alone tends to be discordant and harsh, the signal from the pickup (if large enough) can be almost sinusoidal. Therefore, here we have a ready-made generator for a wide range of organ tonalities—adjustable by altering either the area of the pickup screws or their location and number (see Fig. 207). The reeds must be mounted in a sound-proof box and whilst it might be possible so to arrange them that they could be actuated directly by a playing key, Wurlitzer used small electro-magnets as in Fig. 208. Since each reed must vibrate at only the amplitude required for the pitch, the amount of wind passing is regulated by little swivelling wood mutes controlling the flow as in Fig. 209. Later developments in reed mounting resulted in assemblies like that of

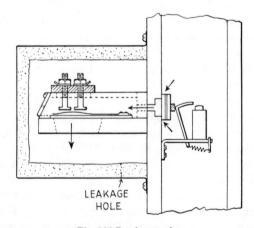

Fig. 208 Reed mounting

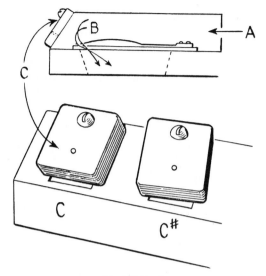

Fig. 209 Reed mutes

to build an electronic organ using reeds which is a constant source of pleasure to those enjoying church or concert organ sound; for, of course, the attack is slow and the sound quite unsuitable for rhythmic music, and some tone colours are unobtainable from reeds.

Reverting now to the latest Wurlitzers, some of which have small synthesizers incorporated, we can take the model 4373 as typical. The most interesting feature is the multiple phase-shift tremolo and tibia circuits. This is an attempt to make the comparatively simple sound as 'sobbing' as possible—characteristic of the theatre organ at which, of course, Wurlitzer were masters of voicing. The signals from the respective dividers are first equalized at the busbars, as in Fig. 211, and then conducted to the tibia filters of Fig. 212. As the smoothed wave forms enter the multiple phase-shift circuits, a vibrato generator of 6 Hz energizes the lamps which actuate the respective photo-cells; each circuit then goes in and out of phase in a random manner, making the remaining harmonics in the tibia tone wander about and so create a richness very difficult to describe. It is a very complicated circuit for a small effect, but Wurlitzer engineering is always complex.

The master oscillator itself is interesting, see Fig. 214. The multiple large-number dividers supply all the wave forms but it will have been

Fig. 210, where one set of pickups above the reeds gave the tuned frequency, whilst another at the ends of the tongues gave twice the frequency—and a somewhat different harmonic content. Remember, too, that reeds stay in tune for years and are still quite easy to obtain from music-house suppliers or Jaquot of Birmingham. A very small fan will supply the necessary wind; one often encounters these on the little commercial reed organs so freely available. It is possible, with a little care,

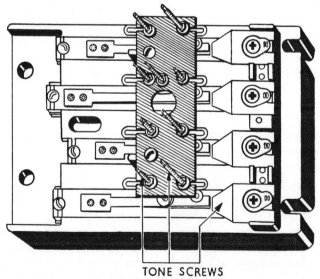

TONE SCREWS
Fig. 210 Wurlitzer type 44 pickups

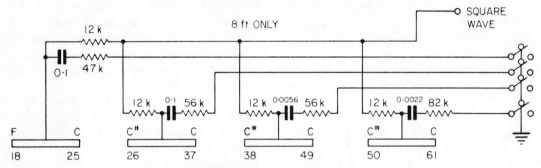

Fig. 211 Part of busbar equalizing network

noticed in Fig. 212 that there are differentiating networks for each octave or less, to clean up the wave forms from the keyers. These latter are very simple circuits as in Fig. 215. Certainly if the diodes have a high enough back resistance, this is much cheaper than using transistor keying. The rhythm circuits in this organ are highly sophisticated, using digital methods with a clock input. It is questionable whether the results are any better than from a simpler circuit as that of Fig. 216. Of course, there are set-up rhythmic tempi on the 'toy counter', as it is called; but since the ICs for the unit are not obtainable on the market, there is little point in describing it in detail. However, we show the simpler rhythm circuit in Fig. 216 and for valve enthusiasts, in Fig. 217.

The Hammond organ

Without doubt the most reliable and hard-working of all electronic instruments, this electro-mechanical organ updates the system invented by Thaddeus Cahill in 1897 (British patents 8,725; 1,903; 3,666A, B, C). Today the reliability can be attained by transistor circuitry and the Hammond company has had to introduce many auxiliary circuits using semiconductors, and even valves in some instances, to fully compete with contemporary competitors using purely electronic methods. Mechanical parts cannot be made and processed in a single operation in the way the integrated circuits can be, therefore the overall labour costs are high and it seems possible that the rotating generators might be superseded in time.

The most interesting part of the generator is the wheel drive. In most organs there are 91 wheels

and possibly one or two blank wheels for mechanical balance. The number of teeth varies from 2, 4, 8, 16, 32, 64, 128 to 192; thus the different spindle speeds and gears are reduced to a minimum. But since the wheels are driven through gears, these cannot be a tight fit so far as meshing goes; there must be play between adjacent teeth. If this is so, then backlash could arise. If one considers that the tone wheels have teeth which approach permanent magnets many times during one revolution, then the action of the magnet will be to try and arrest the movement of the tone wheel every time a high part of the wheel comes under the magnet pole; it will act as a brake. This force is then reflected back on to the gear teeth and so a ripple or vibration can arise which, in an extreme case, could modulate the even turning motion of the tone wheel. To prevent this, and at the same time to filter out any inequality in the drive, the tone wheels are only driven by end friction from spiral springs so arranged that they act as filters. Also, they perform the valuable function of slipping should anything (a particle of hard dust, for instance) fall between the tone wheel and its magnet; the gap here is only 0·005 in. Therefore, in Fig. 218, the brass gear is keyed to the main drive shaft; the Bakelite gear floats on the tone-wheel spindle, and the two tone wheels also float against end shoulders of the shaft, the whole drive being transmitted along the two spiral springs shown. It might be noted that in this figure a double tone wheel is shown on one side; this is now obsolete but other details remain the same. All the tone-wheel spindles run in bronze plain bearings; any other form of bearing produces a noise.

The wave form from these wheels is not quite

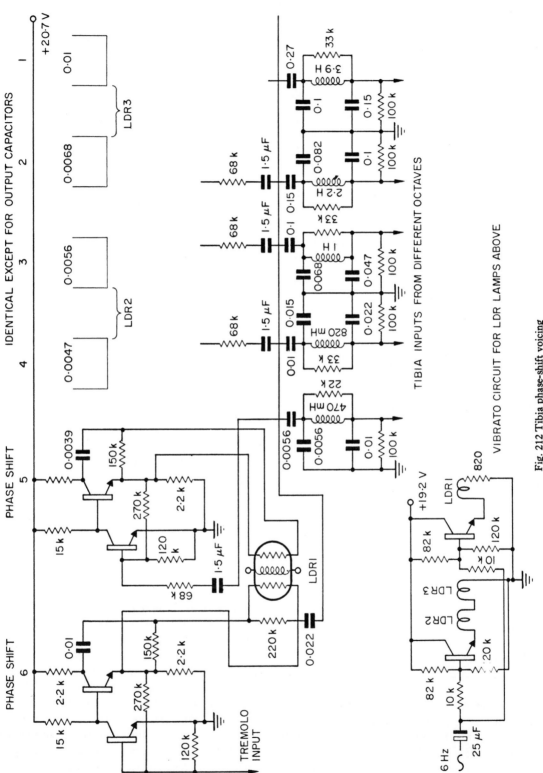

Fig. 212 Tibia phase-shift voicing

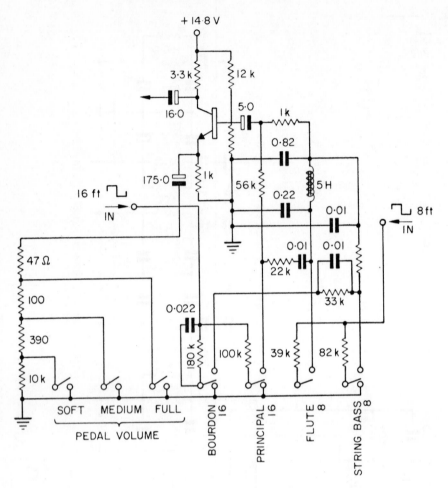

Fig. 213 Wurlitzer pedal tone forming

sinusoidal, therefore filters are fitted to most wheels to ensure this. The arrangements for mixing and keying the signals has been described in Chapter 4, but this is only true of the basic organs and at the present time the Hammond company has other models on the market. However, all organs under £2000 in this country, and with drawbars, use the principles above. Stop keys, if fitted, usually apply to external percussion circuits only.

The other feature of real interest is the line-vibrato device (Fig. 219). This is a phase-shift circuit of an unusual kind and in which an organ signal is made to traverse a transmission line of many sections, each introducing a short delay; the periods so provided can be modified by de-tuning

parts of the line at a rate determined by a multi-section variable capacitor driven by a motor. This effectively changes the frequency of the line sections, and since an instantaneous change in phase in equal to an instantaneous change in frequency, the effect of the line is to raise and lower the frequency in a complex manner. Parts only of the line can be scanned, so that heavy or light vibratos are available at will. Most models have this device, and it is one of the features of a somewhat different Hammond organ which we will now look at.

The G-100 is the largest organ built by this company. Normally it is a two-manual with antiphonal section (playable from swell), and has an extended generator system, all electro-magnetic. There are 33 stops on the swell, 21 on the great and 11 on the

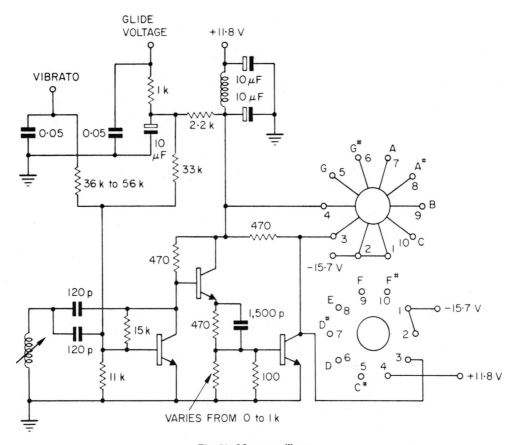

Fig. 214 Master oscillator

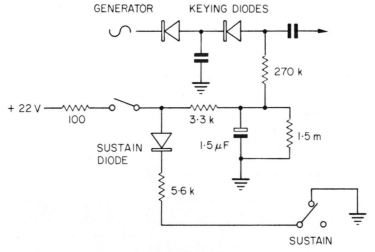

Fig. 215 Keyer circuit

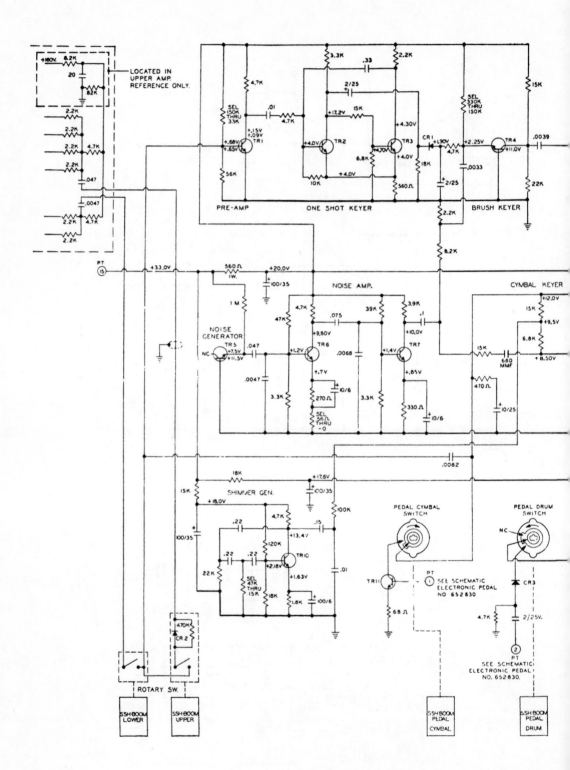

Fig. 216 A transi

SCHEMATIC-SSH BOOM MODEL 4500

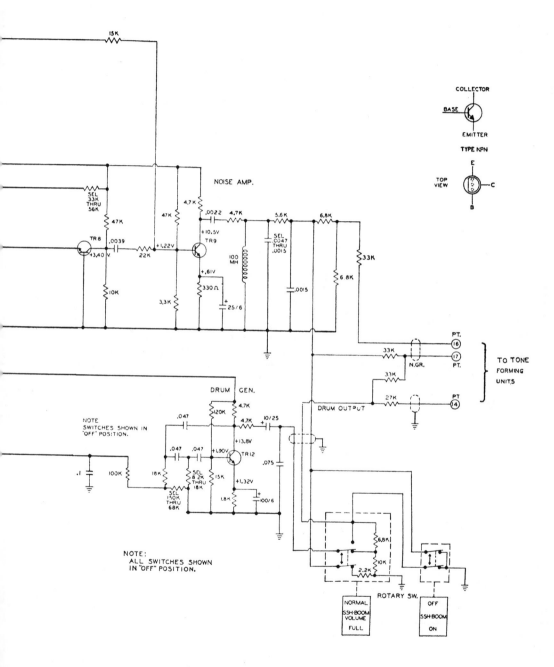

sion of side man

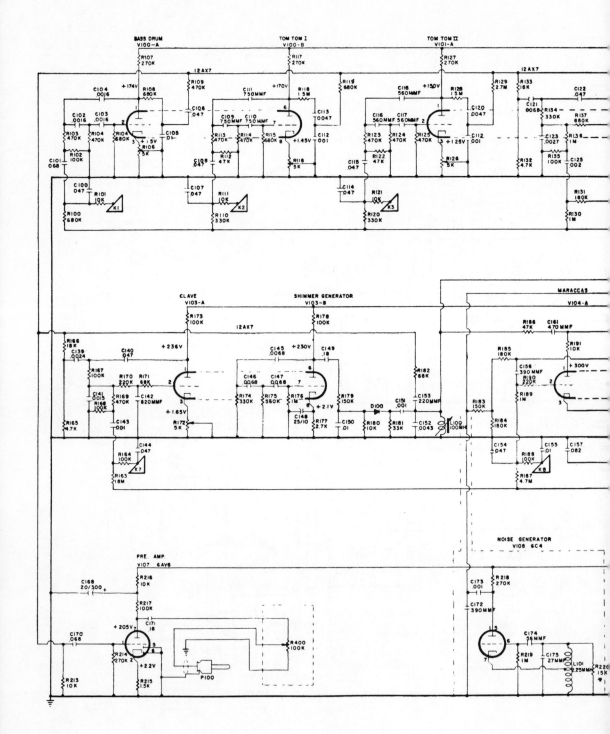

Fig. 217 A

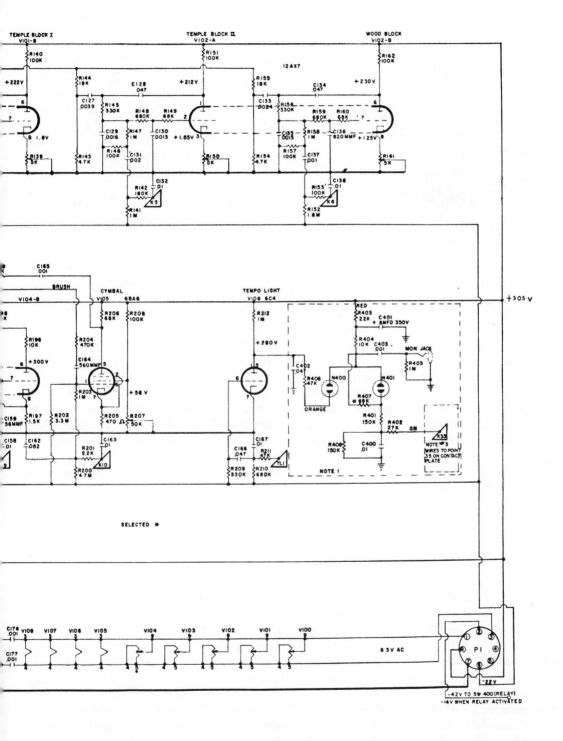

man

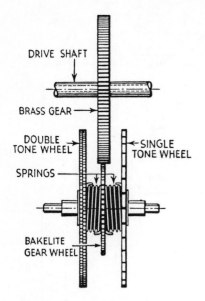

DRIVE SHAFT

BRASS GEAR →

DOUBLE
TONE WHEEL →   ←SINGLE
                               TONE WHEEL

SPRINGS →

BAKELITE
GEAR WHEEL

Fig. 218 Hammond chorus wheel drive

pedal, plus a full complement of couplers. For the first time it has been possible to add stops in the conventional manner on a magnetic-generator organ; indeed, there is no visible sign that this is a Hammond system instrument. A prodigious number of choral and celeste effects are used, calling for a large number of amplifiers; readers may be surprised to learn that many of these are valve circuits, the heater transformer for this alone delivering 20 A. There are very good reasons for not trying transistors in these effects circuits.

The number of harmonics introduced by the key contacts make it necessary to key magnetically and this, coupled with the extreme complexity of the circuitry, makes the console rather large—but certainly not out of keeping with the potential of the organ. It would require a book in itself to adequately describe the whole circuit development of the G-100, therefore one or two interesting sections only are reproduced here. Firstly, the derivation of the tone colours. We show the swell organ, and it will be noted that the original principle is retained, namely synthesis by addition of sine waves. Therefore the values shown would apply to any sine-wave organ and may be useful to the experimenter with such devices. Of course, one must understand that the actual synthesis may be very much modified in the course of subsequent

treatment by amplifiers and especially loud-speakers; but, in general, the networks shown do synthesize very well and can of course be added together; see Fig. 220.

One of the outstanding effects is the celeste chorus, obtainable in varying degrees. The phase differences which make such an effect possible would normally be produced by other ranks of oscillators or pipes slightly detuned flat or sharp to form beats. This device does not really do the same thing but it has the same effect and the ear is certainly not going to stop to analyse the mechanism involved.

In this organ we see a revision of the standard line-vibrato circuit, reproduced in Fig. 219. In this illustration the values of the attenuation obtained are shown for the first time.

The G-100 is only made to order and so few are to be seen; it bristles with interesting circuits, but regrettably it is not possible to find space for further description.

The Hammond Piper Autochord

This small instrument supplants the 'chord' organ and is very similar in size and appearance. The distinguishing features are the split keyboard, the automatic bass and the rhythm unit which can control tone functions as well. Since the smaller organs, and especially those having only one manual and no pedals, cannot simulate or be played as an organ, they have been turned into entertainment machines dependent more on rhythm than on steady tone.

The Piper has 12 master oscillators feeding MOSFET dividers in a staircase fashion (see page 48). The signals from these, which are integrated circuit blocks, pass via transistor keyers to the tone and similar treatment circuits. Many features are similar to those found in other instruments, therefore we show only the circuits of the 'Dynamute', which is a form of wah-wah device operating automatically and without inductors. It produces the effect of a variable mute on a trombone, but each key must be released before the next one is depressed to obtain the proper effect. Also, because such effects are now common on electronic organs, we show the tone filters for the percussion voices, rarely disclosed. Note that all the signals for

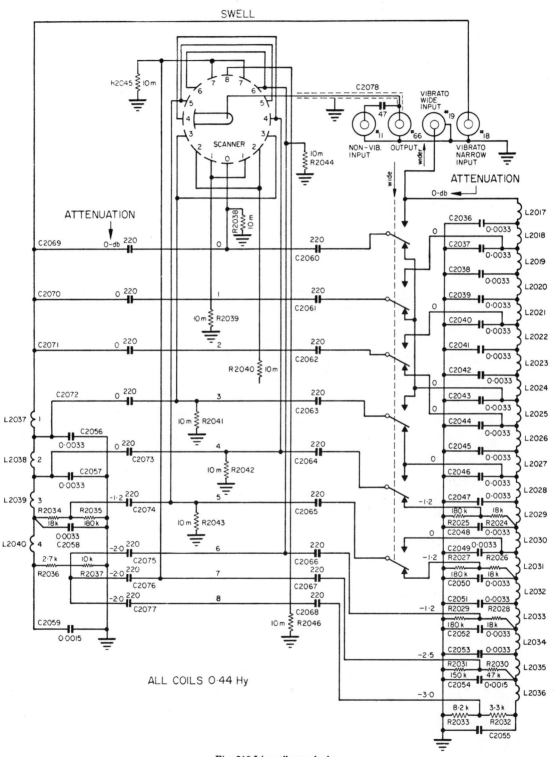

Fig. 219 Line-vibrato device

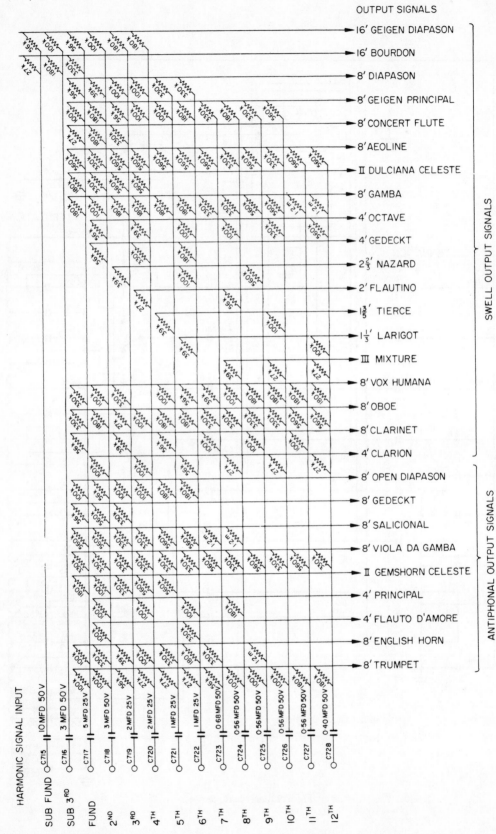

Fig. 220 Scheme of network synthesis

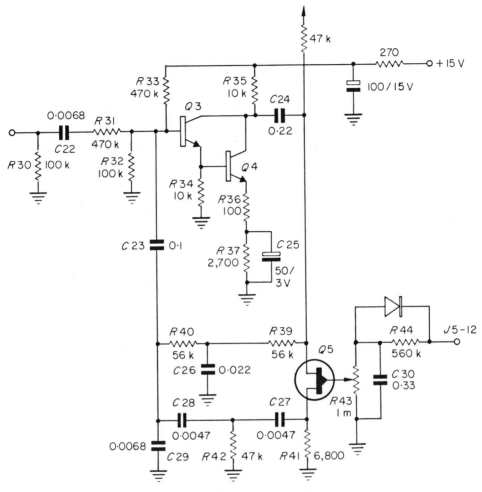

Fig. 221 Piper Dynamute circuit

these come through the percussion keyers from the dividers direct; they then proceed to the gating devices which produce the actual percussive effect.

Fig. 221 shows the Dynamute circuit. The input comes from the generator boards via the key contacts and is developed across R30, C22, R31, R32, and applied to the base of Q3, which is biased from the +15 V supply through R33. R36 and R37 form a voltage divider for the emitter of Q4, the output of which is coupled through C24 to the drain of Q5, a P-channel FET, since Q5 normally conducts. When Q5 is biased off, the signal at the drain is connected to a low-pass filter net, R39, C26, R30 and C29. The output of this filter is coupled

through C23 to the base of Q3 as negative feedback.

Now R43 and R44 form a series voltage divider. Normally there is zero volts on the gate of Q5 until a key is depressed. Under this condition Q5 conducts and signals reaching the drain of Q5 are routed through a high-pass filter, C27, R42 and C28.

When the Dynamute stop key is depressed and a solo key operated, +25 V is connected to J5–12. C30 then charges to the voltage at the junction of R43 and R44, and the gate of Q5 rises to the voltage set by the slider of R43 (about 5 V); at the same time, D1 is reversed biased so that no current

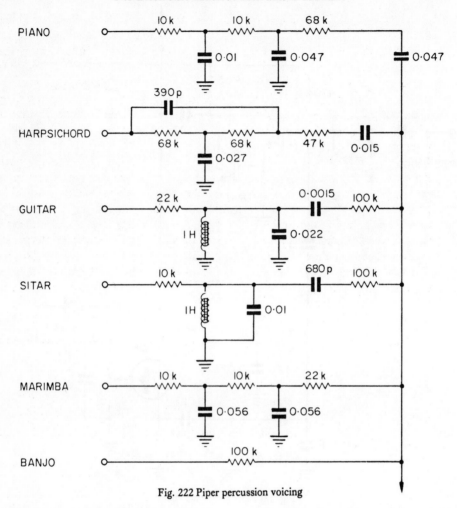

Fig. 222 Piper percussion voicing

flows through it, Q5 being biased off by the voltage from R43, so that signals reaching the drain do not pass to the source but are sent through R39, C26, R40. The action of this low-pass filter alters the negative feedback applied to the base of Q3, thereby changing the frequency response of the circuit.

When all solo keys are released, C30 discharges to ground and the circuit is ready for another key to be depressed.

Figs. 222 and 223 illustrate the formant circuits for the percussion effects of the Piper; we also show a transistor keyer at the input. The filtering resulting from these circuits is apparently

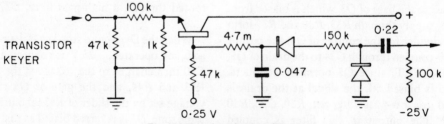

Fig. 223 Transistor keyer at input

sufficient to give a simulation of the sounds shown in the figure.

Other features of this instrument include an automatic bass gating system to pick out the lowest note of any chord played on the accompaniment; an effects device on which seven different rhythmic sequences can be set up; and a slightly delayed vibrato circuit. The bass system above feeds a frequency divider which gives a note an octave lower than that played manually, so simulating an organ-pedal bass.

The Hammond Concorde

This organ represents a complete departure from the tone-wheel concept for a full-size instrument. In common with others already mentioned, it is a 'state of the art' design employing the modern principle of a single master oscillator with sub-

sequent frequency division. The over-riding consideration has been to make both the sound and the control system identical with the tone-wheel instruments, and in this they have succeeded admirably. At the same time, improved keying, superior physical layout for better servicing and the incorporation of a complex rhythm system make the organ lean heavily on electronics rather than mechanics.

The master oscillator employs a crystal as in Fig. 224. It is unlikely that any circuit not using a crystal could hold the frequency to 3·99872 MHz. The output is sinusoidal but for the purpose of division must be made square or at least have a sharp leading edge. This is accomplished in an IC squarer which also divides the prime frequency by 2. The output, now at 1·99936 MHz, is fed into large-number dividers, the ratios ranging from 478

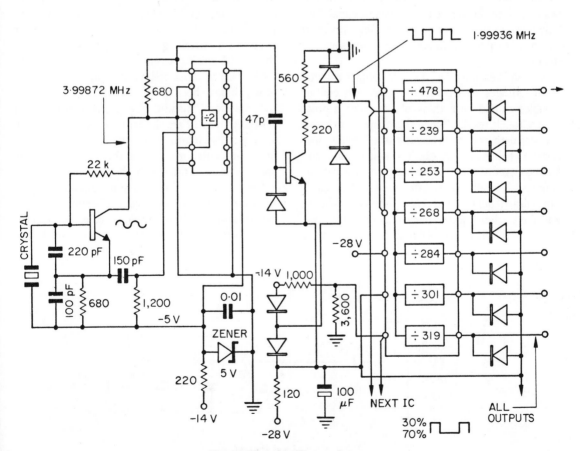

Fig. 224 Master oscillator and squarer

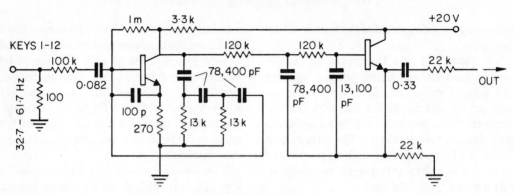

Fig. 225 Sine-wave filters (i)

to 301. Stretched square waves emerge having a mark/space ratio of 30 : 70 and after further extensive division are subsequently turned into sine waves by an elaborate filtering system as in Figs. 225 and 226. This wave form is necessary, of course, because of the drawbar additive mixing system. Note the very exact values of capacitors, only a few of which can be shown. Sine waves are also necessary for the musical percussions such as piano.

Keying is entirely d.c., a single contact controls all the diodes and transistor gates, so contact troubles should be a thing of the past; a much lighter touch results. Since there are no drawbar transformers, mixing is accomplished by a tapped resistor chain as in Fig. 227. The single leaf-spring fixed contact of the drawbar strips is brought into contact with the respective detented busbars as the tab is drawn out by hand. The subdivision of levels and the pitches selected remain as for tone-wheel organs, similarly the pre-set tone-colour keys are at the left hand end of each keyboard; again, only one at a time can be used. This does seem rather a limitation on what otherwise appears to be a versatile design.

The rhythm section is both automatic and manually controlled; in common with many current circuits, the logic system is based on processing clock pulses, but this is only to get over mechanical switching and its high assembly cost, the actual voicing circuits being very similar to those used in other comparable organs, examples of which have been given.

Percussions, sustain, vibrato, reverberation and Leslie equipment are similar for most instruments, although the circuitry varies widely; but it is what one hears which matters. In this organ the Leslie speaker itself rotates and this makes the effect better but is rather slow to start. Surprisingly for such a comprehensive organ, this and two other speakers are built into the console, the applied signal being split by a cross-over network. All are

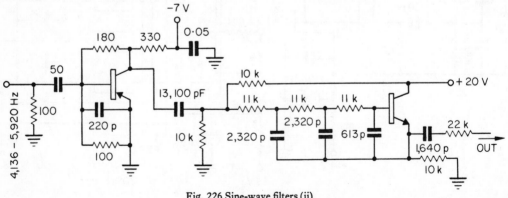

Fig. 226 Sine-wave filters (ii)

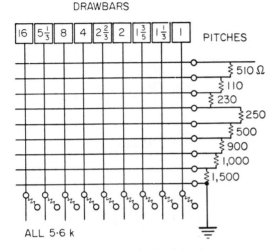

Fig. 227 Drawbar level circuit

controlled by a single expression pedal using photo-cells.

Heinz Ahlborn organ

This modern instrument is analogous with the pipe organ in its system of tone generation. Most legitimate organ voices such as diapason, flute, principal etc. are generated by quite independent ranks of oscillators, using one oscillator for each note. These are directly keyed in the supply lines, but this is subject to carefully scaled time constants over the compass. Because of the multiplicity of ranks and the varying times of attack, the sound is exceptionally rich and solid; the basic organ voices just mentioned require these facilities. The reeds, however, do not need the same energy for the fundamentals, so they are produced by divider circuits keyed through special shaping transistor circuits. Not only are the different ranks keyed with their own time constants, but each rank has its own power amplifiers and loudspeakers. Thus intermodulation is impossible and the units can be placed in the best acoustic situations. The series of Ahlborn organs are quite baroque-like in voicing with incisive upper work and more brilliance than is found in any other organ. It might be added that the actual wave forms required for the foundation tones are directly generated in the oscillators so that tone circuits as usually understood are not used. Thus there is

no distortion, a common fault in the upper registers. Fig. 228 shows an independent oscillator rank and Fig. 229 part of a divider rank with its drive oscillators. These ranks lie above each other in the console and are readily withdrawn, as shown, for attention.

The Yamaha E.5

This is the first time we have been able to examine a modern Japanese organ. Since the American, British and German factories have had many years' experience not only of design but of customer reaction, it is perhaps not surprising that the overall concept of this instrument is tonally conventional. There are, however, one or two interesting circuit features. Firstly it is a divider organ with 12 top frequency master oscillators of quite normal design; in fact, if this arrangement is to be used, one cannot wander very far from convention. But one might note the transistors acting as reactance elements in the vibrato circuits; C_1 is polystyrene, C_2 is Mylar; both are ± 5 per cent. Appended is the information for the tuning range; inductances are in millihenries, top note is $B = 7902$ Hz (see Fig. 230). There are departures from convention in the matter of control, for each stop key is really a four-position switch giving differing degrees of loudness for each voice; this is an admirable idea, if rather difficult to operate. In common with all modern instruments of any pretensions, there is a rhythm section and a good idea here is the button percussion arrangement where four boldly arranged press keys can be hit hard and quickly to bring on equally quick effects like cymbal, block, claves etc. Usually rhythm controls are very small and very hard to operate in a hurry. The sound source for all the percussions is a selected noisy transistor followed as usual by an amplifier and some filtering to get rid of the lower frequencies prior to feeding into circuits such as Fig. 231, in which we show two of the effects, cymbal and triangle.

A new device for organs is the continuous or gliding-tone generator known on this instrument as portamento. Though it is clearly for novelty effects (as witness the squawk, whistle, astro etc. controls), some delightful solo effects are possible. There are four multivibrators, the tuning of which

Fig. 228 Heinz Ahlborn organ—principal rank

Fig. 229 Reed rank

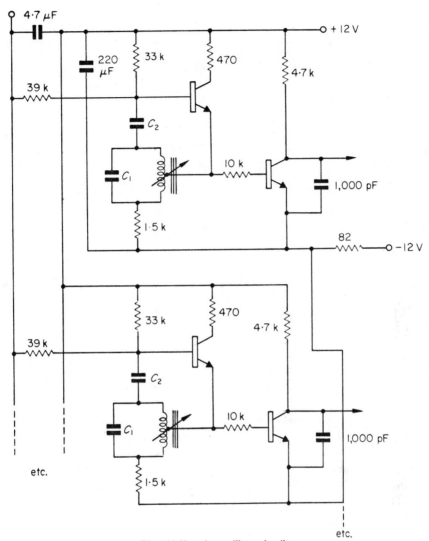

Fig. 230 Yamaha oscillator details

is altered by one part of a variable resistor taking the form of a long strip of material enclosed in an insulating cover and lying above the top keyboard like a flat piece of wood. By touching this at any point, a note is produced depending on the distance from one end, and by stroking the strip the note can be made to glide over nearly three octaves. The circuitry for this seems very complex, as it could have been done equally well with a voltage-controlled oscillator (as in Chapter 7, page 106). However, it would seem its real purpose is to make 'space' sounds.

Note	L	C_1	C_2
C	71 mH	8200 p	0·011 μF
C♯	71 mH	8200 p	0·011 μF
D	71 mH	6200 p	0·1 μF
D♯	71 mH	6200 p	0·1 μF
E	71 mH	5100 p	0·009 μF
F	71 mH	5100 p	0·009 μF
F♯	74 mH	5600 p	0·0082 μF
G	74 mH	5600 p	0·0082 μF
G♯	74 mH	4700 p	0·0068 μF
A	74 mH	4700 p	0·0068 μF
A♯	74 mH	3600 p	0·0062 μF
B	74 mH	3600 p	0·0062 μF

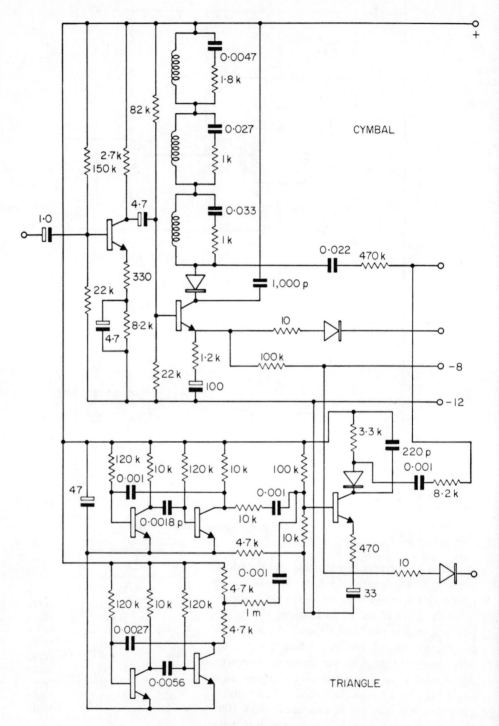

Fig. 231 Yamaha effects circuit

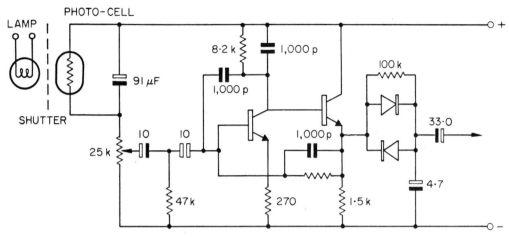

Fig. 232 Yamaha touch vibrato

The other interesting feature in this organ is the touch-sensitive vibrato. By pressing a key slightly from side to side, the vibrato is made to start and follow the movement of the key; it is the same action as a 'cello player would take with his string. Originally invented by Maurice Martenot in 1928 (US patent 1,853,630), it has taken a long time to see the light of day in a modern form. A shutter operated by the keys controls the low-frequency oscillator in Fig. 232 through the agency of a photo-cell and lamp; the circuit is simple and effective. Apart from the above, there is a very full complement of organ voices and a well-balanced specification; though there are smaller models as well.

The Mellotron

This instrument is not strictly an electronic music producer but rather a playing machine. It is included because it is the only example of magnetic tapes for playing under the individual touch and control of the performer. Basically the Mellotron contains two 35-note keyboards side by side (making as it were a continuous keyboard of 70 notes separated by a key slip in the middle). The right-hand section can play $2\frac{3}{4}$ octaves of 18 different instruments, the sounds of which are already recorded on tapes. The left-hand section controls the rhythm and also provides a number of chords to accompany notes played by the right hand. There are 17 different chords and a large number of distinct rhythms. Many different tracks are recorded on these tapes, the heads being moved to select some of these, whilst the actual tapes are divided into sections to further increase the number of sounds available. One of the most satisfactory design aspects of the device is that the playing heads only contact a tape when a playing key is depressed; thus the problem of wear is greatly reduced, if not entirely abolished.

This desirable feature is combined with a pinch roller actuated by a key, so that as well as contacting the replay head any key pressed starts the tape moving. Because of the three tracks recorded side by side on any one tape, the head can also be moved across the tape to scan the correct track; the movements to initiate this are controlled by the appropriate tone button operated by the player. If we imagine the instrument in a starting position, the tape is pulled down over a roller by a spring so that there is none in the take-up box. On pressing a key, the tape is brought into position electronically and the correct sound starts; the tape is then taken into the box whilst keying. If a key is held to the maximum extent, then we have eight seconds of playing time on each tape section before it is drawn back to the starting position. The tape is therefore ferried back and forth by means of the spring and bottom roller, for when the sound is required the capstan roller propels the tape in the right direction; when the sound ceases, the spring pulls the tape back to the starting position. Naturally, the starts of the tape must be set when the machine is prepared for use in the first place.

Tone qualities and rhythms are selected by buttons above the playing keys, and an ingenious electrical system inches the tape along until the correct sound—and at the correct time—is in a position for playing. For example, if a piano is required, it is essential that the key should pick up the start of the note and not half-way along it; electronic registration is used to perform this function. An interesting point is that the capstan motor is driven from an oscillator with a controlled frequency, but the register control motor is caused to rotate from the registering pulses through another amplifier. The capstan frequency can be varied somewhat to tune the instrument to the pitch of other instruments playing with it; this would not of course be possible if the drive was at 50 Hz from the mains.

The mechanics of this device are formidable, but since most of them are buried in the system it is not possible to show the precision and robustness of the workmanship. As an example, the capstan roller extends the whole length of the keyboards, but is ground to the finest limits so that there is no suggestion of 'wow' or flutter at the tape speed of $7\frac{1}{2}$ in. per second.

Fig. 233 shows the general principle of the instrument.

Since the sole sound source is a series of magnetic tapes, it is evident that any kind of sound could be provided; and indeed there are models which produce effects noises only, as well as smaller, less comprehensive instruments.

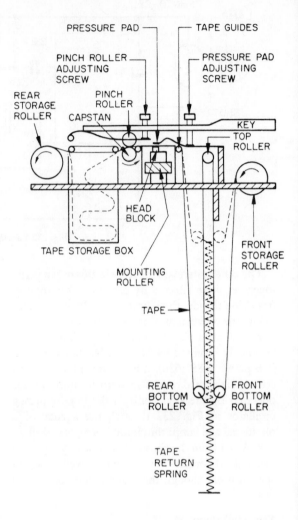

Fig. 233 The Mellotron

8 Experimental Methods

The foregoing subject matter has described the necessary conditions for simulation of musical tones and the way in which these conditions are realized in practical form for commercial production.

The cost of manufacture is the primary consideration in an ever-increasing world of competition. Much ingenuity has been expended in techniques for economical production of components, and the tonal range and general performance of all instruments on the market is strictly related to their cost. As with television and radio, the less costly organs tend to follow the same pattern and this has had some influence in shaping the views of potential constructors. This is not necessarily a good thing, and most of this chapter is devoted to other circuits and devices with which he can experiment. If the reader has now a better understanding of what is required to produce realistic sounds, he may find that a combination of some of these circuits is more effective than any commercial circuit. He has the great advantage that he can take his time and assemble parts as and when he has the inclination and the resources. Many have adopted this policy and assembled real organs in the course of time. However, we do not assume any particular order of subject matter in this chapter.

One of the earliest forms of music generator employed electrically-driven tuning forks. These can, of course, be obtained in a very wide range of pitches so that a frequency coverage of from 32 to over 8000 Hz is quite feasible. The purity of the tone, whilst attractive at first, soon palls, and although the American Rangertone instrument showed some promise, it was found impossible to produce enough tonal variety. Tuning forks are better employed to form percussive sounds like the glockenspiel or celesta, when they can be struck by

a solenoid device as on page 179 and, owing to their low inherent damping, continue to sound for a time after striking; the effect is thus like a chime and can be very attractive. The vibrations can be picked up by a small coil near one tine or by a microphone button lightly touching one tine near the base; any appreciable loading would stop the vibration. It has been suggested that a limited number of forks might be used to supply true as against tempered harmonics in a generating system to reinforce those normally used to form imitative tones. This idea would be useful for truly tuned mixtures; but how do we drive tuning forks? A simple circuit is shown in Fig. 234. Note that the pickup coil is also part of the drive to the buffer stage, usually necessary to prevent the loading of T_1 stopping the fork from oscillating. A simple RC filter will soon produce a good sine wave at the output; alternatively, another pickup coil can be mounted where convenient and taken to a separate amplifier, for the distortion from the buffer arises from the biasing of this stage; the tuning fork itself will always deliver a sine wave unless grossly overdriven. On this subject, whilst the pure wave itself

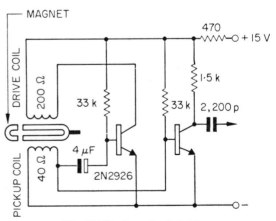

Fig. 234 Simple tuning fork drive

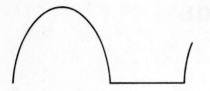

PERCENTAGE OF FUNDAMENTAL

Harmonic No.	2	4	6	8
%	42	8·4	3·6	2·0

Fig. 235 Harmonic content of rectified sine wave

is uninteresting, if it is rectified we get Fig. 235, the harmonic content of which is given below; so this wave is more suitable for flutes etc. which are near to sine waves, but certainly not exactly so.

Earlier it was said that generators having a mechanical origin (i.e. tone wheels, reeds etc.) are not susceptible to electronic vibrato circuits; in such cases there must be a modulator of some other form. An early circuit is shown in Fig. 236 and is for valves only. The small transformer is any step-up type, the primary being the lowest impedance winding. There is provision here to reduce the vibrato towards the bass end of the compass, for it is a general rule that when the vibrato frequency approaches that of the tone frequency it

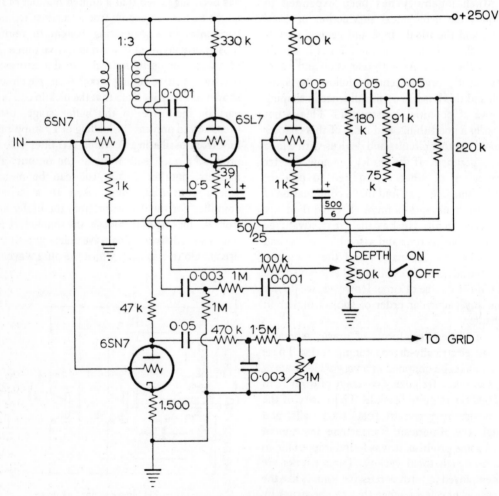

Fig. 236 Phase-shift vibrato circuit

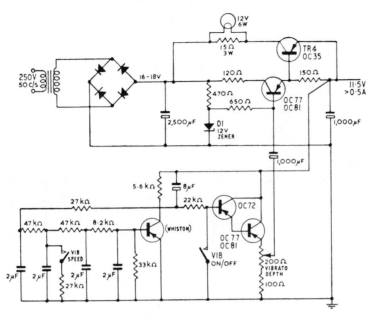

Fig. 237 Resistors 0·5 W unless otherwise shown

becomes most objectionable. For this reason, the vibrato frequency is always below audibility. Yet another way to induce vibrato in oscillators which are reluctant to respond to normal treatment is to modulate the supply line as in Fig. 237. The frequency change brought about by the phase-shift circuit at the foot of the figure is made to control the base conductivity of the main transistor. In this way, a swing of at least 5 V either way can be obtained on the 12-V line, and this is sufficient for many oscillator types.

The earliest kind of rotating acoustic vibrato was the paddle of Fig. 238. Indeed, this device was fitted to all reed organs from about 1850 and has certain uses for small loudspeakers still; the disadvantage is that the paddle may come to rest, largely

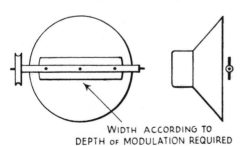

WIDTH ACCORDING TO
DEPTH OF MODULATION REQUIRED

Fig. 238 Loudspeaker paddle

blocking off the radiation from the cone. There is a cyclic change in volume and to some extent in pitch, so that Doppler's formula applies to a degree—

$$f\,(\text{at point of observation}) = \frac{V}{V - V_s}f_s$$

where V = velocity of sound
V_s = velocity of source
f_s = frequency of source.

The sound tends to rise in pitch as the paddle rotates towards the observer and falls when it moves towards the cone. The modulation is only effective at high frequencies.

Now we have dealt with sustain circuits and here we have an example of the opposite: a percussion circuit.

This elegant percussion and wave-shaping circuit is due to Philips and is shown in Fig. 239. There are six transistors, the first two of which are amplifiers for a pulse voltage which is derived from an extra contact on the keyboard. The third and fourth transistors make up a multivibrator which can be either monostable or astable according to the control-switch positions. This part of the circuit is triggered off from the first transistors, and

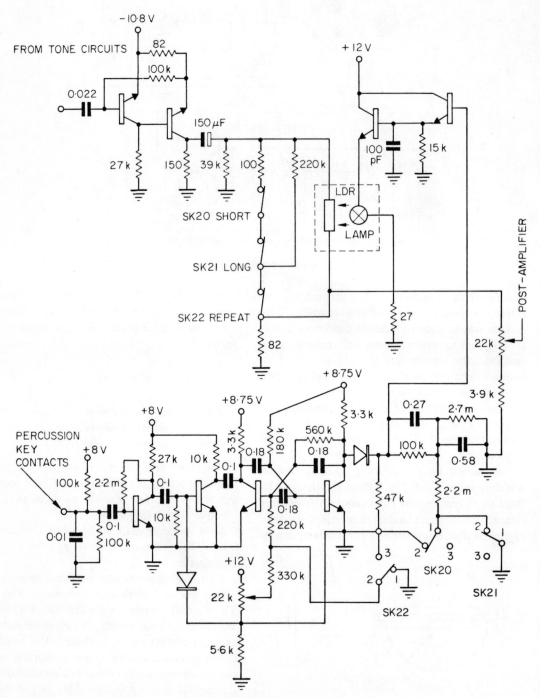

Fig. 239 Philips percussion circuit

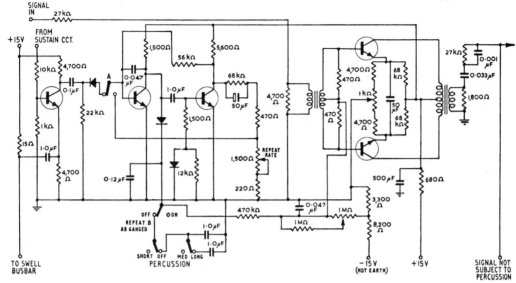

Fig. 240 Percussion circuit

its output voltage is applied to an *RC* network via a diode; then, by means of two emitter followers, this voltage is routed to a lamp which illuminates a light-dependent resistor, acting as a potentiometer circuit of the AF amplifier. Due to the special shape of the voltage which is applied to the lamp, a percussion effect is obtained so long as the multivibrator is connected as a 'one shot' or monostable circuit; but if it is allowed to free-run, then the lamp will be energized at some rate depending on the setting of R.574, which gives a repeat percussion range of from 4–12 Hz. The beauty of this most effective device is that keying the circuit is effected by a simple contact to earth on each key and that the percussion circuit is external to the organ, and therefore the one circuit is common to all notes. The effect can of course be switched off when steady tones are required.

There are other percussion circuits, most of which are inseparable from the instrument in which they exist; however, one other deserves to be mentioned, since it also can be used externally and with any sustained signal source. A pair of transistors in push–pull are biased off so that an injected signal cannot be heard; this bias can be overcome by a strong pulse from a one-shot multivibrator. This is a circuit capable of conducting only once until it is unblocked by some means.

When the bias on the output stages is overcome by the one-shot pulse, a sudden burst of sound is heard and the circuit then is passive until the one-shot is energized again (see Fig. 240).

We have already seen a circuit resembling that of Fig. 241, but this has an additional feature making it useful for percussion. Although the capacitor is charged with 100 V, when the key is released it can only discharge slowly through the 1 m resistor; if now a + voltage is supplied through the neon lamp, this discharges the capacitor very quickly though not instantly; the effect is that of a percussive sound.

A number of sustain circuits have been shown and no doubt the principle is well understood, but

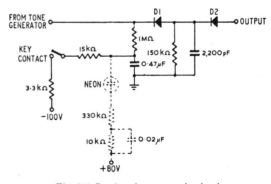

Fig. 241 Semiconductor sustain circuit

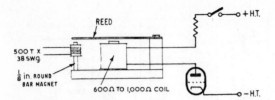

Fig. 242 Mechanical reed sustain device

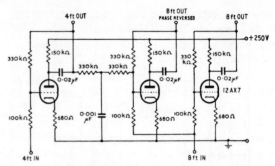

Fig. 243 Phase-reversing circuit

it is possible to have a mechanical sustain as in Fig. 242; it is only applicable to organs having an independent oscillator for each note. The small steel reed is tuned to the oscillator frequency and when the anode current flows through the coil, the reed is caused to oscillate at that frequency. When the key is released, the inertia of the tongue allows it to vibrate for a time, so that if a pickup coil is placed near to it, the tone can be heard. It can either be added to the main tone or used on its own with separate tone-forming networks; this permits reeds of different harmonic content to be tried. Since there is no soundboard or cavity there is no acoustic output and the reed drive causes no audible sound. The reeds can be made from clock spring and carefully filed until they are in tune with the oscillator; though they will pull in if close to that frequency. It has also been suggested that they might be of twice the designed frequency so that when the valve is silenced they tend to revert to

their true frequency; this could give an 'Hawaiian guitar' effect.

It is in the field of experiment that we find people still using valves to some extent, so we give a phase-reversing circuit here which operates in the same way as the transistor device on page 50. Fig. 243 has the correct values of resistor to attenuate the 4-ft signal and the best valves for this circuit are 12AX7 as shown. Applied sawtooth waves appear as 8-ft square waves.

A method evolved some years ago to control overloading of amplifiers in a simple way is reproduced again in Fig. 244; of course it can be applied equally well to transistor circuits. The small lamp is connected, through a regulating resistor, across a loudspeaker speech coil. It is associated with a cadmium sulphide photo-cell

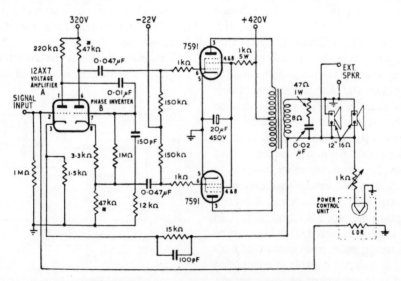

Fig. 244 Method to control overloading of amplifiers

connected between grid and earth—or across the input to the amplifier. When dark the resistance of the cell is very high, therefore it does not affect the gain; but if the lamp lights due to a very loud signal, the cell resistance falls and the input is shunted to ground progressively. When properly adjusted, it is an automatic gain control.

Keying has been discussed at some length, but there are other ways of doing this. Clearly it would not be possible, in any commercial organ but the most expensive, to regulate all the pitch keyers to conform to the way the sound starts in an organ pipe; for we must assume the most costly electronic organs to be pipe-organ imitators. The experimenter could do it, of course, as he is not bound by commercial restrictions. But let us look at what actually happens when a key is pressed on a pipe organ—that is, one in which wind is the motive force for the tone system. When the pipe is at rest, there is a volume of air residing in the conical foot which is the part supporting the speaking tube proper. When a wind valve is operated, this air has to be removed by the wind coming from the supply chest before the pipe can speak, and this takes time, depending on the shape and size of the wind passages and the inertia of the air in the pipe foot, which again depends on the size of the pipe. This random rate of attack or starting tone accounts for much of the mass effect of a number of pipe combinations sounding simultaneously and this, combined with the fact that the sound comes from a wide area, underlines some of the problems the designer of a synthetic instrument has to contend with. Perhaps a gradual contact switch, in which both the rate of making contact and the actual ohmic value of the contact depend on the speed and pressure applied to the key, is the best solution. The original Baldwin graphite unit is shown in Fig. 245, although it is no longer in use. The slotted nylon dolly receives up to three vertically-ganged switches and actuates the curved nickel-silver strip which has two stiffening ribs pressed into it. On depression of a key, the strip meets the wedge-shaped resistance strip at its apex; the resistance here is at least 50 kΩ. Continued pressure unrolls the strip along the resistor until eventually it reaches the silvered end; the resistance is now zero. The fixed part of the

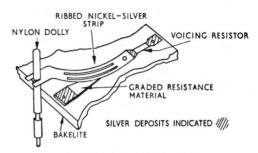

Fig. 245 Baldwin resistance switch

resistor shown at the rear can be adjusted by scraping to equalize the output from each switch. The secret of success in this design lay in the number and manner of coats sprayed on, some hard, some softer; but the life exceeded two million operations. A more recent form of conductive switch not nearly so expensive to make is that shown in Fig. 246; it is made from a silastomer material impregnated with carbon. Carbon made from acetylene black is almost colloidal, that is, has no discernible grain structure, so it makes a smooth dispersion as if it were cream. The ingenious feature of this device is the simple method of ensuring that the round silver wire contact wipes round an arc of the silastomer so as to give a decreasing resistance with an increase in depth of touch. This is achieved as in Fig. 246. It will be seen that the wire, soldered into a grommet or eyelet in the insulating board, is bent at right

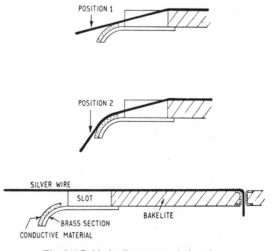

Fig. 246 Baldwin silastomer switch action

angles so as to lie along the top of the board. Where it is to move under the influence of the key dolly, the Bakelite is cut away so that, when the key is pressed, the wire is bent downwards over the sharp edge of the board; it then contacts the extreme edge of the silastomer strip. Further pressure wraps the wire round the radiused angle of the strip, thus allowing the note to sound at full volume.

An interesting pressure-sensitive paint is made by Clark Electronic Laboratories, Palm Springs, California, and is applied in the form of small spots or drops; this material can be obtained in a very wide range of values, both for resistance change and pressure to be applied; one form, type 9A, requires only a few ounces' pressure to change from one megohm to some 50 ohms. A single ounce will make many hundreds of contacts, which is just as well as the price is 20 dollars an ounce.

We have already seen that electrolytic keying is used in the Trautonium by depression of the tone cylinder on to a rubber tube, and this can be applied to organs; though it is not strictly able to provide a wide change in resistance, it nevertheless has an abrupt transition from high to low resistance of just enough duration to get rid of keying transients. Figs. 247–9 illustrate the idea.

One long trough is required for each pitch and the dippers are connected to the tone-generator outlets. A Bakelite strip, *A*, under each key carries as many eyelets, *B*, with long shanks as will cover the number of pitches required. Inserted through *B*, and held by friction, are short pieces of 'soft' pencil lead (graphite), *C*. Below is a Bakelite strip, *E*, extending the length of the keyboard and fitted

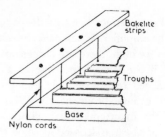

Fig. 248 Trough suspension

with tinplate troughs, *D*. In the bottom of these lie strips of extremely soft foamed plastic, *F*, such as is used for draught-excluding purposes; the troughs are secured by Araldite. The keying strip, *A*, is held in position with an upward bias by a flat spring, *H*, and is depressed at the front end by a button and wire, *G*, screwed into the underside of the keys.

The foam strip is saturated with ethylene glycol antifreeze, but it should be noted that the mixture supplied by Vauxhall Motors is not so effective as it contains other substances. One must, of course, be careful not to spill the mixture, but if the sponge rubber is just saturated there will be little free liquid, although the level may rise and fall a little with changes in humidity of the air. This system is very useful as, owing to the thin section of the troughs, several can be mounted under standard keys. The mountings must, of course, be well insulated to avoid cross-talk, and plastic knitting needles or nylon cords work well in this capacity.

In a more recent development of this idea, devised by A. E. le Boutillier, the troughs are replaced by a thick sheet of Perspex or similar material in which holes are end-milled to contain only a little glycol. Each key is of course above a hole or series of holes according to the number of pitches required, and each hole is joined to the next by a thin strip of nickel silver passing down, across

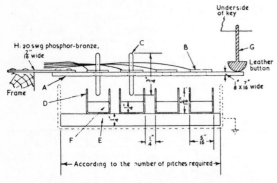

Fig. 247 Liquid-resistance key switches

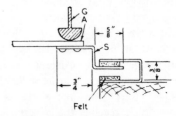

Fig. 249 Touch-limiting device

the bottom and up again to the next hole; the dippers remain the same. In this way, the possibility of spilling the mixture is greatly reduced and all the holes are together so there is not the difficulty of accurately aligning the troughs.

In common with all forms of multiple-pitch keying systems, it is desirable to surround the trough assembly with a sheet tinplate screening box, although the top cannot be enclosed; the box should be earthed.

An ingenious home-made system combines the virtues of direct metal contacts with the advantage of graduated attack. This is an earthing-out connection as in Fig. 250, and a single wire is shown for simplicity. A fixed block on the keyframe holds the wires in such a way that they can be depressed by two actuators made from Perspex and attached to the underside of the keys. To the front of the block is an earthing busbar, to the rear is a strip of graphite-impregnated foam rubber or similar porous material. If now the key is pressed down, the wires will firstly be removed from the earthing bar, then more gradually from the foam strip which has also been earthed; thus the signal will start weakly because the wires are in contact with the foam, but gradually become louder as the pressure on the foam lessens. As the key rises, a reverse action takes place. This kind of connection can only be used if the output from the dividers is taken through capacitors and not directly from the collectors, otherwise the h.t. would be short-circuited to earth.

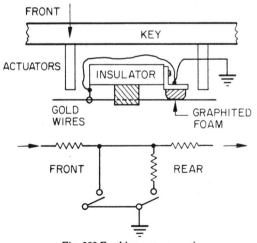

Fig. 250 Earthing-out connection

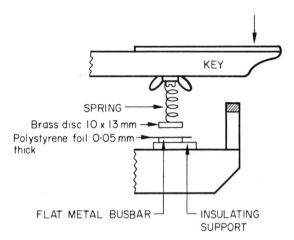

Fig. 251 Capacitive keying system

In Fig. 251 we see a capacitive keyer, developed in Germany. The signal comes to a small metal disc supported beneath a key by a spring. The collecting busbar is a metal strip as shown, covered with a very thin layer of Mylar or similar foil. As the disc approaches the busbar, the signal is gradually heard, finally becoming quite loud—the rate of capacitance change with distance being exponential.

Of course, the whole question of touch sensitivity or graduated attack presumes a new approach to organ tone. Normally, one would not expect any such attributes since the characteristic sound is a steady one; but attempts have been made to confer a degree of expression varying either with the depth of touch or the rate at which the key is depressed. There are several types of capacitive coupling which could be used to bring the sound on gradually, but since this involves a playing technique which is neither that of the organ or the piano it does not seem a very acceptable idea. On the other hand, such attributes as a variable vibrato, for example, might be valuable. A French patent taken out in April 1928 by the pioneer exponent of electronic music, Maurice Martenot, illustrates a scheme by which the playing keys can be moved in directions other than downwards. This is accomplished by mounting the keys with a small gap between each and on a flexible pivot, as in Fig. 252. If pressure is applied from side to side, it is possible to provide a vibrato in exactly the

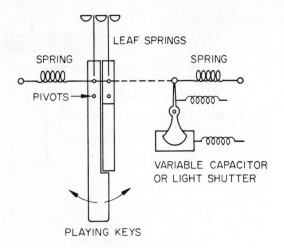

Fig. 252 Touch-sensitive key

same way as a string player does with the finger with which he stops the string. The rear of the key may operate a light-dependent resistor, for instance, controlling the amplitude of a standard vibrato oscillator. Or, by varying the downward pressure on a key, this can cause another LDR system to be controlled, or a variable capacitor, or a carbon or graphite resistor element, or the moveable core of an inductance. In a variation of this patent, several keys were mounted on a metal plate which could be oscillated from side to side, and these displaced the cores of tuning coils which formed part of the oscillator circuits; thus, a chord could provide more than one rate of vibrato if carefully manipulated. The experimenter has a

wide open field here for investigating novel means of control.

A very old idea for touch control is the use of several wire contacts above each other, so arranged that depression of the key makes a wiper contact one after the other; in this way, a series of resistors could be cut in or out thus altering the signal level of a device connected thereto. It has also been used to energize a series of relays in turn.

A standard adjunct of the cinema organ was the double-touch keyboard, a mechanism almost essential for the introduction of effects like cymbal crashes and other forms of extra expression; all theatre organs had this device on at least one keyboard, sometimes on all. It is shown in Fig. 253, and the construction is self-explanatory; a quite strong pressure is required to overcome the resistance of the leaf spring, so making the second contact; of course, other contacts could be fitted to a keyboard of this kind, and the author is surprised that double-touch is unknown on electronic theatre organs; but it would be easy to fit to a pedalboard to introduce drum or cymbal effects from modern rhythm boxes. Highly sophisticated circuits for relating the amplitude of the sound to the rate at which a key is depressed are found in the British VCS-3 electronic music synthesizer; as much as 40 dB change in intensity is achieved by varying the speed of attack.

Closely allied to attack control is the question of noise. Fig. 254 shows how this is related to the onset of the actual tone, although the actual times

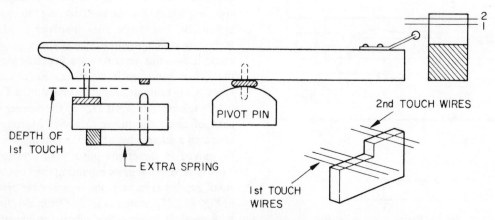

Fig. 253 Double-touch key

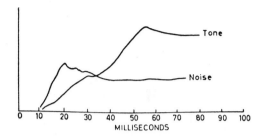

Fig. 254 Relationship between starting noise and tone-diapason

do vary over the compass. The example is taken from about the middle of the range. An ingenious method of solving the noise control is shown in Fig. 255. Instead of the generators being fed from smooth d.c., a noise generator has its output amplified until, after rectification, it has sufficient energy to drive the oscillators. There must then be a noise content along with the tone. But this effect would not be realistic, since the ear hears the noise first and then the tone predominates. So an auxiliary circuit follows the tone generator to give the peculiar transient known to organ builders as a 'chiff'. The choke L_1 is tuned by C_4 to resonate at some harmonic of the oscillator frequency, say the 5th; this will be contained in the noise band. On

keying the circuit, this harmonic energizes the resonant arrangement and is thus accentuated and heard; but by this time, the charge imparted at the same time to C_5C_6 begins to leak away through R_4R_5 so that the diodes conduct and remove the excess voltage from the resonant circuit; the signal level of the 5th and other harmonics now drops to that of the oscillator frequency. Thus the curious starting sound characteristic especially of stopped pipes is imitated; this always consists of odd harmonics, hence the selection of the 5th; the 3rd or 7th would do equally well.

Yet another use for a light-dependent resistor is for attack control of pedal notes (Fig. 256). If derived directly from frequency dividers and keyed with ordinary metal to metal contacts, the note must start abruptly and may produce a thump or click. This can be overcome by taking the signal output busbar and, instead of feeding it directly into the pre-amplifier and tone-shaping network, pass it through an LDR in series with the amplifier input. If, now, contacts common to all pedal keys are made to light a small flashlight bulb, the resistance of the LDR will fall at the rate taken for the filament to heat up, therefore the sound will come on relatively slowly and a much superior effect is obtained. The actual degree of brightness is easily found with a small rheostat in series with the bulb, but once again it must be stressed that the supply has to be very thoroughly filtered if derived from a.c. or an unpleasant hum will be heard with the signal.

In the various organ tone circuits and parts thereof, no mention has been made of the actual physical form of the stop switches. In many cases these are plain wire contacts because if the action of cutting off a voice entails earthing the tone net there will not be any click. In other cases resistance

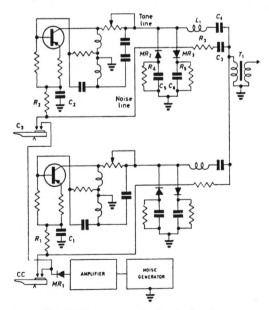

Fig. 255 Starting transient and noise circuit

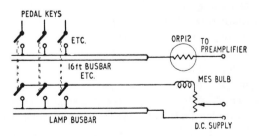

Fig. 256 Pedal attack control

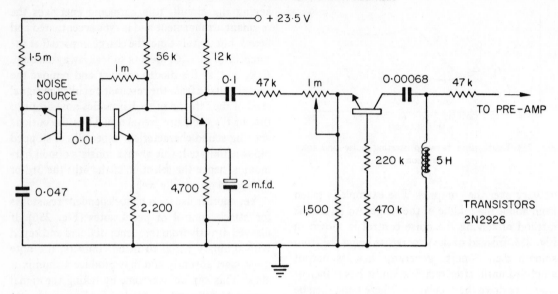

Fig. 257 Conn noise source, cymbal filter on right

switches like the Baldwin design can be used to avoid transients when connecting in to a tone net; and yet again, photo-cells may be placed at the entry to a tone network to earth this when not required; a shutter is operated by the stop arm and this also is a noiseless method. It is only necessary to connect an LDR unit between the intake of the tone filter and earth, then if it is illuminated the net will be shorted to earth; by interposing the shutter, the light is cut off, the resistance rises rapidly and the effective shunt to earth is removed so the tone sounds. There are many possible variants of this system. One advantage is that the tone networks do not have to be close behind the actual stop switches, which may ease layout problems in some cases. Reed switch relays are also used in this manner.

Today nearly every domestic organ has apparatus for generating rhythmic sounds. There are so many ways of designing these 'toy counters', as they are often called, that we could not do justice to all the methods, many of which use special integrated circuits not available on the open market. Some of the devices for automatic rhythmic patterns, e.g. 4/4 time, 3/4, 6/8 etc., and the broken rhythms for modern dances also require clock circuits and so become too complex to detail. However, the basic ingredients of the systems are not too difficult to describe. All high-frequency sounds like triangle or cymbal (Fig. 257) are based on white noise, i.e. noise of a random kind which has had all the lower frequencies removed by filters. Other percussions like drums, claves, blocks etc. are either one-shot multivibrators or similar circuits which paralyse themselves after one cycle of operation. In practical organs, the keying arrangements are sometimes as complex as the rhythm circuits, but we show two ways of obtaining some of the more useful sounds. Firstly, one may note that the noise can be generated by a special Zener diode, an ordinary diode selected because it is noisy; or a transistor with the collector cut off: this is the cheapest method and is used by almost every manufacturer. The degree and nature of the noise varies with the method used to amplify it, and it might be instructive to look at one or two different circuits for doing the same thing (see Figs. 258, 259, 260 and 261). Partly, the differences are due to patents, but on the whole they reflect either the thinking of the designers responsible or they are engineered to use certain parts in common use in the company's products. See also the circuits of Figs. 216 and 217.

Rhythm units must be started at the exact time required for the tempo set up, and this is not easy with some of the controls to be found today. A

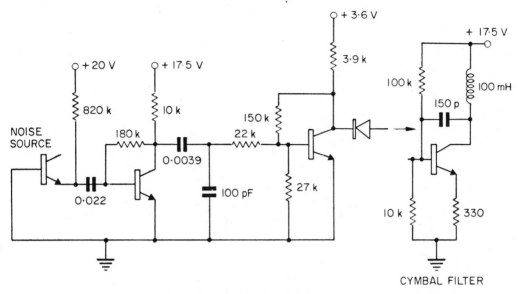

Fig. 258 Wurlitzer noise source

touch switch forms a good arrangement and with a suitable circuit can be made to turn on with one touch, then turn off with the next. A circuit such as in Fig. 260 can be used, the noise potential being influenced by the hand or the bias change as indicated. The advantage of this kind of control is that it can take any physical form; for example, it can be a plate, bar or disc within easy reach of the player; and having a different appearance from a tone stop, it immediately draws attention to itself and needs no searching for.

It must be evident by now that the question of attack, hold and release of a note, if intended to imitate some kind of organ pipe, are all interconnected and in some way dependent on the relative importance of each of these attributes. So if it were possible to combine a keying method with an envelope-shaping circuit, one could simulate some characteristic of specific organ pipes very accurately. The absolute accuracy of this kind of synthesis is held in doubt, partly because if too well done there is a sameness and lack of life; and partly because each and every organ builder has his own ideas on tonal quality. One can therefore only take a general likeness to any given stop as a basis for imitation. But there is no doubt at all about the way in which the tone starts in organ pipes; it has a rising slope as in Fig.

263(A), and this is almost the reverse of the rise slope of a typical diode keyer, Fig. 264. If the constants in the figure are properly chosen, a realistic exponential attack can be used with a simple diode circuit as a gate; and when the key is released the decay operates in the reverse mode, which is exactly like the action of a resonant pipe giving up its energy on the removal of the exciting force. This circuit also removes any trace of transient on operating a playing key (see Fig. 262).

There are occasions when the same kind of curve is needed but without any hold; for it will be recognized that this is the shape of a bell or chime wave form. Such sounds are not continuous but start, rapidly attain maximum energy, then decay more slowly. In other words, the characteristic now required is a complete percussion envelope formed automatically by pressing a key.

The circuit (Fig. 265) gives the details required. When the key is open, C_1 is discharged because of R_1 and R_2. On closing the key, the current through C_1, R_1 and R_2 builds up the voltage across R_2 but this reduces to zero as C_1 charges. Output from R_2 also charges up C_2, and D_2 controls its discharge time. As soon as the key is opened, C_1 discharges through D_1 and R_1. The keying voltage from the emitter follower follows the charge and discharge voltages from the shaper and so allows the signal to

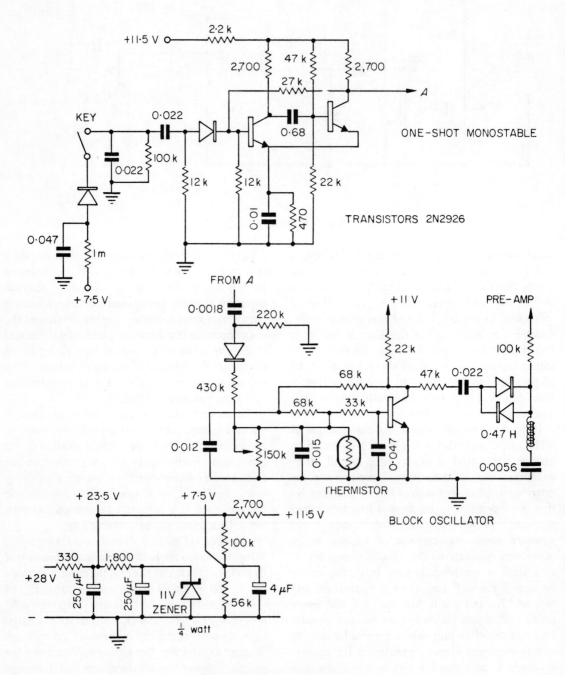

Fig. 259 Wurlitzer noise source

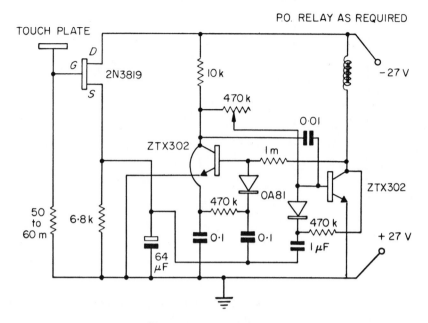

Fig. 260 Touch-sensitive switch

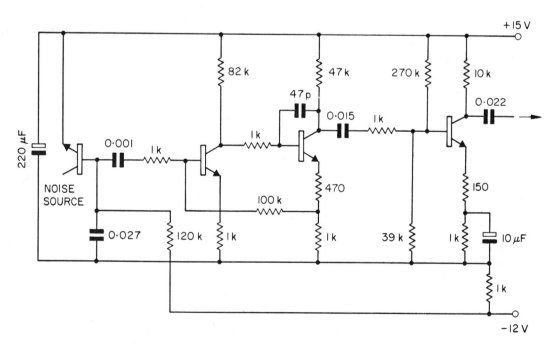

Fig. 261 Yamaha noise source

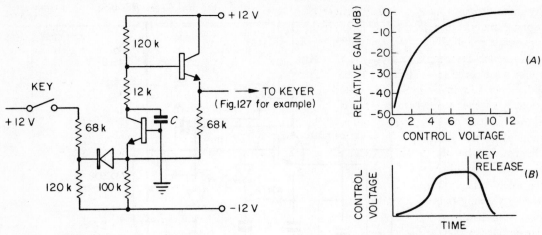

Fig. 262 Envelope-shaping circuit

Fig. 263–4 Comparison of start of tone in (A) organ pipe, and (B) typical diode keyer

pass. Note that the shaper can work on any input wave form, but to stop the 'buzzing' sound of the higher harmonics in the chime output a simple single-section filter is applied to the keyer. Some adjustment for the various frequencies is desirable as the lower notes should decay for longer than the higher ones; values for R_e, R_b and C for the highest (1174 Hz) and lowest (277 Hz) notes keyed are appended. The actual composition of the chime signals is given on page 180.

Of course, the characteristic sounds of many instruments become quite altered if the vibrations

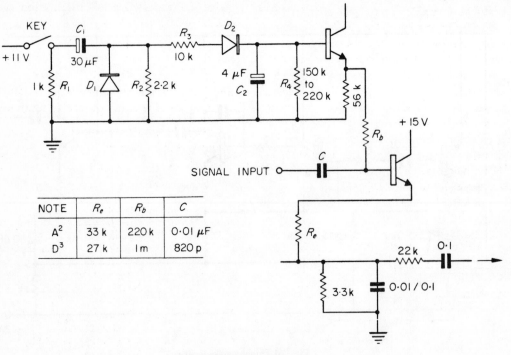

NOTE	R_e	R_b	C
A^2	33 k	220 k	0·01 μF
D^3	27 k	1m	820 p

Fig. 265 Chime envelope circuit

are transformed into an electrical quantity. This may be for many reasons, but is commonly caused by the closer coupling with the air of a harmonic series to which the ear is sensitive. All the other harmonics are there as well; the electrical conversion does not add any, indeed some may be lost; but usually a richer sound results. This is strikingly shown in the case of 16-ft pitch reeds: no amount of careful listening will enable the true fundamental to be heard. But with an electrical pickup, the deep pitch note is at once audible. Thus, many other instruments may be made to yield very pleasing tones if electrically operated.

For instance, the metal bars of the vibraphone, celeste or glockenspiel can be used as shown in Fig. 266. This results in clear bell-like tones of great purity. The impact or clang tone practically disappears and when amplified somewhat the sound is very interesting. Vibrato may be applied by one of the many methods described. Only an extremely small force is needed to strike the bars. Tuning forks are not suitable for this treatment as the sound is dull and lifeless and is readily obscured by any harmonically richer sounds existing at the same time.

It may be desirable to retain the complete harmonic series of the metal bar, as for instance in electrical chimes. To do this, the pickup must be moved from the central position to one end of the bar, as in Fig. 267. This also shows a means of striking the bar; the armature of the solenoid overshoots the central position when energized, thus causing the cork ball to strike the bar once only; for the coil brings the armature to the centre of the field after the first impulse. A more chime-like effect is obtained if the bars are made from cast steel and circular in section.

To calculate the required length of circular steel

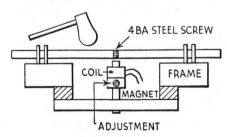

Fig. 266 Vibraphone conversion

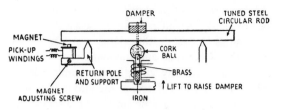

Fig. 267 Electric chime action

bar to resonate at any particular pitch—

$$f = \frac{1 \cdot 33\pi}{l^2} \sqrt{\frac{QK^2}{p}}$$

where f = frequency desired
l = length of bar in centimetres
p = density in grammes per cubic centimetre
Q = Young's modulus, dynes per square centimetre
K = radius of gyration.

For a circular cross-section,

$$K = \tfrac{1}{2}a$$

where a = radius of bar in centimetres.

For a hollow circular cross-section as, for example, a tubular bell—

$$K = \sqrt{\frac{a^2 + a_1^2}{2}}$$

where a = outside radius of tube, in centimetres.
a_1 = inside radius of tube, in centimetres.

The bar should be supported by cords or on knife edges at suitable nodal points.

Bar Free at Both Ends

Number of Tone	Number of Nodes	Distance of Nodes from one end in terms of length of bar	Frequencies as a ratio of Fundamental
1	2	0·2242, 0·7758	f^1
2	3	0·132, 0·50, 0·8679	$3 \cdot 756 f^1$
3	4	0·0944, 0·3558, 0·6442, 0·9056	$5 \cdot 404 f^1$
4	5	0·0734, 0·277, 0·5, 0·723, 0·9266	$8 \cdot 933 f^1$

Of course, all forms of bell and chime sounds can be produced electronically. In no case is it possible to synthesize exactly the sound of a struck bell, since the strike tone and following repercussions involve a constantly changing harmonic pattern which varies from bell to bell and also greatly with the force used to strike the metal. At the same time, a very similar if somewhat smoother replica of bell sounds can be effectively imitated. One way of doing this is to use rotating electrostatic generators with specially engraved wave forms; another method makes use of a group of selected frequencies simultaneously applied to a battery of capacitor discharge circuits having different time constants. The Compton Organ Company had a chime apparatus which could be played from a keyboard, or by mechanical means to provide automatic change-ringing on up to ten bells. Included are the standard changes well known as Westminster, Angelus, Whittington etc.

It is quite possible for the amateur to make his own chimes. The material is cast steel music wire, 11 swg being a suitable size for quite a range of notes, and a piece should be cut off about 8 in. long. One end is then ground to a taper point, rather like sharpening a pencil, and driven into a block of hard wood so that the smallest possible length of the bar to give rigidity is embedded. If the other end or some point along the bar is lightly struck with a cork ball, a note will be heard and tuning consists of shortening the bars by filing until correct. A magnetic pickup may be mounted near the bar, about half-way along its length, and the bars are readily magnetized by stroking with a permanent magnet. It is possible to make a simple hammer escapement operated by playing keys, and a sketch of this is shown in Fig. 268. The device is so short that it could be mounted beneath an organ keyboard if the electrical striking methods are too complicated.

When a downwards pressure is directed to X, the slotted wooden piece S is moved in the direction of the arrow; guides prevent it from wandering. The striker A, held on S by the spring B, engages with the step in the hammer actuator and throws the weighted head upwards. On releasing the key, the striker S skids past the hammer cam and re-sets itself. Pressure is made by

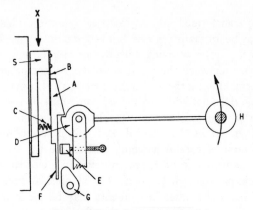

Fig. 268 Simple hammer mechanism

	Carillon Intervals				
Key	1	2	3	4	5
A2	C#3	A3	E4	A4	D5
A#2	D3	A#3	F4	A#4	D#5
B2	D#3	B3	F#4	B4	E5
C3	E3	C4	G4	C5	F5
C#3	F3	C#4	G#4	C#5	F#5
D3	F#3	D4	A4	D5	G5
D#3	G3	D#4	A#4	D#5	G#5
E3	G#3	E4	B4	E5	A5
F3	A3	F4	C5	F5	A#5
F#3	A#3	F#4	C#5	F#5	B5
G3	B3	G4	D5	G5	C6
G#3	C4	G#4	D#5	G#5	
A3	C#4	A4	E5	A5	
A#3	D4	A#4	F5	A#5	
B3	D#4	B4	F#5	B5	
C4	E4	C5	G5	C6	
C#4	F4	C#5	G#5		
D4	F#4	D5	A5		
D#4	G4	D#5	A#5		
E4	G#4	E5	B5		
F4	A4	F5	C6		

the spring C, adjusted by the screwed rod E, to prevent the cam losing contact with A. The other cam bar, G, puts the action off when not required. Recoil of the hammer is assured if the spring C is not too stiff.

Although the aim of this book is to concentrate on the electronic side of tone-colour production, it is not possible to control the manner of operating or playing except by mechanical devices of some sort. Many items are quite standard, such as manual keys for example, and it would be idle to discuss them; but as organs have grown up, so the control methods approximate to those used for many years on pipe organs; but with a difference, the heavy currents used for pipe-organ solenoids etc. could not be switched in electronic generator systems without causing considerable clicks, thumps and other interfering sounds. Accordingly, on the more sophisticated designs, transistor control has become standard for inductive elements; this allows the stop switch, piston or other actuator to carry only a minute current and permits the device controlled by the collector current to be away from sensitive parts of the circuitry. Thus we

find stops which indicate, couplers of all kinds, and even reversible actions such as the indispensable great to pedal coupler, operated by transistors. The action of a simple on or off transistor switch need not be explained, but the reversible systems are interesting because they operate on momentary contact only, and the same contact puts them on or off by successive pressures on the piston which is a simple push-button of strong construction.

A good example of modern circuitry for this purpose is the Conn reverser, Fig. 269. Reference to this shows that it is necessary to associate the

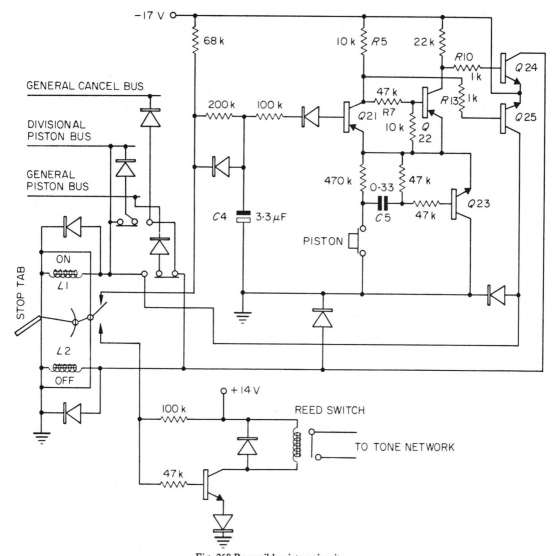

Fig. 269 Reversible piston circuit

piston with the switch it is to control. This is because this switch sets the operating states for the circuit; for instance, if the stop switch is 'off', $C4$ will not be charged. When the stop is 'on', $C4$ will be charged to $-17\,V$. These are the reference parameters which must be set up before the circuit can operate.

In the quiescent state $Q23$ is not conducting and the emitters of $Q21$ and $Q22$ are at approximately $-17\,V$. None of the transistors now conduct and $C4$ is at $0\,V$. $Q23$ is cut off, and until the piston is pressed we assume $C4$ to be discharged. On closing the contact, the base of $Q23$ is grounded through $C5$ and $R10$, causing $Q23$ to conduct. This places the emitters of $Q21$ and $Q22$ near ground potential. As $C5$ charges, a point is reached where $Q23$ will stop conducting, allowing the emitters of $Q21$ and $Q22$ to return to $-17\,V$. When the piston is released, $C5$ discharges through $R6$ and $R9$.

For the short time that the emitters of $Q21$ and $Q22$ are near ground potential, one of these two transistors will conduct. If $C4$ has $-17\,V$ on it (stop switch 'on'), $Q21$ will conduct, holding $Q22$ off because of the low collector potential of $Q21$. This low potential also goes through $R13$ to the base of $Q25$, turning it on; the current from this passes through the 'off' coil $L2$, causing the tab to rise to the off position. This makes the switch contact of this coil position close and so cut off the $-17\,V$ supply to $C4$. Before $C4$ becomes discharged to the point where $Q21$ would stop conducting, and cause $Q22$ to come on, $Q23$ cuts off and this prevents $Q24$ or $Q25$ from becoming active.

So with the tab switch up (off), $C4$ discharges to zero. Now if the piston is closed and $Q23$ conducts, $Q21$ will remain cut off. $Q22$, however, is biased on through $R5$, $R7$ and the $-17\,V$ supply. $Q24$ is next biased on through $R12$ and $Q22$, with $Q24$ current flowing through the 'on' coil, $L1$, so moving the tab to the 'on' position. The switchback contact opens and $C4$ is again allowed to discharge through $R2$, $R3$ and $D3$, and the system is now ready for the next reversal pulse from the toe piston switch. Perhaps we might note in passing that by using thyristors in place of small current transistors, the large action magnets found in pipe organs are controlled by transistor keying nowadays and small

primary chest magnets can be controlled with the kind of transistor shown above. So the trend affects design in many fields and simplifies servicing, apart from the advantages of silence and long life.

A very simple little instrument from which a great deal of satisfaction can be obtained is shown below. Many may also want to make a similar device if only as an introduction to the techniques of organ building. Accordingly a useful circuit is given in Fig. 270, and this produces a square wave just like many frequency dividers; therefore, any of the tone-forming circuits described for these can be applied. In this particular circuit, some three octaves can easily be covered. It would be possible to add a frequency divider if desired. The circuit is a simple multivibrator, tuned by variation of the resistance chain. The initial pitch is set by the rheostat R^1 and each subsequent semitone downwards is adjusted in value until correct. The next interval is then tackled, and so on to the end of the range. The resistor values follow a logarithmic law, being small for high notes and large for low notes. Unfortunately, there is no accurate way of predicting their exact values—and they must be exact; the values must be found by experiment. The pitch can be shifted up or down an octave with the same key resistors by switching the fixed capacitors shown; these will of course have to be trimmed exactly by means of small variables of about 500–1000 pF.

Keying transients are reduced by the simple bias circuit shown. This requires no additional supplies. A continuously variable vibrato is supplied by the second multivibrator. The oscillator must work into a buffer valve, such as the 12AU7 or ECC82.

Of course, transistors have proved very suitable for this kind of instrument and indeed are much easier to use as multivibrators than valves. In Fig. 271 a useful circuit is shown; this is divided into two parts, the vibrato oscillator on the left and the tone circuits next. Just as with the valve circuits, initial tuning is set by the 25 kΩ variable resistor, and other variables are connected as shown to form lower notes. The circuit is suitable for three octaves. It is best to make up a Zener stabilized power supply as suggested on page 91.

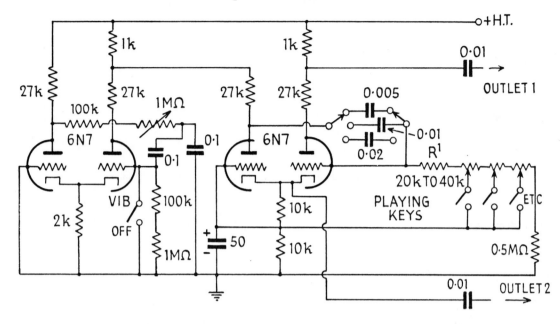

Fig. 270 Simple melodic instrument

As an alternative to the multivibrator, one can use a simple blocking oscillator with a single transistor, as in Fig. 272. Here we show not only the tunable oscillator, but two stages of frequency division. All transistors may be of the same type and an emitter-follower stage isolates the second divider from the first to prevent intermodulation. The transformer can be wound on a core $\frac{3}{8}$ in. by $\frac{3}{8}$ in., simple stalloy or 3·4 to 3·9 per cent silicon iron. Primary 500 turns of 38 swg, secondary 800 turns of the same wire. It may be necessary to adjust the value of the 0·01 μF tuning capacitor and it is difficult to cover more than $2\frac{1}{2}$ octaves

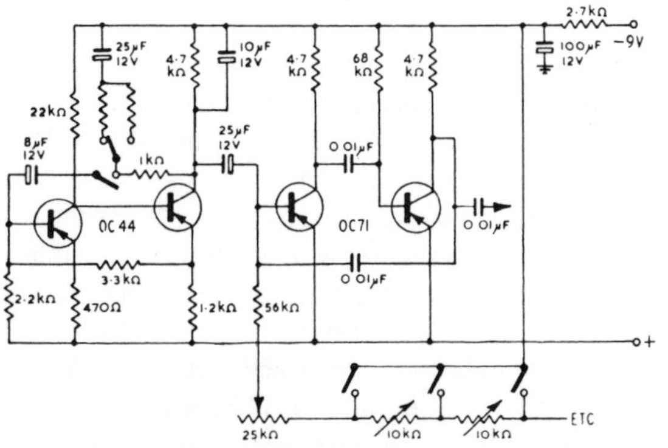

with this circuit. However, it can be made so small that it could be contained in a toy piano, for example. Fine tuning is by the 2kΩ variable resistor shown, and the pitch is not so liable to drift as a multivibrator, so that it could be run from a dry battery.

A useful way to obtain harmonically rich wave forms of more than one kind from an oscillator is shown in Fig. 273. Because the base of the transistor is supplied from a fixed source, it can be so biased that it can be somewhat overdriven. In this case, a square wave appears at the collector and if we then apply a network as previously described in Chapter 4 for conversion to a sawtooth, we can have both types available from the one circuit, so enabling many more experiments in tone forming. It should be pointed out that any bias applied in the manner shown must be stabilized, since variations in the voltage would result in variations in the frequency; this is made use of in Conn organs, where some of the base resistors are so connected (when this effect is required) that alternate notes become slightly sharpened, the others being slightly flattened. This improves the chorus effect when many notes are played at the same time.

Fig. 271 Transistor multivibrator

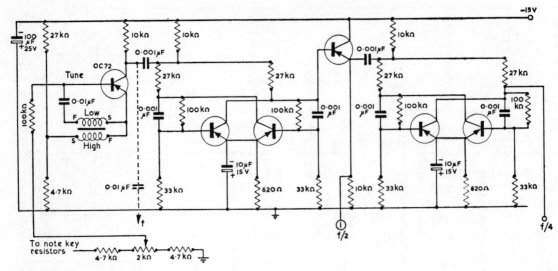

Fig. 272 Complete oscillator and divider circuit

Reverting once more to the use of free reeds as tone sources, in the typical acoustic reed organ the primitive acoustic cavities rather engender the unpleasant harmonics than suppress them; yet the physical limitations of this instrument mask the possibilities inherent in the reed. To produce smoother tones, a magnetic pickup can be applied as in Fig. 83, Chapter 4. All the signal coils can be permanently paralleled so that the impedance match is correct, whilst the relative loudness can be altered by moving the bobbins on the magnets. Practically all the upper harmonics are cut out in this arrangement, which does not interfere with the cyclic motion of the reed tongue.

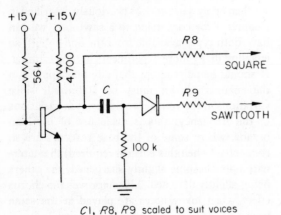

Fig. 273 Simultaneous square and sawtooth generation

The difficulty in obtaining sufficiently smooth or flute-like tones from reeds can be met over most of the scale by attaching very light auxiliary tongues to the main tongue. Thin beryllium-copper strip can be used for this purpose. By careful experiment the centre of the strip can be made to describe almost true simple harmonic motion, thus generating a sine wave, see for example, Fig. 278. A rather refined technique which might be justified in the case of exceptional reeds voiced by an expert, and strongly characteristic (such as a very narrow-tongued string or a French oboe), is to place a single-cell crystal microphone over each reed. Extremely accurate reproduction can be obtained by this means.

It is sometimes found that reeds of 16- or 32-ft pitch are rather slow in speech. This is really a matter of voicing, as by correct treatment it is possible to get almost instant speech. However, a simple generator can be made for, say, a 16-ft pedalboard, on which very rapid passages may be played by arranging the reeds so that they vibrate continuously with only just enough wind to maintain them and keying the signal electrically. The pickup must be electrostatic and the method, with the time delay circuit which eliminates keying clicks, is shown in Fig. 274. The reeds must not be mounted in chromatic order, or serious interference will be experienced due to the formation

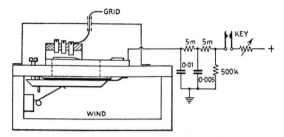

Fig. 274 Continuously vibrating reed arrangement

of beats in the air stream. The acoustic output is greatly reduced by correct setting of the valves, and can be suppressed entirely by a little thick felt screening. There should be a resilient connection to the wind supply, which must be absolutely steady.

Apart from the electrostatic or magnetic methods of extracting the vibrations, it is possible to cement minute etched-foil strain gauges to the reed tongues by means of Araldite. These can all be connected in series and this is a comparatively simple means of cancelling the harmonics and securing the full value of the fundamental frequency of the reed. The gauges are mounted near to the end of the reed where it is clamped, and not near the free end, and then form one arm of a Wheatstone bridge.

All of the foregoing methods possess the advantage that the volume from the reeds can readily be adjusted by electrical means, thus removing one of the greatest drawbacks to the use of free reeds—limitation of output. But, of course, any electrical sound-generating means is much more flexible in this respect than its acoustic counterpart.

Other devices involving electrostatic pickup are shown below.

In the types using a piano mechanism the control is relatively simple. Fig. 275 shows a series of

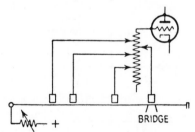

Fig. 275 Electrostatic string pickup

pickup electrodes disposed above a string, and similar sets are provided over the whole of the keyboard. Any or all of these can be inserted into the amplifier circuits by means of switches, and this gives control over the harmonic development. A further measure of control is exercised by electrical formant circuits. The relative strength of any of the harmonics is governed by the polarizing voltage, which can be varied as required. Another pickup on the bridge attempts to convey the starting transients. The relative effects of all the foregoing controls make it possible to extract a considerable variety of tone colours, ranging from the sharp, percussive sounds of the banjo to sustained tones resembling the organ. The soundboard is partially removed to prevent the direct propagation of sound waves; it cannot be entirely removed as the strings would not stop vibrating sufficiently quickly; there would be nothing to absorb energy from them and cause damping.

A simpler form of piano is made from brass reeds struck by a hammer and having an electrostatic pickup, or plucked by an adhesive compound secured to the end of the key shaft as in Fig. 276. By this means, the reed is lifted up until the elastic restoring force of the reed overcomes the adhesion of the compound and this releases the reed tongue which springs back rapidly past a charged pickup point, this producing a percussive sound. With these devices, no soundboard is required, so they can form exceedingly compact instruments for the home. The harmonics in the reeds do not, however, agree with the harmonics in a stretched string, so the sound quality is rather more like the harpsichord than the pianoforte.

The vibrating reed generators do not generate a sufficiently pure wave for direct harmonic combination. It is possible to obtain this by an extensive system of filters, but the very high values of terminating resistance would make the filter complex and expensive. Consequently it is customary to obtain a mixed wave form directly from the

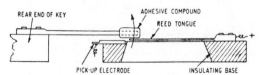

Fig. 276 Simpler form of piano

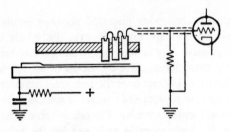

Fig. 277 Electrostatic reed pickup

reeds. This may be done by the means shown in Fig. 277. Here we have a vibrating reed tongue with several pickup electrodes suitably disposed above it. By choosing the position of the screws correctly, and by varying the distance between the screws and the reeds, a surprising range of tonal effects may be obtained. A further control can be exercised by shaping the reed tongue or by attaching an auxiliary vibrating member (Fig. 278). The screws for any reed are connected together, then all the screws for any one set of reeds are paralleled and connected to the grid of an amplifying valve. By correct choice of the polarizing potentials for the reed tongues, varying degrees of loudness are possible.

In the past, great care had to be taken over screening, leads etc. because all electrostatic devices have a high impedance and so are very prone to hum pickup; if the input impedance of the pre-amplifiers is reduced, so is the bass as well as the gain. With the introduction of field-effect transistors, it is easily possible to obtain the gain required as well as the required input impedance to suit electrostatic reed pickups; because the circuit can be made so small, it can be housed close to the reed screws and the risk of hum pickup is overcome to a great extent; though it is still

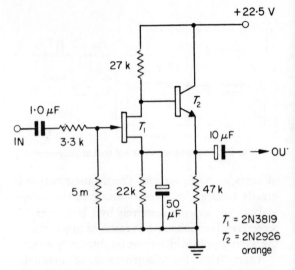

Fig. 279 High input impedance pre-amplifier for reed pickups

recommended to enclose the reeds etc. in a box lined with tinfoil which is earthed. We show a suitable FET circuit in Fig. 279.

There is little doubt that the most effective and distortionless mixing and pre-amplifying today is obtained by the use of an operational amplifier, of which there are now many types. The name has nothing to do with music, it is an expression from computer techniques where this circuit was first employed. Such amplifiers contain a number of elements within a very small case. Their virtue for our purpose is that the input impedance is extremely low—hence the term virtual earth. This means that any number of resistive inputs can be connected together at the input, with good isolation between the signal inputs. The required output response and gain are obtained by feedback from the output to the input; in fact, the gain is the ratio of these two resistors. Fig. 280 shows the basic form but in practice we use an arrangement

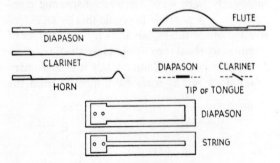

Fig. 278 Shaping of reed tongues

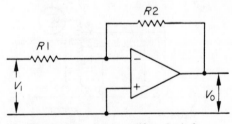

Fig. 280 Operational amplifier—basic form

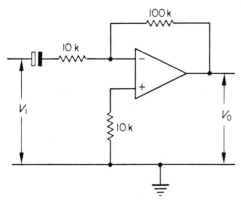

Fig. 281 Arrangement used in practice

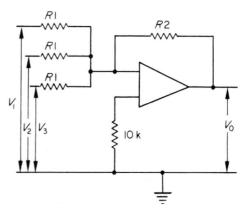

Fig. 282 Gain for several inputs

as in Fig. 281. The gain is $R2/R1$, thus for several separate inputs (Fig. 282)—for which the values of R are chosen to control the input amplitude—we find—

$$V_0 = \left[\left(\frac{R2}{R1} \right) V_1 + \left(\frac{R2}{R1} \right) V_2 + \left(\frac{R2}{R1} \right) V_3 + \dots \right]$$

So, by using such an amplifier, distortion and cross-modulation are avoided and the required gain is realized. However, the way these amplifiers are manufactured makes them very susceptible to damage from external fields, heat, wrong polarity etc.; in which case, the whole package must be thrown away. In addition, some types may introduce noise. A circuit using discrete components and which gives virtually the same results is shown in Fig. 283; the transistors may be 2N2926 or similar. The feedback makes the input impedance very low indeed but one must be careful to have resistance in the input and not try to connect low-impedance sources. This circuit is very quiet and

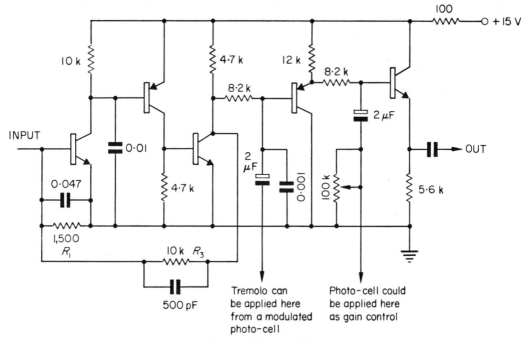

Fig. 283 Busbar amplifier

the gain can be altered by increasing the values of $R1$ and $R3$ in the same ratios.

It has been pointed out (page 122) that a different harmonic series can be extracted from a vibrating string according to the position of the hammer. Many experiments have been carried out with mechanically operated single-string instruments. One arrangement makes use of a string stretched between two posts and carried over a bridge. Small keys are used to 'stop' the string as required to tune it to the correct pitches, and a rotating bone wheel is brought into contact with the string to set it into vibration. The pickup may be electromagnetic, iron wire being wound round the string close to the bridge, or a crystal cartridge under the bridge may be used. In this latter case, however, it may be difficult to eliminate scratching sounds due to the fingers touching or leaving the string. One of the anchoring posts may be moved in either direction by means of a small motor to tune the string, and this post may also be attached to a cam device to produce a vibrato effect. There is no soundboard for the acoustic output should be as small as possible and, since this results in little damping, a felt damper may be used as in Fig. 284. The most pleasing tones seem to be obtained from a violoncello G string; it is clear that this is a purely melodic device.

An electromechanical generator which is suitable for producing pedal tones is seen in Fig. 285. The long conical element is an alloy casting, supported on substantial bearings; the end diameters are in the ratio of approximately 2·5 to 1; around the cone are disposed a number of tone discs driven by friction from the cone; very narrow wheels allow a positive rotating movement without rubbing or sliding friction; the tone wheels can have any shape of tooth but a sawtooth

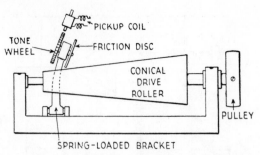

Fig. 285 Variable-pitch magnetic generator

is generally useful; light springs hold the driving discs in contact with the cone; each toothed wheel has its own magnet and pickup coil.

By moving the discs along the cone, tuning to the exact intervals is easily obtained, and for twelve notes all the tone wheels can have the same number of teeth. The cone is provided with a flywheel and rotated by a synchronous motor at a constant speed. Additional tone wheels with more teeth can be fitted to extend the range. Tone-forming circuits of the kind shown on pages 73 and 74 are used to provide the necessary effects.

The more experimentally-minded could try some of the following generating circuits: another unsymmetrical multivibrator, Fig. 286; means for exactly equalizing the wave forms on either side of a multivibrator, Fig. 287; pulse generators from which different kinds of wave can be extracted, Fig. 288; a circuit for silicon transistors only, essentially to produce a sharp spike or pulse for triggering, Fig. 289; lastly a tone generator using a thyristor, enabling a greater output power to be obtained, Fig. 290. The circuit shown in Fig. 289 may prove to be less expensive than a bistable

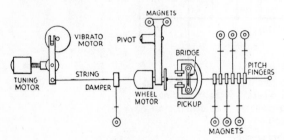

Fig. 284 'Cello device.

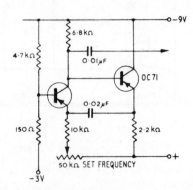

Fig. 286 Unsymmetrical multivibrator

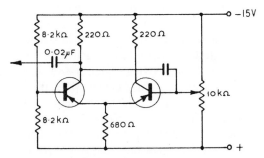

Fig. 287 Multivibrator with adjustment for symmetry

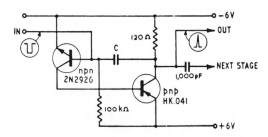

Fig. 289 Pulse generator: may be about 0·0022 for 1000 Hz

divider of conventional type, but the pulse is not suitable for tone forming and should be used to trigger a sawtooth wave-shaping circuit as described on page 83, which also acts as a noiseless keyer. The silicon transistors shown are quite cheap and will no doubt become even cheaper. Because of the very small leakage currents, there is virtually no signal leakage and thus the cross-talk is negligible. A negative input pulse is required for triggering. There are, of course, innumerable other circuits which offer possibilities for the production of musical tones, but many of these can only be used as single units and are therefore unsuitable for a multiple-generator system and quite often extreme precautions have to be taken in the matter of power-supply regulations.

British patent 722,430 discloses a very simple hard-valve sawtooth generator in which the capacitor is charged extremely rapidly and discharged slowly, in contrast to the more usual practice of rapidly discharging the capacitor. Fig. 291 shows the elements of the circuit. The double triode valve

has a series of cascaded resistors, $R_1 R_2 R_3$, etc., in the cathode circuit which can be connected at will to discharge the capacitor C_1 via the cathode resistor R_4 of the second half of the triode. For example, by closing contact S_2, resistor R_1 is introduced into the circuit, while if S_1 is closed instead, resistors R_1 and R_2 are placed in series with the first cathode and so the closing of additional contacts to the left of any one closed contact do not affect the resistance connected in this cathode circuit.

The second anode has an adjustable load resistor VR_1 and there is a fixed resistor in the cathode circuit of V_2. The grid of this valve is returned by resistor R_5 to D, thus making this grid negative with respect to the cathode. The grid of V_1 is directly connected to the anode of V_2. Terminal A is +h.t. and terminal D −h.t.

The circuit works in the following manner. At the beginning of each cycle the capacitor is in a discharged condition and current flows through V_1 to charge it. This charging current flows through the discharge resistor thereby producing a potential difference between the cathode of V_2 and −h.t., such that the cathode is positive with respect to that grid. As the grid of V_2 is electrically connected to −h.t., this has the effect of making this grid

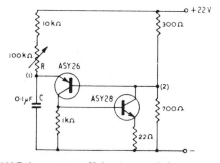

Fig. 288 Pulse generator. Voltage across C rises exponentially depending on time constant RC until voltage at (1) is sufficient to make TR_1 and TR_2 conduct; C then discharges quickly through the 22Ω resistor. This gives a sawtooth at (1) and a pulse at (2)

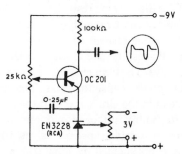

Fig. 290 Thyristor oscillator

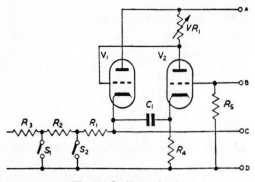

Fig. 291 Oscillator circuit

negative with respect to its cathode, so reducing its anode current. The result of this is to reduce the voltage drop across the anode resistor, so making the first grid more positive, thus speeding up the charging of the capacitor.

This increase of voltage across the capacitor continues until the cathode of the first valve rises to a higher positive potential than its grid, so cutting off the anode current of that valve. No further current then flows into the capacitor. This latter now discharges relatively slowly through the discharge resistors, and this reversal of current also flows through the cathode resistor of the second valve. The phase of the discharge is then such as to increase the anode current of this valve, so making the grid of the first valve still more negative, holding off the charging current until the cathode of the first valve drops to such a voltage that it becomes negative with respect to its grid. The capacitor then begins to charge and the cycle starts again.

Since the frequency of oscillation is proportional to $1/(KCR)$ where K is a constant fixed by the valve-operating parameters, $C =$ the capacitance of the charging capacitor; and $R =$ the combined value of the discharging resistors, it is evident that the frequency can be readily adjusted by varying the higher value resistor of the pair of discharge resistors; that is, the one in the cathode circuit of the first valve. The frequency will vary inversely as the value of the capacitor used. This feature is made use of in the Univox to shift the pitch of the keyboard bodily up or down one octave by switching in suitable capacitor values. In practice these are supplemented by small trimmers on ac-

count of drift with time, due to ageing of the dielectrics etc.

The value of the anode resistor in the second valve controls the amplitude of oscillation because it sets the 'striking' voltage of the first valve; but it performs a more useful function since it can be used to control the oscillation frequency to some extent and is thus a means of exactly tuning the circuit without disturbing the relationship between notes already set up by the cathode series resistors. A pulse can be formed if desired by a diode shaper, see Fig. 292.

There is no reason why experimental generators of the rotary type should not be driven from pulleys by an endless flat belt instead of gears; this greatly simplifies the setting-up of such devices by the amateur. Dimensions for a series of these pulleys to cover one octave of the tempered scale are given in the table.

Pulley Diameters for One Octave

Note	in.
C	2·000
C♯	1·881
D	1·776
D♯	1·677
E	1·583
F	1·495
F♯	1·412
G	1·333
G♯	1·258
A	1·188
A♯	1·121
B	1·059
C	1·000

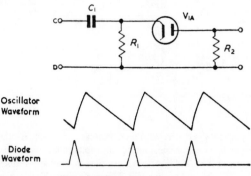

Fig. 292 Effect of diode shaper

The diameter of the motor-driving pulley is obtained from

$$\frac{1 \cdot 188 \times 3300}{\text{r.p.m. of motor}}$$

Pulley Diameters for One Octave

1425 r.p.m. driving shaft pulleys		Generator pulleys to suit	
Note	in.	Note	in.
C	0·716	C	1·147
C♯	0·692	C♯	1·028
D	0·644	D	0·911
D♯	0·698	D♯	0·903
E	0·765	E	0·896
F	0·776	F	0·875
F♯	0·802	F♯	0·831
G	0·824	G	0·803
G♯	0·884	G♯	0·794
A	0·905	A	0·784
A♯	0·870	A♯	0·685
B	0·836	B	0·623

For example, at 3300 r.p.m., 2, 4, 8, 16, 32-tooth wheels give

110, 220, 440, 880, 1760 Hz

The belt may be $\frac{5}{16}$ in. wide and a suitable material is nylon. With such small pulleys, a flywheel on the motor is generally necessary.

Since many single-phase motors in Britain run at 1425 r.p.m. more specific pulley dimensions for the various notes of the equally tempered scale are given (Fig. 293). It is, of course, immaterial what the basic pitch or frequency is.

But if gears are required it is not possible to obtain exactly the intervals of the tempered scale by any simple combination of wheels. The nearest approach is a pair of gears having 89 and 84 teeth. This makes the pitch low by 0·0992 cents (there are 1200 cents in an octave). The next pair of wheels would have 107 and 101 teeth, making the pitch high by 0·0934 cents. Using these pairs alternately, the overall pitch error is kept extremely small and is quite acceptable for any purpose.

The question of initially tuning any instrument sometimes raises problems. Naturally a simple tuning fork of pitch A = 440·000 Hz is the most useful basic tool, and it is simple to arrange to drive this by a valve or microphone buttons; but many people experience great difficulty in tuning all the intervals of the scale, and indeed it is sometimes very hard to tell which octave a note is actually sounding, especially if it contains many harmonics.

A device has been made which visibly indicates on rotating discs the exact tune, or departure from tune, of all the intervals in one octave in any key. A full description of this has been published, but it would seem profitable to build such a tuner into a

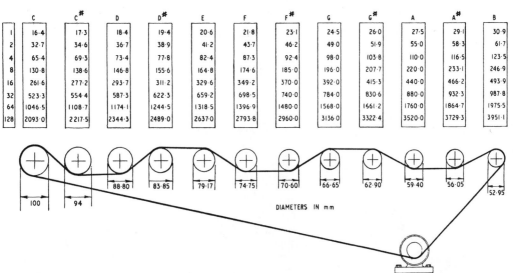

Fig. 293 Pulley diameters for E.T. scale (metric)

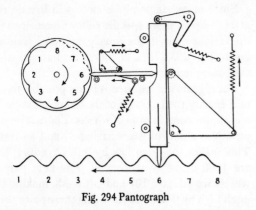

Fig. 294 Pantograph

large electronic instrument as an integral part of the installation; tuning could then be carried out by anyone, and in locations like the tropics this might be a boon.

Experimenters with the Hammond type of tone wheel often experience great difficulty in marking out the tooth profiles. A simple pantograph arrangement of the kind shown in Fig. 294 can be used to mark off any form of wave which can be

drawn out as indicated. It is clear that by adjustment of the cam contours, almost any ratio of dimensions is obtainable. Although this device will mark off any tooth shape, such tone discs still have to be machined. For those with limited workshop facilities, an interesting method of manufacture is shown in Figs. 295 and 296. The soft-iron or fully-annealed mild-steel discs are made as follows—

2- and 4-point tone wheels. These components are of the relative contour shown in Fig. 295, and can be produced by roughing out the blanks from the strip material $1\frac{5}{16}$ in. wide. If two of each of these rough blanks are then finished by hand to the final profile, they can be clamped at each end of the remaining ten blanks on a suitable $\frac{7}{16}$ in. diameter bolt so that all tone wheels of each type are produced to uniform dimensions and shape.

After profiling, the blanks should be separated and all burrs removed, the finished tone wheels being greased lightly to prevent rusting prior to assembly on to their mounting bushes. These mounting bushes are to be produced for all tone

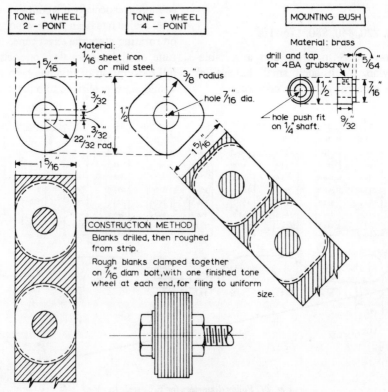

Fig. 295 Constructional details of 2- and 4-point tone wheels

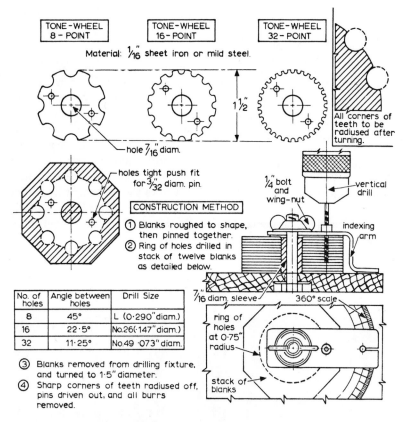

Fig. 296 Method of construction of 8-, 16- and 32-point tone wheels

wheels from brass to the detail dimensions also given in Fig. 295.

8-, 16- *and 32-point tone wheels.* These tone wheels can be produced by the method detailed in Fig. 296, i.e. by drilling a ring of holes in the blanks, then turning away the surplus metal to provide the necessary teeth and gaps of equal width. The diagram shows a simple drilling fixture which will ensure accurate location of the holes at 45°, 22½° and 11¼° spacing, correct size of hole and the size of drill required.

It will be necessary to hold the stack of blanks together by pinning during the drilling operation and subsequent turning to 1·5 in. diameter. After turning, and while still pinned together, the sharp corners of all teeth should be radiused off smoothly, the pins then being driven out and all burrs removed from the finished tone wheels.

Although the tooth form is not the same as that of Hammond wheels, it is quite satisfactory as a music generator.

Whilst on the subject of magnetic generator details, many experimenters are uncertain of the windings for coils using Hammond-type magnets. On the assumption that an 84-note generator will suffice, all the coils can be wound on four sizes of bobbin as shown in Fig. 297. Calling the bottom C of the pedals note No. 1, we have the following windings (see table on page 195).

Although several commercial organs have been described in essence, no attempt has been made to give actual constructional details or dimensions of parts etc. Such information would enormously increase the size and cost of this book and few if any of the instruments shown could really be constructed in their commercial form by the amateur.

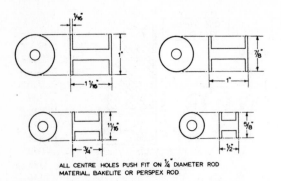

ALL CENTRE HOLES PUSH FIT ON ¼" DIAMETER ROD
MATERIAL, BAKELITE OR PERSPEX ROD

Fig. 297 Bobbins used to wind the generator coils

available in the form of a book entitled *Transistor Electronic Organs for the Amateur* (Pitman); many aspects of organs are covered in the same publication. We have been careful to adhere to standard dimensions of all playing parts and a compact design can be seen from Fig. 298 which shows an organ of this type constructed by an enthusiast with little knowledge of electronics.

It is only possible in a book of this size to outline the more important features of the circuits for the benefit of the experimenter; but intending constructors should benefit by joining the Electronic Organ Constructors Society, of which the author is President; there are members in almost every country.

However, since there is a considerable demand for further details of a small organ, designs, are

Fig. 298 Compact electronic organ constructed by an amateur

Windings for Generator Coils

	Note	No. of Turns	Note	No. of Turns			Note	No. of Turns	Note	No. of Turns
Notes 1–24 inclusive use the largest bobbin. Windings are all 26 swg, S.S.E. wire.	1	830	13	620		Notes 49–72 inclusive use the next bobbin. Windings are all 30 swg, S.S.E. wire.	49	250	61	190
	2	820	14	600			50	243	62	183
	3	800	15	590			51	238	63	180
	4	780	16	580			52	234	64	177
	5	760	17	560			53	227	65	174
	6	740	18	545			54	222	66	170
	7	720	19	535			55	220	67	163
	8	700	20	520			56	216	68	160
	9	680	21	510			57	207	69	157
	10	665	22	500			58	200	70	153
	11	645	23	485			59	198	71	150
	12	635	24	470			60	195	72	143
Notes 25–48 inclusive use the next bobbin. Windings are all 28 swg, S.S.E. wire.	25	455	37	325		Notes 73–84 inclusive use the smallest bobbin. Windings are all 32 swg, S.S.E. wire.	73	142	79	121
	26	440	38	320			74	140	80	119
	27	430	39	317			75	138	81	117
	28	420	40	310			76	137	82	115
	29	410	41	300			77	132	83	112
	30	400	42	297			78	123	84	110
	31	390	43	290						
	32	385	44	282						
	33	370	45	277						
	34	360	46	270						
	35	345	47	263						
	36	339	48	257						

Appendix I

Frequency Table (Hz)

C	C♯	D	D♯		G♯	A	A♯	B
16·351	17·323	18·354	19·445		25·956	27·500	29·135	30·867
32·703	34·647	36·708	38·890		51·913	55·000	58·270	61·735
65·406	69·295	73·416	77·781		103·826	110·000	116·540	123·470
130·812	138·591	146·832	155·563		207·652	220·000	233·081	246·941
261·625	277·182	293·664	311·126		415·304	440·000	466·163	493·883
523·251	554·365	587·329	622·253		830·609	880·000	932·327	987·766
1046·502	1108·730	1174·059	1244·507		1661·218	1760·000	1864·654	1975·532
2093·004	2217·460	2344·318	2489·014		3322·436	3520·000	3729·308	3951·064
4186·008	4434·920	4698·636	4978·028		6644·872	7040·000	7458·616	7902·128
8372·016	8869·840	9397·272	9956·056		13289·744	14080·000	14917·232	15804·256
16744·032								

CCCC	16·351 Hz is the lowest note of 32 ft pitch.
CCC	32·703 Hz is the lowest note of 16 ft pitch.
CC	65·406 Hz is the lowest note of 8 ft pitch.
C	261·625 Hz is the so-called middle C of the keyboard.

E	F	F♯	G
20·601	21·826	23·124	24·499
41·203	43·653	46·249	48·999
82·406	87·307	92·498	97·998
164·813	174·614	184·997	195·997
329·627	349·228	369·994	391·995
659·255	698·456	739·988	783·991
1318·510	1396·912	1479·976	1567·982
2637·020	2793·824	2959·952	3135·964
5274·040	5587·648	5919·904	6270·928
10548·080	11175·296	11839·808	12541·856

Appendix II

Colour code for carbon resistors

The distinguishing colours are always read in the following order: body, tip, dot.

There are two different methods of marking the colours—

(a) The whole of the body is one colour; the tip, or one end, is another colour; and the dot may be an actual dot or a narrow band.

(b) The body is a neutral colour, buff or white. The 'body' colour is then the broad band at one end; the 'tip' is the next narrow band; and the 'dot' is an adjacent narrow band.

In addition to the significant colours, there may be, near the centre, the following colours—

Gold	This means ± 5 per cent tolerance
Silver	This means ± 10 per cent tolerance
No colour	This means ± 20 per cent tolerance

A pink band means the resistor is of a high-stability type. The colours used are—

Black	0	Green	5
Brown	1	Blue	6
Red	2	Violet	7
Orange	3	Grey	8
Yellow	4	White	9

Examples. The body colour is the first significant figure; the tip, the next figure; the dot, the multiplying factor, i.e. number of zeroes.

Body	Tip	Dot	
Green	Black	Red	
5	0	2	= 5000 Ω
Green	Green	Green	
5	5	5	= 5,500,000 Ω
Yellow	Violet	Orange	
4	7	3	= 47,000 Ω